William Doxford & Sons Ltd.

of Sunderland

Shipbuilders and Engineers
1837-1988

Patricia Richardson

Other books by the author
Addington, The Life Story of a Kentish Village, 2012
Felix Calvert & Company, A Capital Brewing Family, 2015

ISBN 978-0-9574465-2-6

Design and layout by John Hawtin
Published by Patricia Richardson, St. Vincents, Addington, West Malling, Kent ME19 5BW
0044 7876 102 572 email: richardsonbooks@btinternet.com
Printed by Remous Limited, Sherborne, Dorset.

Front Cover:
The Montcalm (837) under the overhead gantries in Pallion West Yard, 8 March 1960.
Courtesy of Dr. Ian Buxton

Back cover:
Doxford engine 67PT6, just prior to testing at Pallion Engineering Works, 1962.
Courtesy of Jack Jordan

The West Gatehouse with bunting for the visit by HRH Edward, Prince of Wales, 3 July 1930.
Courtesy of the Sunderland Antiquarian Society

Frame of the second turret ship, Turret Age (219) under construction at Pallion East Yard, 1893.
The Engineer, 16 March 1894.

Contents

Male Descendants of William Doxford of Dalton-le-Dale, Co. Durham

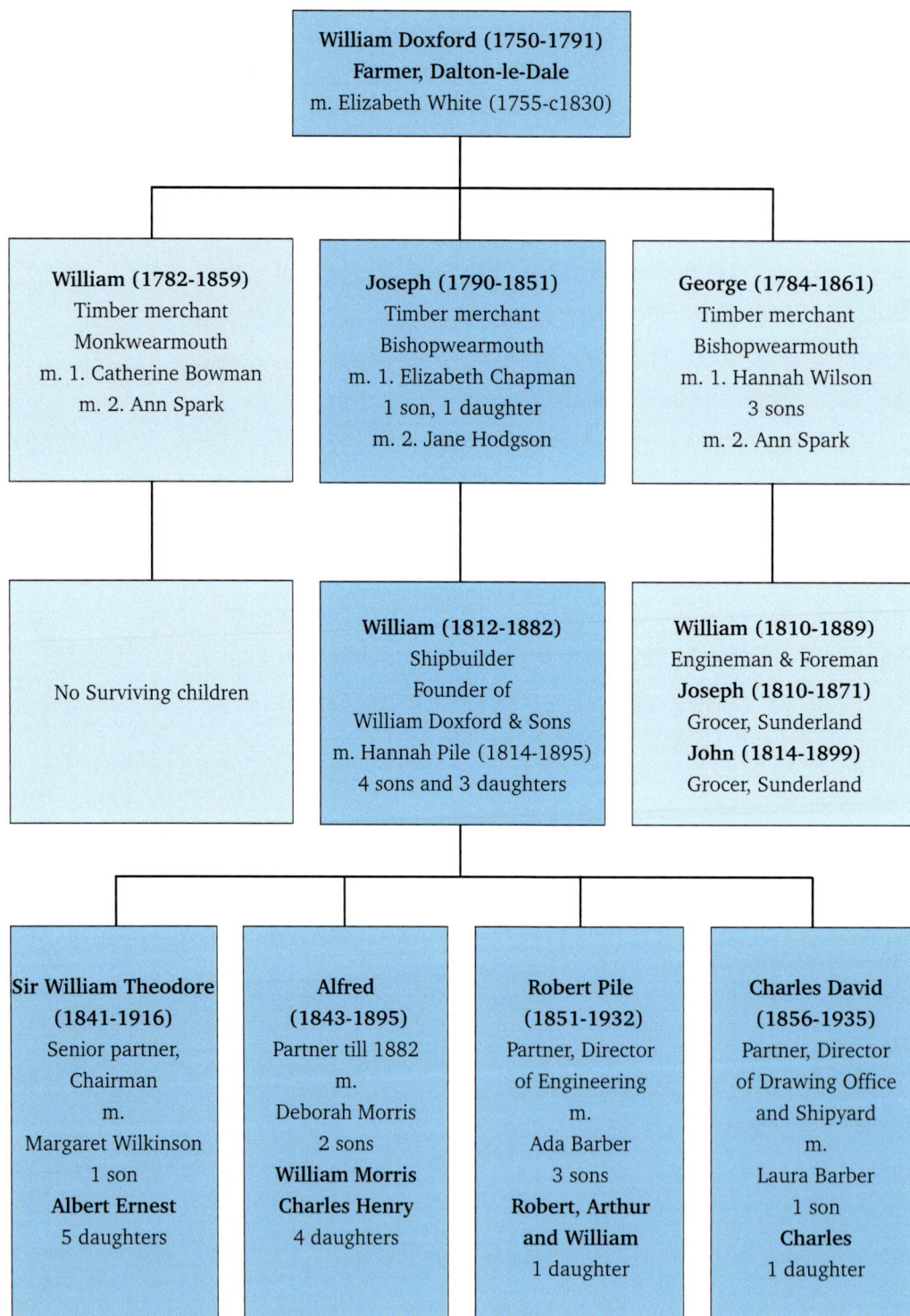

William Doxford (1750-1791)
Farmer, Dalton-le-Dale
m. Elizabeth White (1755-c1830)

William (1782-1859)
Timber merchant
Monkwearmouth
m. 1. Catherine Bowman
m. 2. Ann Spark

Joseph (1790-1851)
Timber merchant
Bishopwearmouth
m. 1. Elizabeth Chapman
1 son, 1 daughter
m. 2. Jane Hodgson

George (1784-1861)
Timber merchant
Bishopwearmouth
m. 1. Hannah Wilson
3 sons
m. 2. Ann Spark

No Surviving children

William (1812-1882)
Shipbuilder
Founder of
William Doxford & Sons
m. Hannah Pile (1814-1895)
4 sons and 3 daughters

William (1810-1889)
Engineman & Foreman
Joseph (1810-1871)
Grocer, Sunderland
John (1814-1899)
Grocer, Sunderland

Sir William Theodore
(1841-1916)
Senior partner,
Chairman
m.
Margaret Wilkinson
1 son
Albert Ernest
5 daughters

Alfred
(1843-1895)
Partner till 1882
m.
Deborah Morris
2 sons
William Morris
Charles Henry
4 daughters

Robert Pile
(1851-1932)
Partner, Director
of Engineering
m.
Ada Barber
3 sons
Robert, Arthur
and William
1 daughter

Charles David
(1856-1935)
Partner, Director
of Drawing Office
and Shipyard
m.
Laura Barber
1 son
Charles
1 daughter

Illustrations

Credits are given in the text of the book.

Introduction and Acknowledgements

This is the story of a family business of shipbuilders and marine engineers at Sunderland. In 1837 William Doxford built a small wooden ship on the River Wear for the coastal trade. After a shaky start, he moved to Pallion, about three miles upriver from the docks, where he was joined in partnership by his four sons. After William's death, three of the brothers took the business from strength to strength and brought in the third generation. William Doxford & Sons (latterly under successor names) traded for 150 years, establishing an enviable reputation. As well as describing their ships and engines, I have concentrated on the narrative of the business and the people who made things happen. I have not gone into great technical detail.

The book follows the twists and turns of the shipbuilding industry on Wearside throughout the 20th century, until its final demise at the end of the 1980s. After selling their family concern in 1919, the two surviving brothers continued in post and steered the Company through the recessions of the 1920s and 1930s. Doxford then became the most prolific provider of merchant ships during the Second World War. When the post war boom faltered, the Company joined a consortium that moved in and out of public control. Pallion was one of two surviving shipyards on the River Wear when it finally closed in 1988.

I would like to record my thanks to all who have helped me. My husband, Michael, great-great-grandson of the founder, has been my fellow researcher and editor. Francis Hanson Doxford Budden and William Henry Warren Davis, two fellow descendants of William, have shared their family archives. Francis has also given invaluable help as proof checker. My thanks go to Douglas Smith, President of the Sunderland Antiquarian Society, Jack Jordan, past officer at Pallion and member of the Doxford Engine Friends Association, fellow members at the World Ship Society, staff at the Tyne & Wear Archive Service, Peter Searle of www.searlecanada.org and George of www.sunderlandships.com. I owe a special debt to my cousin, Dr. Ian Buxton, retired visiting professor at the School of Marine Sciences and Technology at Newcastle University. Ian encouraged my efforts, pointed me in the right direction and corrected my errors. Finally, my grateful thanks go to John Hawtin, friend and retired graphic designer, who has generously designed this book for me.

I have made every effort to contact the copyright owners of the illustrations in the book, but have failed in some instances. I have credited the photographer, wherever possible. Owing to the age and source of some of the images, reproduction has been affected.

Patricia Richardson, 2019

Frontispiece: The River Wear, 1837, the year that William Doxford built his first ship. Family print adjusted by Patricia Richardson.

Chapter One

The Doxford Family of Northumberland

The family who later built ships at Sunderland on the River Wear took their name from the Northumberland hamlet where they were living in the early Norman period. According to Kenneth Cameron's 'English Place Names', Doxford gained its name from a pre-Norman owner call 'Docc' and the ford that he controlled. P. H. Reaney, writing in 'The Origin of English Surnames', confirms that Doxford falls into the category of the place a person came from. This map gives the relative distances between the villages where the first members of the Doxford family lived. Most were in the modern, and extensive parish of Embleton, which lies between Alnwick and Bamburgh, just east of the A1 trunk road to Berwick. Embleton stretches inland from the coast to Christon Bank and Ellingham, where the hamlet of Doxford once stood. This has now vanished, but is remembered by the house known as Doxford Hall.

1. Map of the area of Northumberland showing the villages where the Doxford family first lived.

Drawn by C. & J. Greenwood 1827/8.

Image Courtesy of University of Glasgow Library.

At the turn of the 20th century Charles David Doxford (1856-1935) commissioned a family tree from a researcher who suggested that his family was descended from a Norman family called de Gaugi. The researcher alleged that a certain Sir Adam de Gaugi (d. 1209) took the name de Doxford from the lands he held in Northumberland. Charles Doxford was a subscriber to the extensive genealogy books compiled by James Watson Corder (1867-1953), the noted family and local historian of Sunderland. Corder recorded the births, deaths and marriages of all the local families and also made detailed notes about their businesses.[1] Whatever he personally thought, Corder was not in a position to challenge the family tree presented to him by his friend and this has remained in the public domain ever since, despite the doubts of the wider Doxford family.

The de Gaugi family certainly held lands in Northumberland, including Doxford, and also in the southern counties of England. Their name appears in manorial documents dating from the 12th century. In 'A History of Northumberland, Vol. II', (1865) the hamlet of Doxford is described as part of the parish of Ellingham. The author, John Hodgson, recorded a succession of Doxfords who held 'Dochesefordam' from 1304. Prior to this the hamlet was held as a part of the barony of Gaugi by the de Mering family, who were descended from an Alice de Gaugi. The Norman family vanished from the records at the turn of the fourteenth century, and a Thomas de Doxford, appears on the Subsidy Roll of 1296, paying the largest dues in the hamlet to the barony. This seems to confirm that their name came from the area in which they lived, rather than as a descendant of the de Gaugi family.

Hodgson wrote that

> "The Doxfords did not attain to the degree of gentry, but belonged to the yeoman class of small freeholders, who frequently adhered to their patrimonial estate more tenaciously than the larger landed proprietors".

As yeomen they were not subject to an 'inquisition post mortem', so Hodgson could not establish a reliable family tree. However, he did mention a connection to an Adam de Gaugi who died in 1286, leaving no descendants. This de Gaugi appears in the earlier 'Synopsis of the Peerage of England', published in 1825 by Nicholas Harris Nicolas. Nicolas recorded that Adam's cousin Roger de Clifford "was found to be his heir",[2] and Hodgson notes that the Doxfords became free (rather than customary) tenants of the Earl of Northumberland following the confiscation of the estate of a John de Clifford at the end of the fourteenth century.

Hodgson located a rental dated 1488 stating that a Henry Doxford (1430-1496) held 105 acres in Doxford, 'a hamelette of Ellingham'.[3] This Henry was married to Alice Beadnall, whose name comes from another village nearby. Henry and Alice were ancestors of the Sunderland Doxfords, but Hodgson's family descended from the eldest son and diverged from the Sunderland line produced for Charles David

Doxford. The senior line held land at Doxford until the death of Robert Doxford in 1635. Robert was childless, so some of his land passed to his cousin, Gilbert Swinhoe of Berrington. Robert Doxford's will, quoted in Hodgson's work, states that his lands in Doxford had been lately in the hands of Nicholas Forster. This is the family name of wives of the Doxford family of Sunderland.

The junior line, who became the Doxfords of Sunderland descend from John, (b 1470) a younger son of Henry and Alice. John married Elizabeth Swinhoe. Their grandson, Renold (1540-1611), who lived all his life at Beadnall, married Isabel Forster. Renold left a will, registered at Durham, and his inventory stated that his estate was worth £30 15s. He and Isabel had a son, named George (1570-1630). George married Elizabeth Forster, who was perhaps his cousin, and moved his family to Ellingham. George's son Edward (1600-1660) was born in Ellingham, but died at Embleton. According to the records of the Church of Latter Day Saints[4], during the seventeenth and eighteenth centuries the Doxford family were overwhelming based in the Northumberland villages of Embleton, Rothbury, Howick, Bamburgh, Bothal with Hebburn, Tynemouth and Earsdon. Most can be found in the family tree of William Doxford the first shipbuilder. The sons' names used more than once were Henry, John (7), Matthew, Ralph, Richard and William (7). The daughters were mainly Ann (4), Eleanor, Elizabeth, Isabel(la) (5), Jane, Margaret and Mary.

2. The 1752 gravestone of Ralph Doxford in Embleton churchyard.

Photograph by Patricia Richardson

Four generations passed, led by Henry Edward (1630-1699), William (1655-1715), John (1682-1736) and John (1715-1776). This John Doxford was baptised at Holy Trinity, Embleton on 15 January 1715 and married Elizabeth Gair at the same church on 1 June 1735. Elizabeth was aged about sixteen. A family tradition states that in 1745, "to avoid trouble over the border" John and Elizabeth Doxford moved their family from Embleton to Dalton-le-Dale, just south of Sunderland in the county of Durham. However, this could not have happened. There are no records of a Doxford baptism or burial at Dalton-le-Dale until 1782. It was their son, William (1750-1791), who made the move. Additionally, William's older brother, Ralph, who was born in 1743, was buried in Embleton churchyard on 23 January 1752/3. In the burial record, Ralph's place of abode was given as Craster Laugh, then a hamlet within the parish. A substantial gravestone with finely carved lettering was erected in the child's memory in Embleton churchyard, suggesting that the family were established farmers.

Of John and Elizabeth's family of eight only the last four survived to adulthood. As a convention I will mark those who reached adulthood in bold throughout the text.

The family were:

1. John (1736-1750) born and died at Embleton.

2. William (1738-1750) baptised 26 March 1738, Embleton.

3. Isabel (1740-?) born and died at Embleton.

4. Ralph (1743-1752/3) baptised 27 August 1743, Embleton, died 23 Jan 1752/3 "Aged 9 Years and 6 Months."

5. **Arthur (1746-after 1775)** baptised 4 May 1746 at Embleton. Arthur married Jane Watson at Lesbury on 16 October 1764. Their four children were born in Lesbury, but left no descendants.

6. **Henry (1748-1791)** baptised 16 December 1748 at Howick. Henry married Barbara Summers (1739-1809). Of their six children, their son Henry (1775-1830) was a miller, who married Barbara Hedley. Their family of eight were born in Northumberland but the family then moved to Whitburn, near Sunderland. His son, another Henry (1809-1887), married Mary Dobson and is noted as a 'mason's labourer' in the 1861 census. Like his forebears, he had a large family.

7. **William (1750-1791)** born in Howick, died at Kinley Law House, Cold Hesledon, Dalton-le Dale, Co. Durham. His grandson founded the shipbuilding firm of William Doxford and Sons.

8. **Isabel (1757-1792)** did not marry. She also moved to Dalton-le-Dale, where she was buried.

As can be seen above, John and Elizabeth had moved to Howick by 1748, as their sixth child, Henry, was baptised there on 16 December. John was buried in Howick churchyard on 15 December 1776. His wife survived him for fourteen years. She was buried at Embleton on 15 November 1790.

3. Holy Trinity, Embleton. The gravestone is facing the porch. Photograph by Patricia Richardson

William Doxford of Howick and Dalton-le-Dale (1759-1791)

William was the second child of this name born to John and Elizabeth Doxford, their seventh child and youngest son. He was born in Howick, where he was baptised on 27 April 1750. He probably spent his childhood and early manhood

4. The area of Durham to which William Doxford (1751-1790) moved.

From the map of Durham Drawn by C. & J. Greenwood 1819-20.

Image Courtesy of University of Glasgow Library.

in the parish. His father died in 1776, by which time his older brothers were married. How William was earning his living at this point is unclear. It may be that he had already left Howick, but his marriage suggests that he moved to Co. Durham at about that time. On 13 May 1779 William married Elizabeth White at St. Michael's church, Bishopwearmouth. At that time there were three parishes in the future metropolis of Sunderland: Monkwearmouth, on the north bank of the Wear, Bishopwearmouth on the south bank and Sunderland parish itself, then a fishing settlement at the mouth of the river. With the growth of industry on the Wear they merged together and became the municipal borough of Sunderland in 1835.

At his marriage, William was aged 29 and Elizabeth, who was born at South Shields, on the Tyne, was 24. Their first child, Jane, was baptised at Bishopwearmouth on 25 June 1780. The couple left Sunderland shortly after this and lived briefly at Farnton Hill, Dalton-le-Dale, after which they moved to Kinley Law House, Cold

Hesledon, still in the same parish. 'Law' means 'Hill' and Kinley Hill overlooks the sea to the south of Dalton. The farm was given as their abode at each of the subsequent five baptisms. William died aged 41 and was buried at Dalton-le-Dale on 27 September 1791. He left a widow with an eleven year old daughter, and three sons aged nine, seven and one.

5. The Kinley Law area of Cold Hesledon, south of Dalton-le-Dale, overlooking the North Sea, where William Doxford farmed.

Photograph by Patricia Richardson.

William and Elizabeth Doxford's children were:

1. **Jane (1780-1800)** died unmarried at Dalton-le-Dale.

2. **William (1782-1859)** baptised 28 July 1782 at Dalton-le-Dale, William married twice. He was a timber merchant at Monkwearmouth.

3. **George (1784-1859)** baptised 23 May 1784 at Dalton-le-Dale. George lived in Bishopwearmouth, and was a timber merchant. He married Hannah Wilson and had eight children. His sons, John and Joseph were grocers and wine merchants at 98, High Street, Sunderland. This line continued into the twentieth century, and is recorded below.

4. John (1786-?) baptised 16 April 1786, Dalton-le-Dale. Died as a child.

5. Isabel (1788-?) baptised 8 June 1788, Dalton-le-Dale. Died as a child.

6. **Joseph (1790-1851)** baptised 11 July 1790, Dalton-le-Dale. He was a timber merchant, see below. His son founded the shipbuilding business.

Elizabeth Doxford remained at Dalton-le-Dale. As none of her children were of working age the family may have suffered financially. Her sons seem to have served apprenticeships as wood workers. She was a widow for thirteen years. By the time she remarried, on 1 May 1804, all her sons were living in Sunderland. Her second husband was also widowed. George Storey was an unskilled worker, who gave his profession as 'labourer' on the marriage certificate. Elizabeth is reputed to have died in 1830.

6. St. Andrew. Dalton-le-Dale.

Old Postcard

Although neither William nor George Doxford, the elder sons of William and Elizabeth, are central to the shipbuilding story, it is helpful to record their lives, as they shared some of the family businesses and appear in trade directories for Sunderland.

William Doxford of Dalton-le-Dale and Sunderland (1782-1859) timber merchant

William and Elizabeth's eldest son moved to Sunderland and established a business on North Bridge Street, Monkwearmouth shore. William's first wife was Catherine Bowman, by whom he had no children. Catherine died in 1844. Six years later, aged 66, William married Anne Norris, who was 34. He and Anne had a daughter, known as Annie, who died in her teens. At his death, William appointed his nephew, John Doxford, son of George, as one of his executors. His residual legatees were all his nephews, including William Doxford, the shipbuilder, showing that the families were still in communication with each other. William was buried in the cemetery of St. Andrew's, Dalton-le-Dale.[5]

George Doxford of Dalton-le-Dale and Sunderland (1784-1861) sawyer and timber merchant

George was a sawyer who moved from Dalton-le-Dale to Pittington, five miles inland. There he married Hannah Wilson (or Moore), who was five years his junior. Corder gives Hannah's father as William Wilson. She may have been a young widow, as her burial record suggests that her surname was 'Moore'.

George and Hannah's first child, **William (1810-1889)** was baptised at Pittington

7

church. The couple then moved to Sunderland, perhaps to join his elder brother, William. Their following two children, **John (1814-1899)** and Elizabeth (1816-1829), were baptised at St. Peter's church, Monkwearmouth, where William had his yard. The family later moved across the river, making their home in Littlegate, Bishopwearmouth. Hannah (1819), Hannah (1820-1834), Esther (1823), **Jane (1825-1896)**, who married William John Finlay and left two daughters, and **Joseph (1830-1871)** were all baptised at St. Michael's, Bishopwearmouth. George set up on his own account as a sawyer and timber merchant and took his younger brother, Joseph (1791-1851), into partnership. Their yard was in Walton Place, close to the High Street and to Joseph's home.[6]

At the 1833 election that followed the Reform Act, George and Hannah had been married for over twenty years and he was in his late forties. According to the Poll Book they were living in Drury Street. He qualified as an elector as the proprietor of houses, rather than one house. Street names have changed, but a Drury Lane runs into Lombard Street, parallel and south of the High Street.

Shortly after this, they moved to Walton Place, next to the timber yard. Hannah, their daughter, died there in 1834 and Hannah, George's wife in 1836, aged 47. Both were buried in Galley's Gill Cemetery, Bishopwearmouth churchyard. George re-married. His second wife was Sarah Stark. She was thirteen years his junior, so would have been in her thirties at the time of this marriage, but there were no further children. At the 1841 census the couple were in Union Street, with George's occupation given as 'Male Servant', implying that the partnership with his brother had ended. At the 1851 census, George and Sarah were living at 33 George Street (or 34 as it is given in 1861), still in the same area. In 1851 he gave his occupation as 'retired from business' and in 1861 as 'proprietor of houses'. At both censuses their home contained two schedules, so they had sublet part of the property. In 1851 George and Hannah's youngest son was still at home. Joseph had not followed his father's trade as a sawyer. Instead, he was starting a partnership as a grocer with his older brother, John.

George died in George Street on 6 December 1861, aged 77. His burial took place at Bishopwearmouth cemetery, which had opened as a municipal facility in 1856. Sarah lived for a further twenty two years. She was still in George Street at the 1871 census, giving her occupation as 'income from rents'. She later moved to 6 Blandford Street.[7] In both cases her home was part of a multiple occupancy. Sarah Doxford died on 22 October 1883, aged 86 and was buried with her husband.

George and Hannah's eldest son, William, married twice and had eight children, though not all survived. His first wife, Isabella Forster, was buried in Galley's Gill Cemetery with one of their children. At the 1841 census he had recently been widowed and was working as a sawyer, probably with his father. He re-married in 1843, his second wife being Anne Spark (1812-1877). After his father retired from business, William moved from job to job and from home to home, according to subsequent census records. He was working as a porter in 1851, an engineman in 1861 and by 1871 was a foreman. He died in 1889, aged 78 and was buried in Bishopwearmouth Cemetery, next to his second wife.

Doxford & Co., Grocers and Wine merchants

John Doxford, George and Hannah's second son, and his brother Joseph, were in partnership at 98 High Street, Sunderland, trading as J. Doxford & Co. They were grocers, tea dealers, wine, ale, porter and spirit merchants.[8] John married a Welsh girl, Mary, but she died in 1859, leaving no children. His second wife was Mary Wilson, who had been born in Leeds. They married at Bishopwearmouth on 2 August 1864 and lived in Azalea Terrace, in the Ashbrooke area of Bishopwearmouth.[9] John ran his business until his death in 1899, aged 84. He was a respected local figure who was appointed a governor of Sunderland Infirmary at its foundation in 1867.

7. John Doxford, (1814-1899)
Grocer, Sunderland High Street

John and Mary had one son, John George Doxford (1865-1946). The family joined the Wesleyans; father and son funded the establishment of new premises in Sunderland. However, John George had moved to Hill House, Bodenham, Herefordshire, by the time of his marriage in 1888.[10] John George and his wife, Elizabeth Walker, had four daughters, two of whom married. I could not trace whether either left children. He died at Bickley in Kent.

John's brother and partner, Joseph, lived at 15 Waterloo Place. He was married to Sarah Jane Baldwin, the daughter of a local shipowner. Joseph played a major role in the local masonic lodge and was a director of the Industrial and Provident Building Society. He died at the beginning of January 1841, aged 40, after a long illness.[11] He and Sarah had nine children. Of these, Joseph Junior and Albert William left descendants. Joseph Doxford junior (1856-1935) was a marine engine fitter and remained in Sunderland. He and his wife, Elizabeth Jane Levi, had a large family. One of their sons, Rowland Doxford, trained as a chartered accountant and emigrated to Canada, where his descendants now live. Others remained in the North East. Albert William (1857-1936), a naval architect, lived in Newcastle-upon-Tyne. He married Eleanor Russell and had a family of three. Another son, Alfred Ernest, worked as a shipbroker's clerk in Sunderland and then lived for a time in Richmond, Surrey. He died unmarried in Derbyshire in 1901, aged 39.[12]

Joseph Doxford of Dalton-le-Dale and Sunderland (1790-1851), Sawyer and Timber merchant

William Doxford of Dalton-le-Dale's youngest child was named Joseph. He was born at Kinley Law House and was baptised on 11 July 1790. He was a toddler when his father died in September 1791. Joseph was apprenticed as a sawyer at Easington. It was there that he met his wife, Elizabeth Chapman (1785-1845). She came from Greatham, near Bishop Auckland, further down the coast. They were married at St. Mary's church, Easington on Christmas Eve, 1809. Joseph signed his name, but Elizabeth made her mark. Both gave Easington as their parish, so it is likely that Elizabeth was a servant on a local farm. Elizabeth was a few years older than her husband, according to census records.

The couple's first child was born at Easington in 1810, after which the family moved to Sunderland. They lived firstly in Monkwearmouth, so Joseph probably joined his oldest brother. The family then crossed the Wear to Bishopwearmouth where he set up his own business.

The family was as follows:

1. **Elizabeth (1810-1883)** baptised at Easington on 6 May 1810. In 1833 she married John Doughty, a mariner, and lived in Bishopwearmouth. They had four children: Elizabeth Hannah, William John, Mary Jane and John George Doxford Doughty. All married, and descendants can be traced for the youngest two.

2. **William (1812-1882)** transformed his father's timber business into a great shipbuilding firm. His life is described in Chapter Two.

3. Joseph (1814)

4. **John (1815-1842)** baptised at St. Michael, Bishopwearmouth on 24 December 1815. John became a printer's compositor.[13] He was not married.

5. Mary Jane (1820-1824)

6. Thomas (1825)

Although trained as a sawyer, Joseph developed a substantial business as a timber

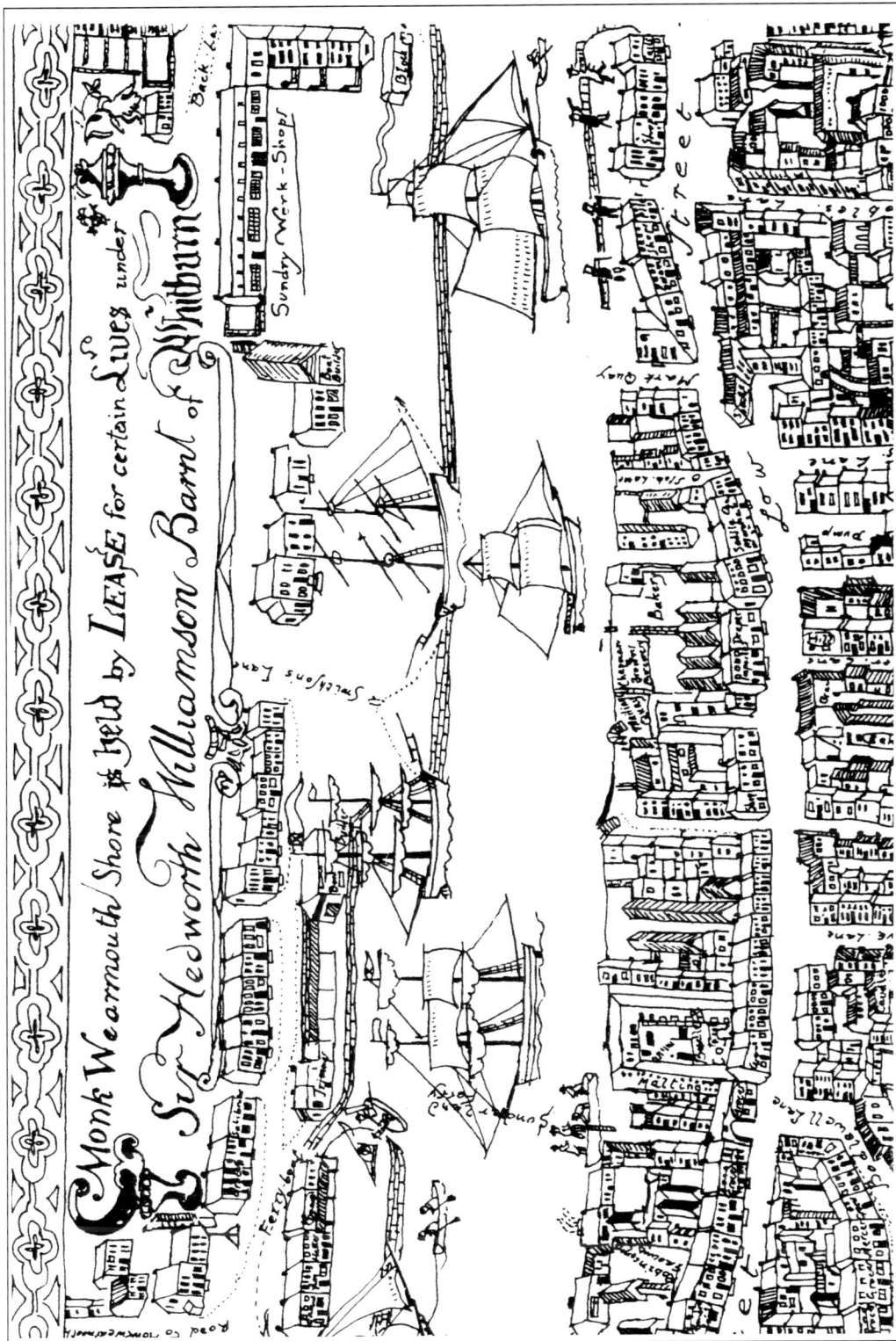

8. Plate A6 of John Rain's 'Eye Plan of Sunderland and Bishopwearmouth', published in 1790. It shows the area of Monkwearmouth Shore where Joseph first set up business as a sawyer, and Low Street, where Robert Pile, the glass engraver, was living. Hannah Pile, Robert's daughter, married Joseph's son, William.

merchant. He may well have financed the building of small wooden ships, as this was an associated business of such merchants. Corder gave the location of Joseph's yard as in Walton Place.[14] His entry in the Poll Book of 1833 gives his address as Walton Street, nearby. His qualification to vote was as the proprietor of a single house.

At the 1841 census Joseph was 50 and Elizabeth was 55. They had by then moved to a substantial house at 8 Bedford Street, a dog-legged street running into Bridge Street, very close to the river. It is now separated from this by the ring road and is a commercial area. With them that night were John, their younger son, Elizabeth Doughty, their daughter, with her husband and two children, and just one servant. This was Elizabeth Mills, aged fifteen. Joseph gave his occupation as shipbuilder, having recently bailed out his eldest son, William, whose first concern had failed. Joseph returned to his business as a mahogany and timber merchant, and was also a shipowner. He had moved his premises to Walworth Street by 1850.[15] Elizabeth Doxford died in 1845. In July 1848 Joseph remarried at Roker. His second wife was Jane Hodgson, a widow.

In character, Joseph Doxford was an upstanding member of the community, who taught at the Bethel Sunday School, attached to the Chapel in Villiers Street. This implies that he had non-conformist beliefs, though he brought his children to the Church of England for baptism. He was aged sixty when he died in early 1851. His widow, Jane, was given a life interest in their home in Bedford Street, and the timber business was left jointly to his two surviving children, Elizabeth Doughty and William Doxford. William was appointed sole executor. Family records give Joseph's death as 21 January 1851, but his will and grant of probate, dated 14 June 1855 and lodged at Durham, states that it occurred on 18 February. The value of his estate was "not more than £200".[16]

Chapter Two

1812-1882
William Doxford of Pallion, Shipbuilder

William was born at Monkwearmouth on 1 March 1812 and was baptised at the church of St. Peter on 5 April. He was Joseph and Elizabeth Doxford's second child and their first son. Having moved from Easington, Joseph was establishing himself as a sawyer and timber merchant. William's education is unknown. He probably joined his father at a young age as an apprentice and later trained as a shipwright. William was 22 when he married Hannah Pile (1814-1895) on 28 April 1834 at St. Michael's church, Bishopwearmouth. Hannah's portrait shows her as an attractive young woman. She was the ninth child (of ten) of Robert Pile, a glass engraver of Low Street, Bishopwearmouth, and his wife Ann Chrisp. There seems to be no connection with the local family of shipbuilders, William Pyle & Sons. Robert Pile was born at Wallsend and married in Gateshead, his wife's parish. Since the eighteenth century her family had lived in Lamesley, now a suburb of Gateshead. Robert and Ann came to Sunderland in about 1807.

9. William and Hannah Doxford, c. 1838, with their two eldest surviving daughters, Elizabeth and Catherine. Family portrait.

The portraits of William and Hannah show that they were slightly built. William was probably about five feet seven inches tall. They began their married life in Bishopwearmouth, on the southern side of the River Wear. They lived firstly on Wear Street and then moved to Bridge Street.[1] They had a large family. Of their twelve children, eight survived to adulthood and most left families. The four sons became partners in the family shipbuilding empire, bringing their individual skills and strengths to the enterprise. Their first child, Elizabeth Ann, was born on 25 November 1834. The last death amongst the family was that of the second youngest child, Eveline Ritson. This occurred on 18 May 1949, giving a single generation span of 115 years. 113 years passed between the first and the last death.

Their family were:

1. **Elizabeth Anne (1834-1925)** who was baptised at Bishopwearmouth church on 21 December 1834. She married Joseph James Spraggon (1834-1903), then farming at Carville, Northumberland, at the Ebenezer Chapel, Sunderland. They became Quakers. They later farmed seventy acres at Wallsend, Northumberland and 123 acres at Hayston Hill, Offerton, co. Durham. They had no children. On retirement, they lived at 1 Egerton Street, Sunderland. Joseph was buried in the Friends' Burial Ground in Bishopwearmouth Cemetery on 6 April 1903.[2] Elizabeth was 90 when she died on 19 September 1925. She left £5,374 in her will, of which £1,200 was bequeathed to her nephew, William Harrison Crosby "in recognition of his work during the whole of the Great War."[3] Her executors were her brother, Robert Pile Doxford and her nephew, Albert Ernest Doxford.

2. Sarah Jane (1836-1836)

3. **Catherine Hannah (1837-1911)** The family were still living on Wear Street when Catherine was born in July 1937. She married Harrison Crosby (or Crosbie), a shipping agent, and left two daughters and a son, William Harrison Crosby, who served as a Lieutenant with the Durham Light Infantry during World War I (WWI). Their son married but had no children. The daughters did not marry.

4. Mary Hannah (1839-1840)

5. **William Theodore (1841-1916)** Senior Partner, William Doxford & Sons. Known by his second name. Married Margaret Wilkinson and left a son and five daughters. Living descendants. See Chapter Five.

6. **Alfred (1842-1895)** Partner. Married Deborah Morris and left two sons and four daughters. Living descendants. See Chapter Six.

7. Sarah Jane (1845-1860)

8. Emily (1847-1850)

9. **Mary Katherine (1849-1937)** married Colonel Edwin Vaux, son of Cuthbert Vaux, brewer and spirit merchant. Their daughter, Ethel, married Edward Cheke. Living descendants.

10. **Robert Pile (1851-1932)** Engineer and Partner. Married Ada Barber and left three sons and one daughter. Living descendants, including the author's husband. See Chapter Seven.

11. **Eveline (1854-1949)** married Francis William Ritson, shipowner and broker, on 8 June 1881. His grandfather, John Ritson, a chemist in Sunderland, had invested in ships as the Nautilus Steam Company. Frank's father and uncle set up F. & W. Ritson to manage the fleet.[4] The Ritsons lived at Dane Holme, Ashbrooke, Sunderland. They had four sons and a daughter. Their descendants now live in Western Australia.

12. **Charles David (1856-1935)** Partner, later managing director. Married Laura Barber and left a son and a daughter. Living descendants through his son. See Chapter Eight.

William Doxford's first shipbuilding ventures

William progressed from working as a sawyer, shipwright and timber merchant to building ships. Existing business histories state that he began in 1840 at Coxgreen, (spelled on this map Cooks Green) a few miles upriver from Sunderland, but where the River Wear is still tidal.

10. Sunderland c 1820, drawn by C. & J. Greenwood. Image Courtesy of University of Glasgow Library.

Captain John Landels and a small team of volunteers compiled worldwide shipyard lists on behalf of the World Ship Society.[5] His list for the Doxford yards states that eight registered ships were built at Coxgreen between 1837 and 1841. The first two were the William and Catherine, 196 gross tonnage (grt), registered in 1837 to himself and the Betsey & Jane, 147 grt, registered to Delavel & (-----), Newcastle, in 1839. It is, however, possible that the first two ships were constructed at different locations. The gap of two years may also indicate a change of yard. George Almond, of Sunderland Technical College, undertook research into William Doxford & Sons during the 1970s. Almond believed that William's first yard was at North Dock, Monkwearmouth, and that his second was at Hylton, also on the north bank.[6] This seems likely, as at the 1841 census the family were living in Howick Street, Monkwearmouth. In a publicity leaflet issued by the new owners of William Doxford & Sons in 1921 to celebrate the installation of the first opposed piston marine oil engine, 1840 was given as the start of the business. This has subsequently become the accepted date, but they may have been unaware of the two early Lloyd's registered ships.

11. Sunderland in 1832, showing the first, bowed iron bridge and typical houses that William and Hannah may have occupied in the first years of their marriage. Ships were then constructed on the foreshore. The smoking chimney is that of a bottle factory. Author's collection.

The tonnage of cargo ships is calculated by either capacity, or weight. The 'gross registered tonnage' (grt) refers to a hull volume of approximately 100 cubic feet, the word deriving from a wine 'tun' (barrel). This is the overall volume within a ship's hull, whereas deadweight tonnage of ship, cargo, fuel, etc. was measured in tons of 2,240 lb (today in tonnes of 1,000 kg), so is a higher figure. The gross registered tonnage is considered the best measure of a 'ship size'. It does not give her length and breadth, but follows certain averages. I have used this throughout the book, except where the deadweight is the only figure available.

By 1840, William Doxford had moved his yard to Coxgreen where he increased production. He built small wooden sailing vessels that plied the coastal trade. These first ships probably carried coal and grain round the coast, often as far as

London. On the return journey, the 'cargo' was often sand or gravel, as ballast, but sometimes also used in the many glass works that stood along the banks of the Wear.

The ships built at this period on the Wear had typically two to three masts. The illustration is of a barque (sometimes spelt bark), which was a square rigged ship, i.e. a sail and rigging arrangement in which the primary driving sails are carried on horizontal spars (known as yards) thus 'square' to the masts and keel.[7] Some of the different riggings were barque, brig, brigantine, snow and ship. The ship was full rigged, i.e. without triangular sheets fore and aft.

12. A typical small barque of the period.

Courtesy of the Sunderland Antiquarian Society.

Within a year William built six ships.[8]
* 1840 Jane and Isabella, 204 grt, for Christopher Elliott, Robert Reed and Thomas Smith, Sunderland
* 1840 Swallow, 185 grt, for John Thompson, Sunderland
* 1840 Robert and Ann, 275 grt, for Clay and Co., Newcastle
* 1840 Bee's Wing, brigantine, 155 grt, for John Robson, John Crosby and William Walker, Sunderland
* 1841 Nestor, brig, 288 grt, for R.G. Adams, Newcastle
* 1841 Gateshead Park, barque, 317 grt, for Abbott & Co., Newcastle

Bankruptcy

However, this early venture had a short life. 1841 saw a widespread downturn in the national economy. The following years became known as the 'hungry forties' and included the famine in Ireland. The Government had been running a significant deficit for three years. This had a serious retrograde effect on trade, and in consequence on shipbuilding. According to 'Where Ships Are Born' by J.W. Smith and T. S. Holden, written in 1947, thirty to forty local concerns went out of business in these years, including William Doxford. J. F. Clarke, on whose two volumes on shipbuilding on the North East coast I have drawn with gratitude, counted more than forty, most of which never revived.[9] The bankruptcy notice for "William Doxford of Bishopwearmouth and Monkwearmouth, ship dealer and chapman",[10] was announced in the Sunderland and Durham County Herald on 7 May 1841. His final ship from Coxgreen, the Amelia Mary, 237 grt, was launched mid-year, but by William's father. This ship was classed at Lloyd's by Joseph Doxford for Joseph Culliford, (b. 1810), of Murton Street, Bishopwearmouth and John Wolstenholme, a grocer.[11] Culliford subsequently became a major Sunderland shipowner. It is possible that Joseph tried to run the business but found he had neither the skills nor the enthusiasm. She was the only ship that he built and, in August that year, he announced a sale on Monkwearmouth Dock in the newspaper above: "of the whole of the stock and materials of Joseph Doxford who is declining the business." The Amelia Mary was lost at sea in 1859, according to Corder. Many ships of the period had a similar lifespan.

It is clear that William continued to work as a shipwright, as he received his certificate as a shipbuilder at the end of 1841.[12] On 18 January 1842, according to the London Gazette, William had fulfilled the terms of his bankruptcy order and was discharged.[13] His address on the discharge announcement names him as of 'Bishopwearmouth and of Monkwearmouth shore, Ship Builder'.

Doxford & Crown, Low Southwick

William did not register a ship during the following two years, but on 17 September 1844, he was in a position to sign an agreement with John Hafford Esq. and Mr. Ogle Collins to take premises at Low Southwick "lately occupied by a Mr. Barker". The lease until 23 September was for £5 after which, for $2\frac{1}{2}$ years, the rental was £40 per annum, payable half yearly. Joseph Doxford stood surety for his son.[14] William took Clement William Crown (1812-1889) into partnership, and the new concern traded as Doxford & Crown. Low Southwick lies in the west of Monkwearmouth, near to Howick Street where William Doxford was then living. William Crown was a younger son of Luke Crown, one of the major Sunderland shipbuilders. His elder brother, John, had also established a shipyard at Low Southwick. John Crown's yard survived for over a century before being subsumed into J. L. Thompson and Co.

Doxford & Crown's first ship, the Dolphin, was a snow of 255 grt. The word 'snow' comes from an old Dutch word for beak, as this type of vessel had a long sharp bow. The Dolphin was launched in April 1845 and registered by J. Culliford & Co., Sunderland, to whom Joseph Doxford had sold the Amelia Mary. The start of the enterprise was bumpy, but he and Crown seem to have survived a hearing announced in the Northern Star and National Trades Journal of Leeds on 17 January 1846 to take place in the bankruptcy court on 3 February, as no bankruptcy order was made. They built sixteen ships between 1845 and 1851, nine registered at Sunderland and three at Newcastle. The largest was the Duke of Northumberland, a barque of 571 grt, built at the end of the partnership for Nicholson, Sunderland.

There were numerous shipowners on the North East coast at that period. Ships were owned in 64 parts, so it was easy to build up a portfolio of shares in several ships from small beginnings. Investors were both men and women. Some individuals later ran major shipping lines, trading all over the world, but most remained small investors. There were few other speculative opportunities for placing money, apart from railways. At the 1851 census, in the division of Monkwearmouth where William lived, there were six shipowners, whose ages ranged from 38 to 75. Two were women. Shipownership was not necessarily their primary income. John Davison, aged 34, at 15 Howick Street, gave his occupation as a shipowner, grocer and baker (but with shipowner first). William and his family were still in Howick Street, at number 44.[15] At number 43 lived yet another shipowner, Mary Hunter, aged 75. William's business had grown, as he gave his occupation as a shipbuilder, employing thirty men and boys. His partner, William Crown lived at Ogle Terrace, Southwick. He gave his occupation as a shipwright, so seems to have been second in command. However, the partnership was struggling and was wound up later that year. Their last ship, the Refuge, a snow, 253 grt, was launched in May 1851, but found no buyer. William Doxford registered her under his sole name. When both men restarted in business, the partnership was not revived.

The further life of the ships that William Doxford built in partnership with William Crown can be traced through Corder's notes and through various websites. Three of their ships are known to have foundered during the 1850s. It seems that the attrition rate at the time could reach 5% per annum. Ships were sometimes badly or over loaded and some foundered in storms, but losses were not necessarily sustained whilst on the high seas. The approach to harbour was a renowned hazard, due to inadequate surveying, the difficulty of berthing a sailing ship in poor weather and human error.

Between 1851 and 1858 William Doxford built no ships, but it seems that he was supplying and financing other shipwrights in addition to acting as a timber merchant, having inherited his father's yard. Contemporary local directories show that he had fingers in a number of pies. Hagar's Directory of 1850 gives William's name as treasurer to the Monkwearmouth Savings Bank on Barclay Street and records that he was also a ship broker, insurance broker, shipowner and timber merchant at 34 North Bridge Street. Ship broking is another occupation which appears frequently in the census records. Like shipowning, it was a 'low cost entry' profession. Brokers not only offered insurance for ships and cargoes, but also sought cargoes for owners and looked after the paperwork. J. F. Clarke studied William's timber accounts from 1851 to 1858. These showed that he was selling timber to yards at Coxgreen, where he had first set up in business. William gave advances to three shipwrights there on a regular basis.[16] He may then have arranged for investment in these ships through his ship broking and insurance business. Messrs. Reay, W. Johnson and Jobling each built ships that appear in the Doxford timber account books. The amounts loaned were significant. Between 1851 and 1856, Reay received £16,965, whilst W. Johnson received £2,305 between January 1854 and August 1857, this being when William Doxford opened his Pallion yard. Jobling received £2,531 between January 1856 and May 1857. Clarke also discovered that a William Johnson became the chief shipwright foreman at Pallion, so may have been the same man. Johnson's ship the Alacrity was a barque of 317 grt. She was one of the last ships financed by Doxford and was owned by Thomas Todd of London. The Alacrity sailed on the London to South Africa run, but for less than ten years. She was wrecked on 17 May 1865 whilst anchored off Table Bay; one of eighteen ships driven ashore by a violent storm.[17]

On a personal level, William and Hannah's family grew as the decade progressed. Hannah was 43 when Charles David, their twelfth and final child, was born in 1856. The family was complete by the time William returned to shipbuilding.

13. Howick Street, home to the Doxford Family in the early 1840s.
Courtesy of the Sunderland Antiquarian Society

1857: The move to Pallion

In 1857 William established a new shipbuilding yard. This was at Pallion, on the south side of the Wear, about three miles from the mouth of the river. He now traded as W. Doxford, Pallion, Sunderland. His first yard, with five berths, was to the west of its later position and at least part was leased from Christopher Maling Webster of Pallion Hall.[18]

20

14. Map of The River Wear mid 19th century, showing Doxford yard, Pallion Hall, and no Queen Alexandra Bridge. Author's collection and image.

In 1857 William Fordyce published 'A History of Durham'. He stated that:

> "From the entrance of the harbour up to Hylton Ferry, the banks of the Wear, on both sides, are crowded with shipbuilding yards and docks, presenting, in a most striking point of view, an exemplification of the enterprise and industry which have so effectively conduced to the prosperity of the port. Scarcely an opening on the shore of the river, or a nook or crevice in the limestone rocks which overhang it, can be found in which a ship of large or small dimensions is not in course of erection. Sunderland is emphatically the first shipbuilding port in the world."

William Doxford's yard at Pallion, therefore, joined many others on the river. Most quickly vanished, but this time William's enterprise succeeded. In the early years, according to Corder, he was financed by a William Briggs, whose name for a period was written on the yard gates.[19] William Briggs had a business at the Exchange on the High Street, as merchants, shipbuilders and ship brokers. The next door yard was T.R. Oswald & Co., also founded in the 1850's on the site of an earlier yard.[20]

The next generation

William Doxford now brought his sons into the business with him.

In 1858, as a teenager of seventeen, William Theodore joined his father at the new yard, in training to take over the management. The second son, Alfred, came into the business shortly after. Alfred's occupation at the 1861 census was given as a ship's carpenter, i.e. a shipwright. The youngest son, Charles David, entered the drawing office in 1873, also at seventeen. The third son, Robert Pile, trained and worked elsewhere, and did not join his brothers until 1878.

21

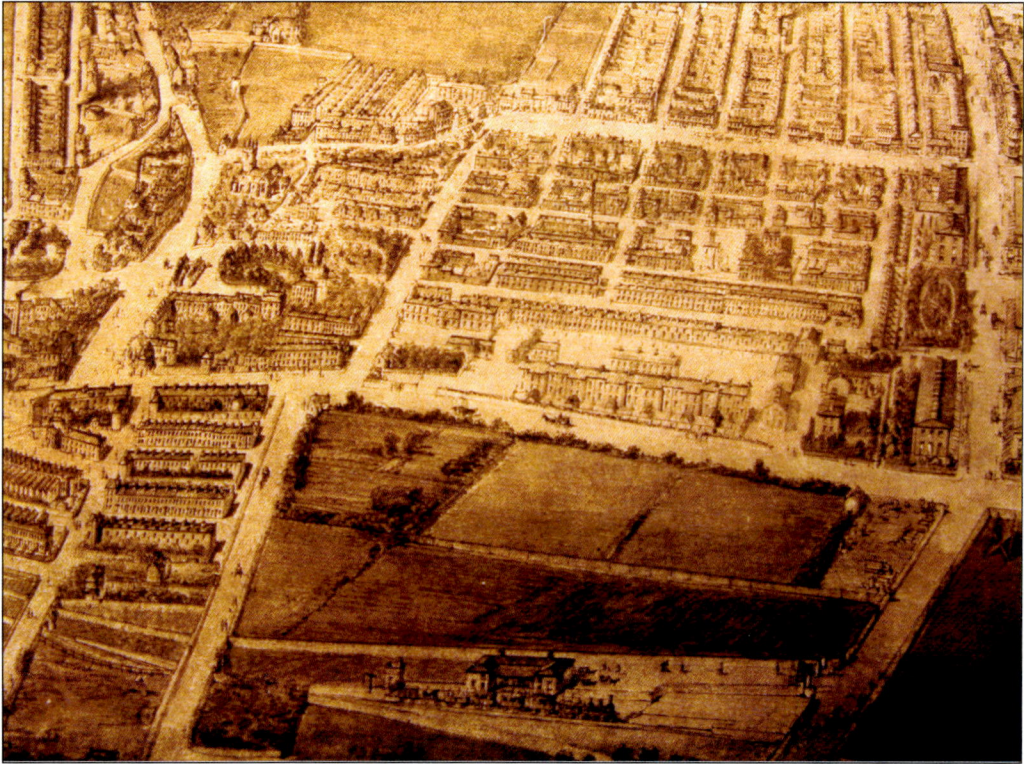

15. Aerial View of Bishopwearmouth in 1857, showing the open area laid out as Mowbray Park with the Winter Gardens, now part of Sunderland Museum. Courtesy of the Sunderland Antiquarian Society.

To be close to their new yard, William and Hannah Doxford left their terraced house in Howick Street, and moved across the river to a substantial property in New Pallion. This move raised William's social status. On 1 September 1860 their eldest daughter, Elizabeth Ann, married Joseph Spraggon. In the announcement of her marriage in the Newcastle Courant of 7 September, William styled himself 'Esquire'.

The 1861 census gives a vivid snapshot of the locality where the family lived. Their home was not only close to Pallion Hall, but also to the new railway station.[21] It was surrounded by terrace upon terrace of homes housing their workers, and those of the other Pallion yards.

In their home at Pallion that night were all their surviving children. These were Elizabeth Spraggon (27), Catherine (23), William Theodore (20), clerk, Alfred (18), ship carpenter, Mary (12), Robert Pile (9), Eveline (6) and Charles David (4). Despite ten family members, only one female house servant was at the premises with them. Theodore and Alfred had joined their father and the younger children were noted as scholars.

16. William Doxford as Senior Partner of William Doxford & Sons.

William Doxford was still building his ships in wood, but this was the beginning of iron shipbuilding on the Wear, with steam engines being installed alongside sail to power the vessels. Steam power was already used for static engines in the shipyards and was soon introduced for the locomotives that shunted goods around the yard. Though most breadwinners in the neighbourhood were shipwrights, block makers and sawyers, others were in new occupations as engine makers, boiler smiths and iron ship workers.

In 1861, of the forty six shipbuilding concerns on the river Wear, ten lay in Pallion.[22] W. Doxford, Pallion was employing twenty five men and twenty boys. Of his near contemporaries in age, Robert Thompson Junior, at Southwick, employed forty five men and thirty boys, but George Short, at Mowbray Quay, had only one man and twelve boys. From Parliamentary Returns studied by J. F. Clarke for a paper he wrote in 1980, the average number of men employed in a shipyard on the Wear that year was sixty four, so William was still a middle player.[23] Although Short and Thompson were the same age as William, the average age of shipbuilders on the Wear was surprisingly low. Boys joined a yard and from sixteen they started long

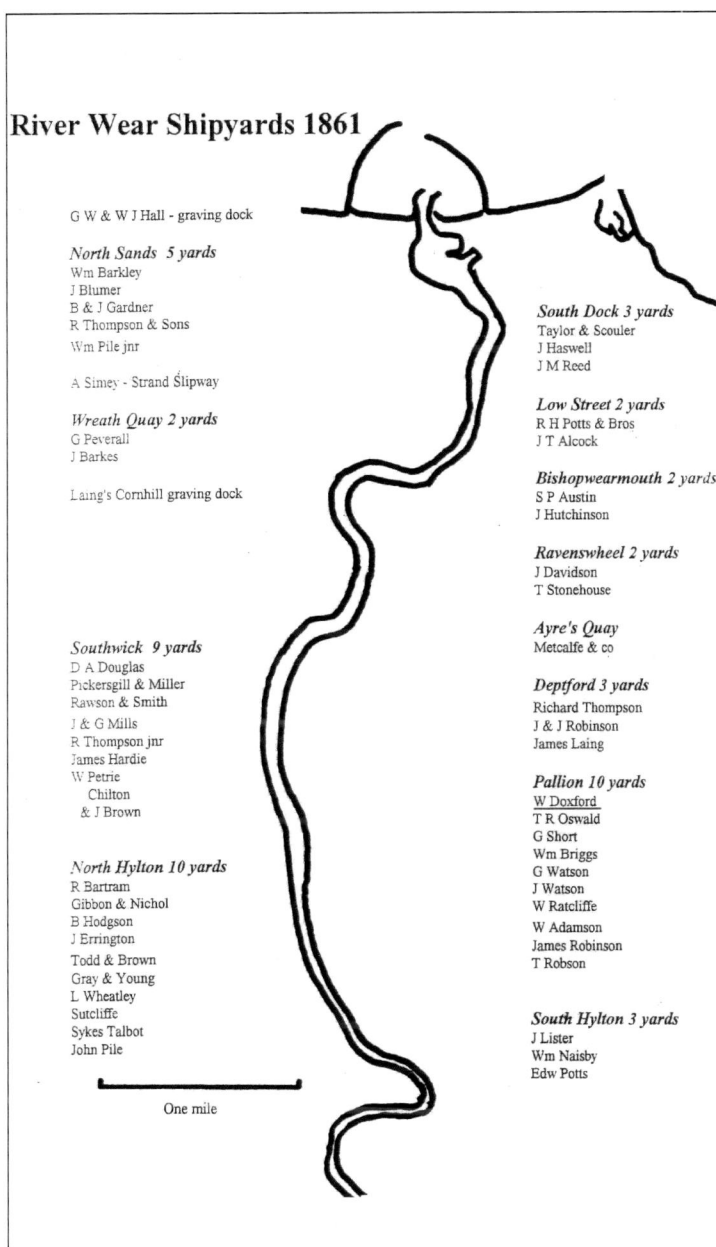

River Wear Shipyards 1861

G W & W J Hall - graving dock

North Sands 5 yards
Wm Barkley
J Blumer
B & J Gardner
R Thompson & Sons
Wm Pile jnr

A Simey - Strand Slipway

Wreath Quay 2 yards
G Peverall
J Barkes

Laing's Cornhill graving dock

Southwick 9 yards
D A Douglas
Pickersgill & Miller
Rawson & Smith
J & G Mills
R Thompson jnr
James Hardie
W Petrie
   Chilton
   & J Brown

North Hylton 10 yards
R Bartram
Gibbon & Nichol
B Hodgson
J Errington
Todd & Brown
Gray & Young
L Wheatley
Sutcliffe
Sykes Talbot
John Pile

One mile

South Dock 3 yards
Taylor & Scouler
J Haswell
J M Reed

Low Street 2 yards
R H Potts & Bros
J T Alcock

Bishopwearmouth 2 yards
S P Austin
J Hutchinson

Ravenswheel 2 yards
J Davidson
T Stonehouse

Ayre's Quay
Metcalfe & co

Deptford 3 yards
Richard Thompson
J & J Robinson
James Laing

Pallion 10 yards
W Doxford
T R Oswald
G Short
Wm Briggs
G Watson
J Watson
W Ratcliffe
W Adamson
James Robinson
T Robson

South Hylton 3 yards
J Lister
Wm Naisby
Edw Potts

17. The Shipyards on the River Wear in 1861. From Building Ships on the NE Coast, Part 1, p 92

apprenticeships. Having finally qualified as master, they preferred to work for themselves. They were highly skilled craftsmen who produced small wooden ships of a fairly low Lloyd's classification (i.e. ten years and below) to keep the price competitive. The majority sailed from north eastern ports such as the Tyne, but a significant proportion of the Wear output was registered by London owners.[24]

From 1857 to 1864, the yard made modest progress. Doxford launched just seventeen ships, though these were considerably larger than those built by Doxford and Crown at Southwick. His ships were wood and almost invariably square rigged. The first to be launched at Pallion was a barque called the Royal Bride, 526 grt, built for Ray & Sons of Portsmouth and registered on 15 April 1858. Although the Elizabeth Ray, also owned by Ray and Sons of London, was a small brig of only 160 grt, the others ranged from 259 to 898 grt. The average tonnage was 470.

Their ships were for general cargo use, but some also transported passengers. The Belgravia, a full rigged ship, 889 grt, was built in 1862, and owned by Joseph Somes & Sons, London. Belgravia's first two voyages were from London, via India to Auckland, New Zealand. According to the website on Crimean war veterans who travelled to Western Australia,[25] she then underwent repairs in 1863 and was copper bottomed. Her next three voyages were to Western Australia, carrying convicts.[26] On her fifth and final voyage she sailed from Portland, Dorset on 7 April 1866 carrying one of the last shipments of male convicts to Western Australia: the thirty fourth voyage out of thirty seven.[27]

The Belgravia arrived in Fremantle on 4 July 1866, carrying 106 passengers and 275 convicts, only two having died on route. Of the passengers, thirty were men who were pensioners from the Crimean War of 1854-56. For a free passage, these men guarded the convicts and were accompanied by their wives and families. Additionally, there were four warders, a clergyman, three women and two children. One of the warders was a medical doctor. His care of the convicts must have been a factor in their health and by that time there was virtually no use of the lash. The journey must have been harrowing, as the ship was only 169 ft by 34 ft 6 in. This was the last journey that the Belgravia undertook. She was wrecked on the Coromandel Coast on 2 October 1866 whilst returning to the United Kingdom.

An interesting anecdote of this journey is that one of the prisoners on board became the last survivor of eighty years of transportation to Australia.[28] He was Samuel Speed, born around 1843, who passed away in November 1938. He is reputed to have fallen on hard times in England, due to poor sight. He and a friend were so hungry that they set fire to a hayrick, hoping to be arrested and fed. They were prepared to be transported if that would achieve a better life. Speed served his time, gaining his certificate of freedom in 1871. He never reoffended in his long life so maybe the story is true. He eventually lost his sight completely and died in Clermont Old Men's home, Karrakata, his age being given as 95.

The changeover to iron

On 9 April 1863, William and Hannah's oldest son, Theodore, married Margaret Wilkinson. His marriage seems to have galvanised Theodore's ambitions for his father's business. Only two ships left Pallion in 1862, but six were built the following year. The sixth was the first Doxford ship to be built in iron. Their last fully wooden ship was launched in July 1864. This was the barque Hesperia, 448 grt, Lloyds no. 47271, owned by E. Jarvis, Salcombe. She was re-registered later as Dalhousie. The Hesperia was the last Doxford ship without a yard number.

Late in 1863, Theodore encouraged his father to turn to iron for all production. Iron ships had been built on the Tyne since the early 1840s, and by the mid 1850s comprised about 50% of the Tyne output, but in 1863 only three other yards on the Wear had taken the plunge. This decision proved a successful one, leading to a rapid increase in business. The size of a wooden ship was constrained because of the stresses on the framework and the difficulty of making strong joints. Additionally, timber frames were heavy and took up a lot of space, limiting the amount of cargo that could be carried. Iron ships could be constructed on a larger scale and capacity, and needed less maintenance. Doxford's early iron ships were powered by sail, though static steam driven engines were already operating in the works at Pallion. The output in 1864 was five ships with a total grt of 3,910. The four iron ships were: 993, 500, 699 and 1,270 grt respectively. Doxford were one of only seven out of fifty seven shipyards then open on the Wear to build five or more ships that year, but still stood well below J. L. Thompson and James Laing & Sons.[29] The crucial turning

18. The Antrim (C2), 1864, the second iron ship in the Doxford yard list. Lloyd's number 50277.
Note the steam powered tug behind her in the river.

25

point for Sunderland shipbuilders to embrace iron construction occurred in 1868. By 1872 production of iron ships leapt from c 40,000 tons to over 120,000 tons, whilst that of wooden ships dropped to less than 10,000 tons.

Using the new material led Doxford to begin a formal yard list. In the minutes of the Company, these are given the prefix C for Contract, so I will use this to denote the yard numbers. C1, for instance, was the iron barque, Golden Sunset, 628 grt, launched on 10 November 1863 and completed later that year for H.T. Wilson & Chambers, Liverpool. Only three of the first ten numbered ships were built for Sunderland shipowners, indicating that embracing iron meant that the yard could expand its customer base. C2 is shown on page 25. This was the ship rigged, Antrim, 993 grt, for Moore and Co. of Liverpool, launched on 7 March 1864. The photograph shows her passing beneath the Clifton Bridge at Bristol. In May and June two more iron ships were launched, but in the early hours of Saturday, 25 August, Doxford suffered a setback when a large fire broke out at about three o'clock. The night watchman quickly raised the alarm, but the blaze spread rapidly. Two fire engines attended the scene, and a floating barge was deployed to douse the flames with water from the river. Although they prevented the damage from spreading to the adjacent Oswald yard, they only brought the blaze under control the following morning. The events were described in great detail by the Newcastle Chronicle,[30] giving a picture of the layout of the yard at that period, and the materials used in fitting out a new ship.

> "The western portion of the yard is devoted to the building of ships on the stocks, whilst the east side was (sic) covered by a very extensive range of sheds and buildings, comprising blacksmiths, joiners, and blockmakers' shops, the block being continued by the extensive saw mills, extending down almost to the edge of the river. In the saw mills were two boilers and an engine driving two frame saws and three circular saws, besides planing and grooving machines, and in a shed adjoining were some valuable machines for iron work – machines for drilling, cutting and punching. In and about the joiners' shops was a large quantity of wood, one large teak balk,[31] and a great deal of mahogany and other wood wrought up into ceiling and fittings for one of the vessels in course of construction. Besides all this, there was a large and valuable collection of tools belonging to the workmen employed in the joiners and blockmakers' shops."

The damage was estimated at between £4,000-5,000, shared between William Doxford & Sons for his stock and the landowner, Christopher Webster, for the buildings. The article stated that both were fully insured and that Doxford used the Royal Insurance Company.

A further description of the yard comes from the rating valuation for the 'Township' of Bishopwearmouth of 1866, held at the Tyne and Wear Archives. William Doxford was assessed on his "Ship Building Yard, Workshops, Counting House, Warehouses, Saw Mill and Erections" at Pallion, which did not become a separate parish until two years later. The gross estimated rental was assessed as £265, and the rates payable were £221. For comparison, James Laing was assessed for two separate yards at Deptford. The first had a shipbuilding yard, graving dock, quays, workshops, warehouses, cranes and other plant, and the second, another shipbuilding yard, contained workshops, a draughting loft, counting house, stable cottage, land and machinery. Laing's combined rates were £1,338. Additionally, Laing was leasing saw and planing mills and a timber yard at Deptford for an estimated £184 jointly to Alfred Oswald and Frederick George Boyton. By 1882 Doxford surpassed Laings in both the number of ships launched and their gross tonnage and eventually survived the demise of the Laing enterprise.

A year later, in 1867, William Doxford appointed John Holey (1842-1933) as the secretary to the Partnership. Holey was born near Selby, in North Yorkshire and came to Sunderland as a young man. He married Mary Ann Cole in Sunderland in 1866. Holey served firstly the Partnership, secondly the Private and thirdly the Public Company, finally retiring in 1917 after 48 years' service. He and Mary Ann had six children. Two of their sons, John Thomas and Arthur, also joined the firm. John Thomas, a naval architect, served an astounding 61 years before retiring in 1944, aged 74. Arthur, who died in 1943, was the Company Accountant. John Walton Holey, Arthur's son, also served as Company Secretary, so the family's involvement with Doxford did not cease until 1973, 106 years later.

Another fire was reported at the yard four years later, on Saturday, 13 August 1868. A night-watchman had been told to apply the dampers to a number of furnaces, but to keep them alight over the weekend. A flame shot out the front of one of the furnaces, being unable to escape up the chimney, and caused the loss of a blacksmiths' shop. It was reported that:

> "Hundreds of workpeople were soon on the spot, but as it was Saturday night, a great portion of them were in a state of intoxication, and were comparatively useless. By the aid of two fire engines, which did not arrive until late, the neighbouring property was saved, and had not a dead calm prevailed, a large number of ships in course of erection must also have been burned down."[32]

Again, the damage of £1,000 was covered by insurance, but it was also reported that the yard would be closed for repairs and workmen laid off, as well as losing their tools. Nevertheless, production barely faltered.

Their first ship of over one thousand gross registered tonnage was launched on 15 November 1864. She was also their first single screw steam ship, SS Adalia (C4), 1,270 grt, eventually owned by Chapple and Dutton, London.[33] From the James Laing & Sons ledger, it seems that they were the original purchasers. Laings were diversifying into ship owning in addition to their shipbuilding concern.[34] They paid £17,550 for her on 21 January 1865, plus £1,400 for a spar deck. Laings then sold 3/8 to Gourlay Brothers, Dundee for £7,106, 2/8 to Christopher Webster (Pallion Hall) for £4,738 and 3/8 to Chapple for £9,187, making a profit of £1,736. No doubt this was quite a typical on-sale at the time.

SS Adalia carried passengers as well as cargo and was also powered by sails. She had a short life. She sailed from Plymouth on 5 June 1872,[35] en route to Quebec, and was wrecked on St. Paul's Island, Nova Scotia, at the entrance of the St. Lawrence and known as 'The Graveyard of the Gulf'. The passengers and crew were rescued by the SS Pictou, a Canadian vessel and arrived at Quebec on 4 July. This very dramatic depiction of the rescue was sketched by an Officer on the Pictou.[36]

The output in 1864 reached 3,400 grt, from four ships. Five were registered in 1865, but then production quickened. The average registered tonnage between 1866 and 1869 (25 ships) was 521.5. However, the individual tonnage remained varied, and even in 1866 half were below 250 grt. The smallest, at 239 grt, was the brig Alice Scott (C16), 1866, owned by D. Cooper Scott, London. She was one of four similar sized iron ships built for the same owner, the other three being brigantines. The

19. The wreck of SS Adalia (C4) off St. Paul's Island 1872. First Doxford ship of 1,000 tons.
Courtesy of the Nova Scotia Archives.

largest ship was built in 1868. This was the barque, Gloria (C26), 729 grt, an iron ship owned by the Spanish group, Olana, Larrinaga & Co., Liverpool.

In 1869 Doxford built their first two ships for a foreign registered owner. These were the Catalina (C27), 500 grt, an iron barque, and the Arina (C30), 249 grt, an iron single screw ship, both for Ylurriaga, Bilbao.

Two further Doxford marriages took place during the 1860s. Alfred married Deborah Morris in the spring of 1865 and Catherine Hannah married Harrison Crosby (or Crosbie), a shipping agent, on 24 April 1869. The Crosbys lived at 11 Cresswell Street, Bishopwearmouth. Catherine was widowed in 1884, but remained in Cresswell Street for the rest of her life. Their son, William Harrison Crosby (1879-1955), became a naval architect and ship's draughtsman. The 1911 census suggests that he may have joined the family shipyard, but he and his wife later moved to Knowle Bawdrip, near Bridgewater in Somerset.

Before the end of the decade William and Hannah Doxford left Pallion and moved back to the centre of Bishopwearmouth. The new suburb of Ashbrooke was developed to the south of Fawcett Street in the 1850s, and had doubled in size by 1865. This had become a fashionable area, with new homes, and local business owners moved away from their yards and warehouses. At the 1871 census their address was given as 1 Kensington Esplanade. This may have been the first house that they owned outright. It lay close to Mowbray Park, just off the Ryhope Road. With William and Hannah were their younger sons, Robert Pile, (19) and Charles

20. & 21. 1 The Esplanade, Bishopwearmouth, the substantial home of William and Hannah Doxford during the 1860's. Insert taken 24 April 1871, Courtesy of the Sunderland Antiquarian Society. In colour, Author's photograph September 2018

David, (14). Their two younger daughters, Mary (21) and Eveline (16), and Catherine Crosby were also with them that night. The shipyard had grown substantially in the past ten years and William was now recorded as employing 340 men and 60 boys, a remarkable achievement, but still well surpassed by J. L. Thompson, whose yard employed 624 men and 20 boys. The family still had only two maids living with them. Neither were born locally. Mary Stockdale (55) came from Lincolnshire and was probably their cook. Ann Allison (22), the housemaid, was from Stockton. The 1871 Christie's Directory shows W. Doxford & Sons, iron shipbuilders, Pallion, with William living at 1 The Esplanade and William Theodore at 10 Esplanade West, across the road from this photograph.

The new yard

The move to iron not only meant training the workforce in different skills, but brought the need for a larger yard into sharp focus. The Suez Canal opened in 1869, so journey times to the East Indies were greatly reduced and trade increased. This led to new opportunities for shipbuilders and shipowners. Ships again began to grow in size and also to change in shape to accommodate passage through the canal. In 1870 William, Theodore and Alfred gave up the first yard and moved the business to a larger site to the east of the village of Pallion. The new site was made up of several redundant shipbuilding yards and rubbish tips. Behind these was a deep limestone quarry. The land was levelled and a yard with five berths was laid out. This was later known as the West Yard, as further adjacent land was acquired to the east. By 1902 the site covered 36 acres (14.5 hectares). Their ships were now regularly over a thousand gross registered tonnage, but iron hulls and steam engines did not necessarily ensure a safe passage on every journey. SS Consort (C39), 1,074 grt, was registered by W. Swainston & Sons, Newcastle, on 23 January 1871. She was stranded near Trondheim, Norway on 20 February.[37] Luckily she was salvaged and continued in service until at least 1884.[38] SS Silkstone (C34), built for Pope and Pearson, Hull sank on 8 August 1882 after a collision in Waterford Harbour with the SS Reginald. M. J. Cox, Waterford, had bought her the year before.[39]

In 1872 Doxford received four Admiralty orders: three gunboats and a corvette. The first was, HMS Cygnet (C60), launched on 30 May 1874 and commissioned in 1875. She was a Forester Class composite gunboat of 455 tons displacement, with auxiliary steam power. As one of five gunboats in a fleet of fifteen naval vessels, HMS Cygnet assisted at the bombardment of Alexandria on 11 July 1882, in response to the uprising under Urabi Pasha.[40] She was followed by HMS Express (C61), (commissioned 1875, sold in 1889), HMS Contest (C62), (1875 to 1889), and HMS Magicienne(1875), later Opal (C63), an Emerald Class Corvette of 2120 tons displacement, whose sleek lines and steam funnel are shown here. HMS Opal's first armament was 14 muzzle-loading 64-pounder rifled guns, but after five years on the Pacific Station she was re-rigged as a barque, and her armament was reduced by two. She was broken up in 1892 at Sheerness.

22. HMS Opal, formerly Magicienne. (C63) Corvette built for the Admiralty in 1875. This image is post 1880, as she is rigged as barque. From Shipping World. 9 September 1936

The Admiralty orders gave the firm a heightened reputation and ensured that the yard went from strength to strength. The orders for their commercial ships came mainly from Liverpool, Newport, Caernarvon and London, though others were commissioned from further afield, including Antwerp and Bilbao. The enlarged yard launched eighty ships during the 1870s. The tonnage continued to grow; only the Rosamond (C112), built in 1879 for R. Thomson, London, was registered below 500 grt. Most were between 1,000 and 2,500 grt. The largest was SS Victoria (C72), 2909 grt, launched on 10 October 1875 for Olano, Larrinaga & Co., Bilbao.

William Doxford & Sons had no predominant buyer but, by 1877, they were one of the leading shipyards on the River Wear, rivalled only by James Laing & Sons, Short Brothers and Robert Thompson. William's grand-children married into all three of these families.

23. SS Victoria (C72) Iron, Full rigged. 1875

The marine engineering department 1878

The firm became marine engine builders the following year. From the 1850s three primarily marine engineering firms had been established on the river Wear. These were John Dickinson & Sons, Monkwearmouth (1852), George Clark's Southwick Engine Works (1848) and the Sunderland Engine Works of the North East Marine

Engineering Co. (1866), at South Dock (NEM). On embracing steam power, Doxford purchased their engines and boilers from Clark or NEM. Two early ships Phoenix (C33) and Silkstone (C34), built in 1869 for Pile & Co., Sunderland, had simple engines, but after this all engines were compound. This involved the steam from the boiler passing through a high pressure cylinder followed by a low pressure cylinder to extract the maximum power from the steam. Robert Pile Doxford, aged 27, now joined his father and brothers in the business to found a marine engineering department. Robert had been working at NEM under its general manager, William Allan, who founded the Scotia Engine Works in 1888.[41] It was a compelling decision

24. The Doxford Compound engine of 1879, fitted to the SS. Grecian (C116) The man standing beside the engine demonstrates its great size.

to bring this in hand - a ship's machinery cost 30% of the total. This basic design of compound engine with one high pressure and one low pressure cylinder was used by Doxford until the mid-1880s, afterwhich Robert oversaw the development of triple expansion reciprocating steam engines.

The first ship fitted with a Doxford steam engine came into service in 1879, within a year of Robert joining his father and brothers. This was installed into the Alava (C110), 2,244 grt of 250 nominal horsepower (nhp). (Nominal hp was calculated from a formula that bore little relationship to the actual power, which around this time was four to five times greater.) She was launched on 9 January 1879, and registered to Olano Larrinaga & Co., Bilbao, who had purchased earlier ships from Doxford. The illustration is of the engine fitted to SS Grecian (C116) later that year, of 400 nhp.[42]

Doxford's relative position to its rivals on the Wear

The Newcastle Chronicle of 27 December 1880 published a chart giving a gross registered tonnage output of 116,227 from the thirteen shipyards then operating on the river. Doxford, in fourth position, produced 16,132 grt,[43] only 1,748 beneath the leader, J. L. Thompson at 17,880. Bartram Haswell & Co. and Robert Thompson followed at 10,473 and 10,471 respectively. Two yards produced less than 2,000 grt. George Almond, at Sunderland College of Education, included these figures in his thesis and analysed local information further. He found that from 1853 to 1880 the average tonnage per ship more than doubled, from 500 to 1,000 grt, but that the number of ships built halved, from just over 150 to 75 per year. Doxford built seven ships in 1880, five steam powered, and two barques, with an average 2,304 grt, so their ships were well above the mean. In fact, the J. L. Thompson output was eleven ships, all steam powered, but only two of these were over 2,000 grt, their average being 1,642 grt.

25. SS Catterthun, (C125), 1881, fitted with a 250 hp twin cylinder engine powered by two coal-fired boilers. Extracted from the Doxford archives in 1976 by George Almond.

The Catterthun (C125) was launched in April 1881, for the Eastern and Australasian Steamship Company. She was powered by a 250 bhp 2 cylinder Doxford engine powered by two coal fired boilers. She carried cargoes of gold from Australia to China, returning with tea, with a mainly Chinese crew, though others were freed East African slaves. She also accommodated about forty passengers. On the night of 8 August 1895 she foundered during a storm off Seal Rocks, between Sydney and Brisbane, with the loss of fifty five passengers and crew, though twenty eight managed to survive by launching two of the lifeboats. For obvious reasons, a salvage operation was rapidly mounted, but 1,000 of the 8,000 gold coins on board were never traced, the suggestion being that they had been withheld by the divers. Further unsuccessful attempts were made in the mid twentieth century to find the coins, and the wreck site, at sixty metres, is a popular site for recreational divers.

William Doxford in retirement

Towards the end of the 1870s, William (71) and Hannah moved into Grindon Lodge, just off the road from Sunderland to Chester-le-Street. The house was on the boundary of two new parishes, South Hylton and Silksworth, but stood in Silksworth. It was an old manor house, standing in its own small park. Those at Grindon at the 1881 census were William and Hannah, Charles David, 24, and Eveline, 26 (incorrectly recorded as Caroline), both still unmarried. Their three servants: a cook, waiting maid and housemaid, had all been born in Co. Durham. William was probably now in semi or full retirement. He died at Grindon on 26 April 1882, and was buried in Bishowearmouth cemetery. William Doxford did not leave a will, so the administration of his personal estate was granted to Theodore on 22 June. This was originally valued at £8,738 5s 8d, but was re-sworn as £12,174 7s 7d in October.

26. William Doxford in retirement. Courtesy of William Warren Davis.

William Doxford had been a skilled craftsman and a man of strong personal drive and ambition, both for himself and for his family. Although a cautious man, he had embraced change as iron replaced wood in navigation and had thus developed and enlarged his business. Working with his four sons, he brought his shipbuilding concern to prominence by introducing a marine engineering shop to the shipyard. On a personal level, William and Hannah remained within the close community of shipbuilders, professional people and business owners of Sunderland. All their children married within that society, but William had risen from fairly humble beginnings to be a respected leader in the new metropolis. He left a thriving shipbuilding business that met the challenges at the end of the 19th century.

Hannah Doxford moved to 1 Grange Crescent. Her youngest daughter, Eveline Ritson, and her family, were there with her at the 1891 census. She died at Grange Crescent on 7 March 1895, aged 80, and was buried with her husband in Bishopwearmouth Cemetery.

Chapter Three

1882-1900 Three Doxford brothers develop Turret Ships

Alfred Doxford, the second son, left the partnership on 30 June 1882, three months after William's death. The announcement in the Sunderland Daily Echo of 24 August 1882 described the business as 'Shipbuilders, Ship Repairers, and Marine Engineers', and stated that the partnership had been dissolved by mutual consent.

Of the three remaining brothers, William Theodore became the lead, Robert Pile was the Managing Director of the marine engineering department and Charles David of the shipyard. Theodore, as senior partner, was the driving force in the partnership's development as commercial shipbuilders. The business was now one of the leading yards of Sunderland. On 27 December 1882 the Northern Echo of Darlington published a table of ship launches on the Wear. Compared with the figures of 1880 given in Chapter Two, this shows that output on the river had nearly doubled in the previous two years. The four leading yards had been particularly successful. Doxford was still in fourth position, from a cohort of sixteen, but had produced twice the number of ships as in 1880. Their average tonnage had, however, dropped.

A YEAR'S SHIPBUILDING ON THE WEAR (1882)

Name of firm	No of ships	H.P. (nhp)[1]	Grt	Average grt
J. L.Thompson & Sons	13	2,625	27,811	2,145
Short Brothers	15	2,430	26,385	1,779
James Laing & Sons	9	2,590	23,004	2,556
William Doxford & Sons	14	1,795	22,231	1,587
Robert Thompson & Sons	11	1,849	19,947	2,216
Sunderland Shipbuilding Co.	7	1,820	17,419	2,488
John Blumer & Sons	8	1,230	14,660	1,833
Bartram, Haswell & Co	6	1,260	12,195	2,033
Osbourne, Graham & Co,	7	890	11,882	1,626
W. Pickersgill & Sons	6	760	8,868	1,477
Strand Slipway	8	540	7,647	956
S. P. Austin & Sons	5	570	5,125	1,105
Kish, Boolds & Co.	4	500	5,150	2,288
North of England Shipbuilding Co.	2	430	4,165	2,083
Baxter & Co.	5	420	3,018	604
Priestman & Co.	3	318	2,084	695
Totals	123	20,027	212,491	1,717

In 1883 the output on the Wear was 212,313 grt, and this figure was not matched until the end of the decade. The total combined output between 1885 and 1887 was 10,000 less than this figure. By 1884 another depression in trade was in place. Despite this, Doxford increased production that year, to 19,868 up from 14,083 grt in 1883, though the number of ships that left the yard was nine in both years. Theirs was the only Wear yard to increase its output, though most of the orders would have been received before the freight market slump. Doxford built only four ships in 1885, and 7,000 men were out of work in Sunderland.[2] At this time of pressure, shipbuilders and marine engineering firms on the Tyne, Wear and Tees came together to form the North East Coast Institution of Engineers and Shipbuilders. The Doxford brothers joined the new institution, and William Theodore Doxford became its second President. Meetings were held regularly in Sunderland. The Institution established scholarships to enable talented young men to attend university and gain a degree in naval architecture or marine engineering.

Doxford were still relatively small in terms of employment. The wage books for staff and skilled men survive at the Tyne and Wear Archives from the 1880s right up to the late 1930s. In 1882 the weekly wage bill was £32 4s 9d. Doxford employed sixteen 'officials', whose total of £28 14s 0d gives an average of £1 15s 11d. The four draughtsmen were paid a total of £5 10s 9d per week, i.e. an average wage of just over £1 2s. The highest man received £3 15s, whilst the apprentice's pay packet contained only four shillings. An extra staff member and a further draughtsman were recruited the following year, bringing the total weekly remuneration to £38 11s 4d, implying that the directors were increasing the skill levels of their workforce.

As the 1880s began, Doxford were not in the forefront of changing construction from iron to steel. Up to 1880, this was considerably more expensive than iron, £25 per ton as opposed to £9, and steel could not be produced locally. However, as early as 1882, the cost dropped to £13 per ton as against £7 10s for iron, and Doxford built their first ship in steel that year. This was Kirkmichael (C142), 933 grt, for the aptly named J. Steel & Sons, Liverpool. The steel for this ship was manufactured by Beardmore of Glasgow. However, due to the downturn in trade, steel remained uneconomical for general tramp steamers and ships for the next five years, during which Doxford built only six steel ships from a total output of twenty five. In fact, in 1885 they built only four small ships, and these were all powered by sail. The four masted ship pictured here was clad in iron. The Kate Thomas (C163), was launched on 15 June 1885 and delivered later that year to W. Thomas & Co., Liverpool. She was in service until 4 April 1910, when she sank after a collision twenty two nautical miles north of the Pendeen Lighthouse, off Landsend. The tragedy was that the steamer that sank her, the India, had no lookout so remained unaware of the collision and continued her voyage. The Kate Thomas sank within eight minutes, resulting in the loss of virtually all the nineteen on board, including wives of both the captain and the chief officer. The only survivor was a young apprentice, who was picked up by a passing tug.

27. The Kate Thomas (C163), full rigged ship, 1885. The fifth last ship powered only by sail to be built at Pallion.

The recession deepened even further in 1886, causing immense distress amongst Sunderland's residents. Many were laid off, though the foremen were retained. Fortunately, this particular slow down eased fairly quickly, and all production at Doxford went over to steel in 1887. The photograph below was taken on 18 March 1889 and shows nineteen foremen, all who worked in the shipyard, rather than the engine works.

28. Doxford foremen of the Shipyard Department, photographed in 1889.

Courtesy of the Sunderland Antiquarian Society.

By 1888, all the shipyards on the Wear were building only in steel and, in 1889, William Beardmore, who had supplied the steel for the Kirkmichael, opened a steelworks at Castletown, outside Sunderland.

Despite such difficult trading conditions, seventy five ships built by Doxford were completed during the 1880s, though some were delayed until the end of the decade by their purchasers. This number was only slightly lower than in the 1870s and, as the ships were larger, output actually expanded. In addition, the marine engineering division was supplying other shipyards. Their early engines were generally compound reciprocating marine steam engines. Such engines used two or more

29. SS Warrego (C147),1884, lying in the Brisbane River, with government buildings behind her. She carried both cargo and passengers. Public Domain

stages of steam expansion. By introducing further cylinders, and recycling the steam, less coal (later oil) was needed. The exhaust steam passed from the first high pressure cylinder to one or more larger, low pressure cylinders, thus making the engine more powerful and efficient. The steam was generated by a Scotch fire tube boiler, which consisted of a squat horizontal cylinder, with one or more cylindrical furnaces in the lower part of the shell and numerous small-diameter fire-tubes, set in water, above these. After the gases and smoke from the furnace passed to the back of the boiler, they returned through the small tubes and up and out of the funnel. Because the gases returned on themselves, the boilers were halved in length compared to earlier versions, and were more suitable for marine use. The output was still constrained by the boilers, though, until their further development meant that they could achieve 60lb per square inch, reducing coal consumption to 2½ lb per horsepower per hour.[3] Once triple expansion engines were the norm, sailing ships could no longer compete, especially after coal bunkering depots developed along the shipping routes. By 1892, the engine output on the Wear exceeded 100,000 ihp (indicated horse power) for the first time and, according to J. F. Clarke, by 1897 the engine output from Doxford challenged that of the dedicated marine engineers, reaching 28% of those built in Sunderland, and surpassing that of George Clark & Sons.[4]

 At that period most Australian ships were built in the British Isles. SS Warrego (C147), 1,552 grt, a steel steamship registered in 1883 to the Queensland Steam Ship Co., London, took passengers and freight up and down the Australian coast. She had a thirty year career until, in 1912, she was laid up and sold to the Australian Navy, for use as a store ship. In October 1913, she was towed to lie off a Darwin

38

beach, but, despite having 600 tons on coal on board, a cyclone that hit the coast in 1919 left her high and dry near the Darwin wharf. As if that wasn't enough, she was subjected to a Japanese bombing raid in 1942. In 1960, the wreck still lay on the beach, but the land was required for a power station. The ship's final remains were covered over, and lie hidden there still.[5]

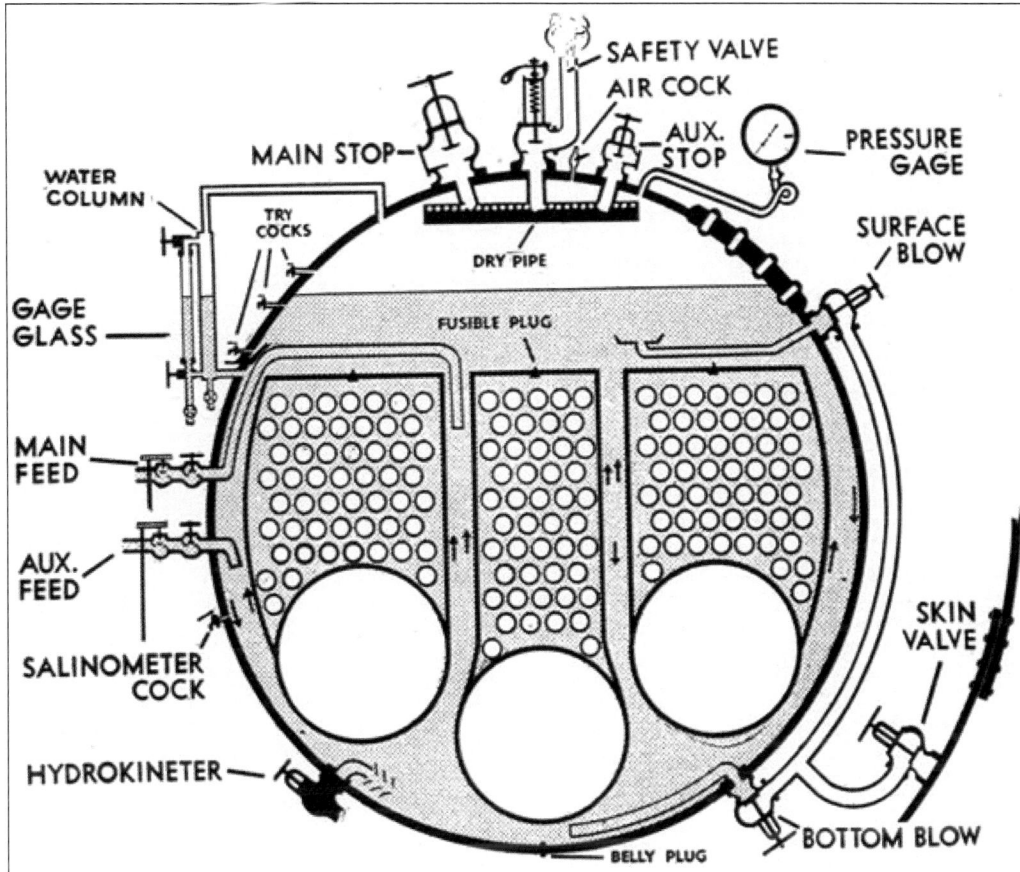

30. Plan of a typical Scotch Boiler.

In their flexibility over shipbuilding, in 1887 Doxford built two very dissimilar ships. The first was the huge cargo and passenger ship, SS Golconda (C166), (firstly named Nulli Secunda), 6,037 grt, which was owned by the British India Steam Navigation Company. She had a triple expansion engine, two funnels, a single screw and four masts. In 1915 she carried six hundred German civilian internees from a camp in Ahmednagar to London, after which they were repatriated via the neutral Netherlands, followed by a further five hundred the following year. This kindness was not rewarded, as the ship was mined in the North Sea on 3 June 1916, off the coast of Suffolk, with the loss of nineteen lives.

The second ship was a single-screw torpedo boat, (C169), built on a speculative basis after encouragement from the Admiralty. This was a ship of only 85 tons displacement. She made 21 knots on trial, an amazing speed for the time. During this she was powered by a coal-burning locomotive boiler, but shortly afterwards

she converted to oil-burning. Trials on this new fuel were successful. However, she was ahead of her time, and the Admiralty declined to take her. She was sold privately, taken to Nicaragua and renamed the El Rayo.

32. The experimental torpedo boat (C169) 1887, ordered by the Admiralty. Later renamed El Rayo.
© Sunderland Museum and Art Gallery.

The size of the Golconda was exceptional. Though, by the late 1880s, the majority of Doxford ships were over 2,000 grt, only a few topped 3,000. One was the Mamari (C186), 3,583 grt, one of the first refrigerated cargo ships. She was delivered to Shaw, Savill & Albion Co. Ltd., Sunderland in June 1889.[6] Her contract price was £44,000, a considerable sum, calculated by the materials, the build costs and a fee to the builder. The engine and auxiliary machinery were a significant portion of this cost, some 25-30%.

Another innovative ship was the Fee Cheu (C171), 1,034 grt, built for J. Whittal, London in 1887. She was designed for laying and repairing submarine telegraph cables between Formosa (now Taiwan) and mainland China. She also carried six guns, so could be used as a naval vessel. She had a set of triple expansion engines generating 1,100 nhp, and could achieve 13 knots.[7]

In January 1890, SS Maori King (C192), 3,807 grt, was completed for W. Ross & Co., London. This ship had an unfortunate early history and a sad end. According to the official report, she approached the port of Brisbane on the night of 7 December 1890. The pilot, Aspland, boarded the vessel and a tug was attached. However, the Maori King's engines ceased to engage. She had difficulty rounding Harris Point and struck rocks at Barker's Quarry. Luckily, by re-engaging her engines, she got off the rocks, and with some difficulty entered port. It is clear that such large vessels needed careful handling when approaching harbour. The Maori King was in service for nearly twenty years, but was lost on 17 September 1909. She was on the coastal route from the northern port of Chingwantao (now Qinhuangdao) to Hong Kong with a cargo of coal, when she struck rocks and ran aground near Ningpo (now Ningbo).[8]

The last ships built by Doxford as a partnership were launched in 1890. One was the Réaumur (C196), just 1,540 grt, for D'Orbigny & Faustin Fils, La Rochelle. The Réaumur, as reported in the Marine Engineer of 1 June 1890, was an A1 Class steel ship, length 250 ft, breadth 35 ft, depth 18 ft, 6 in. She had a cellular double bottom both fore and aft. Her engines were triple-expansion, three cranks, from the Doxford engine shop. The cylinders were supplied with high pressure steam from oversized boilers. Her steering gear was built by Bow McLachlan of Paisley and the propellers by Crawford Bros. of Monkwearmouth. Winches were by Welford Bros of Pallion. These names show the strength and number of subsidiary trades on the Wear. Nearly all the industrial work in Sunderland was generated by the shipbuilding or coal industry. Réaumur's sister ship, Valin (C198), 1,549 grt, was launched at about the same time.

The Private Limited Company

Throughout the 19th century, partnerships in all types of enterprises converted to limited companies. A series of Acts passed through Parliament, introducing the principle of limited liability, beginning with the Joint Stock Companies Act of 1844. This was replaced by further Acts in 1856 and 1862, which allowed seven or more members to form a registered joint stock company, with liability limited to each shareholding and a minimum capital. Several amendments to the 1856 Act were consolidated as the 1862 Companies Act, the first company law statute to take that title. The 1862 Act dealt with accounts and disclosure, financial statements on statutory forms audited by the Board of Trade, rights of shareholders over meetings and inspections and procedures for appointing directors. It allowed partnerships to enlarge by offering shares to outsiders, either privately or publicly, thus bringing extra capital into an enterprise, but the Act still restricted the partners to twenty.

On 1 January 1891, the Doxford brothers created a Private Limited Company under the name William Doxford & Sons Ltd.[9] This acquired the Partnership of iron shipbuilders and marine engineers, with a capital of £200,000, as 20,000 shares at £10 each, of which 17,300 shares were allotted to the new Directors, Theodore,

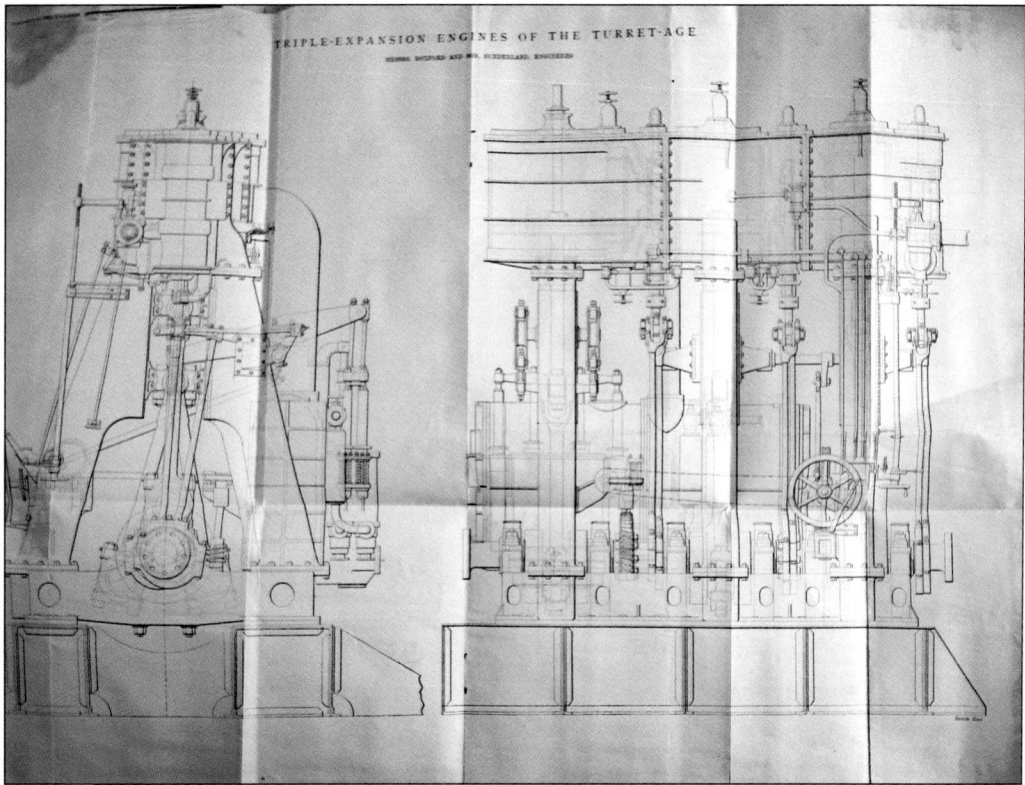

33. Plan for the Triple Expansion engine that powered Doxford ships from the 1880's to 1921. This one was installed in SS Turret Age, 1894. Published in The Engineer of 4 May 1894.

Robert and Charles Doxford, to their wives and to Theodore's son, Albert Ernest. Ernest Doxford (b. 1867) had joined the partnership in 1890, but was not yet a Director. Theodore Doxford was elected its Managing Director at the first Directors' Meeting held on 19 January 1891. A. O. Hedley, Theodore's son-in-law, was appointed the Company Solicitor. The National Provincial Bank became the Company's bank in September. A local accountant, Henry Rawlings, was the auditor and John Holey was appointed Company Secretary at the First General Meeting, held the following day. His salary was £350 per annum. The Directors' salaries were set at £2,000 for Theodore and £1,500 each for his two brothers.

The shares were distributed as follows within the Doxford family:[10]

Name	Share nos.	Shares
William Theodore (Cert. no.1)	1-6,500	6,500
Robert Pile (no. 2)	6,501-11,500	5,000
Charles David (no. 3)	11,501-16,500	5,000
Albert Ernest (no. 4)	16,501-17,000	500
Margaret, wife of Theodore (no. 5)	17,001-17,100	100
Ada, wife of Robert (no. 6)	17,101-17,200	100
Laura, wife of Charles (no. 7)	17,201-17,300	100

n.b. Certificate no. 4: was cancelled in May 1893 and reissued as No. 8: 300 shares 16,701-17,000 in the names of Charles Doxford and Octavius Hedley, and no. 9: 200 shares, nos. 16,501-16,700 in the name of Ernest Doxford.[11] The three Directors agreed to create seventy five £1,000 debentures at 4½% to raise some working capital. The first thirty nine were acquired by Messrs. William John Dundas and George Dalziel, solicitors, and Spencer Campbell Thompson, an insurance actuary, all of Edinburgh. Shortly afterwards, the three men took a further sixteen of these debentures, leaving twenty unallocated.

The Pallion site now covered 52 acres (c. 21 hectares) and had a 1,500 foot (457 metre) frontage along the River Wear. The shipyard and engine works, owned as freehold, were conveyed from the Partnership to the Limited Company for £80,793, the brass foundry for £9,645 and the perpetual and ground rents on land at adjacent Deptford for £150, making a total of £90,588.

The new Company was immediately in dispute with W. H. Tyzer, of Tyzer & Co., London, who refused to agree that he had a contract with the new entity for two ships, C209 and C210. This affected the handover of, SS Hawkes Bay (C201), 4,583 grt, a refrigerated cargo vessel, ready for delivery. This ship was, with difficulty, handed over on 21 January for dry docking, but the sea trial was delayed until mid-February, due to the Tyzer's intransigence. She had a triple expansion engine, with a single screw. Her dimensions were: length 364 ft, breadth 48 ft and depth of hold 32 ft 6in. Her hull had an overlapping plate system. Although this meant she had a less smooth side, it suited their shipyard production better and gave greater strength to the hull. She could achieve an average 10 knots. Coal consumption was 30-32 tons per day. On her maiden voyage she took on a cargo at Antwerp for New Zealand ports, arriving in May 1891. The Southland Times, Invercargill, South Island of 16 June 1891, praised her lines and accommodation, and said that she was the largest ship to enter Bluff Harbour. The Hawkes Bay was built for the frozen meat trade, and the first and second holds were specially insulated for this, with the refrigeration provided by Hall's. The insulated space held 65,000 mutton carcases. Additionally, electric light was installed in the vessel, principally to facilitate cargo discharge. She still had sails, though, and was schooner rigged.[12] Such a large cargo needed fast loading and unloading. One of Doxford's innovations was the facilitation of discharge. There were winches at every hatch, and Doxford patented their derricks. However, this was the last ship they built for this company. Mr. Tyzer continued in dispute with Doxford, as he alleged that the refrigeration units were faulty. The original quotation had included £62,500 for the two outstanding ships. After lengthy arguments, W. H. Tyzer agreed to pay £3,000 in compensation, and C209 and C210 were eventually built as SS Dominion for the Dominion Shipbuilding Co., Liverpool and SS Darwin for H.W.H. Stevens, Melbourne, but not until the end of 1891, and at a considerably reduced price.

The first ship produced by the Private Company was launched on 9 February 1891. This was the Honresfield (C202), a steel barque, 3,025 grt, and completed that month for J. Joyce, Liverpool. 1891 also saw the first ships built by Doxford for Cayzer, Irvine & Co., Glasgow, founded as C.W. Cayzer & Co. in 1877 by Sir Charles Cayzer (1843-1916). They were run under Clan Line Steamers Ltd., and all ships had this prefix. The vessels were the SS Clan MacNeil (C203), Clan MacLeod (C204) and Clan MacIntyre (C205), all 2,512 grt. This company became one of Doxford's major customers, especially once turret ships were an accepted shape. (See below, this Chapter) From the Board of Directors' minutes of 13 October 1891, the approximate cost of the Clan MacNeil was £47,000. The agreements for payment on ships under construction at the time were quite complicated, and designed to keep income flowing into the shipbuilder's accounts. During the recession of the 1920s, shipowners asked to pay cash on delivery, causing almost unresolvable problems. On a contract agreed at £39,000, for instance, payments were normally made as follows:

On signing of contract	£1,000
When keel is laid	£1,000
When framed	£7,000
When plated	£10,000
When launched	£10,000
When completed	£10,000
	£39,000

As reported at the second General Meeting, during its first year of trading the Limited Company incurred a loss of £16,828 15s 2d. This was in part due to the dispute with W. H. Tyzer, but losses on the steamers and sailing barques built at Pallion that year amounted to an astounding £23,318 10s 11d, whilst salaries, interest and depreciation amounted to a further £9,529 8s 9d. Some profit, fortunately, had been made on new vessels, repairs and departmental accounts, alleviating this.

Turret ships

In the second half of the 19th century numerous new designs of ship were tried out to improve efficiency and economy and to facilitate the loading and discharging of cargos. The regulations first introduced in the Merchant Shipping Act of 1873 (known as the Plimsoll Act), but amended in the Merchant Shipping Load Line Act in 1890, laid down official rules for freeboard tables and calculations. The regulations became necessary because many ships had been lost through overloading. Shipbuilders sought the ideal combination of deadweight, capacity, stability, strength and speed, by rearranging the number and layout of decks and superstructures. Theodore Doxford was approached with an opportunity to improve the design of their ships. An innovative shape developed by an American was altered with great success by Doxford. The following description of the development of turret ships is adapted from 'The Doxford Turret Ships' written by Leonard Gray and John Lingwood in 1975.

In 1891, the Charles W. Wetmore, built by Captain Alexander MacDougall of Duluth, Minnesota, docked at Liverpool.[13] She was in service on the Great Lakes. Her principal 'whale back design' was a cigar shaped ship with a cambered upper deck, on which stood vertical steel cylinders, which MacDougall had named 'turrets'. These turrets supported a walkway, as seas could break over the deck.

34. The American whaleback Charles W. Wetmore, that stimulated Doxford to develop the turret ship design. Note the walkway on top of the deck with its open turrets. Public Domain.

The Charles W. Wetmore attracted numerous visitors, its owners charging them one shilling to board. A shipping manager, William Johnston of Liverpool, asked C.A. Lichtenberg, a local agent, to approach Theodore over a potential order for a ship based on the Wetmore, but with modifications to make it suitable for use as a collier as well as holding general cargo. Theodore Doxford had kept small notebooks since 1864. In these he recorded details of approaches and quotations for ships. On page 23 of his second volume, he notes the discussed dimensions as "310' x 42' x 262'; Modified Whaleback; 1% commission."[14] He quoted £27,000 for the order on 11

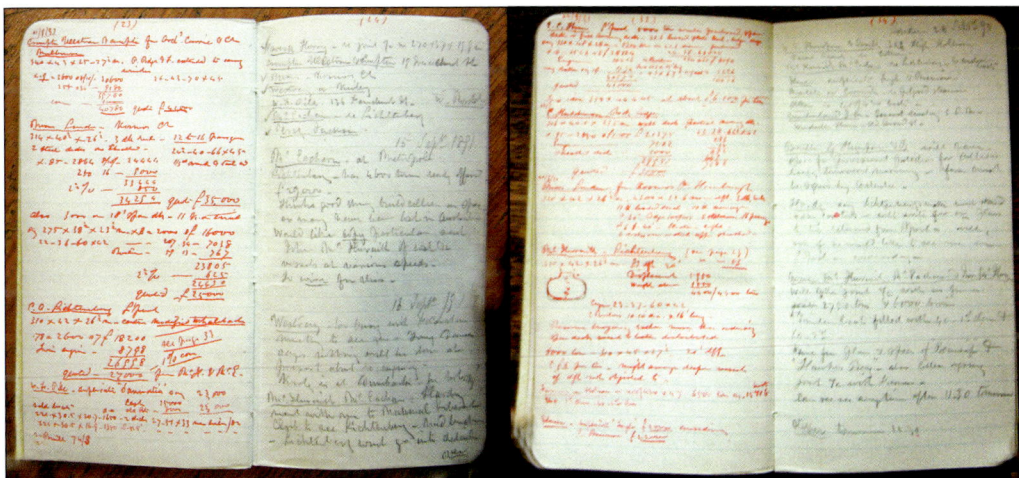

35. & 36. W.T. Doxford's notebook for 1891, pages 23 and 33, recording the quotation given for a modified whaleback design, 11 Sept 1891. Ref: DS.DOX 2/5/2 © Tyne & Wear Archive Service.

September 1891: £8,798 for the twin engines and £18,200 for the ship itself. On 15 September, (page 24), he visited London and discussed the modifications with another agent, Messrs McIlwraith, McEacharn & Co., with whom Doxford had previously done business.[15] Andrew McIlwraith requested that particulars be sent to his brother, John, "of cost of vessels at various speeds. So wire this." McIlwraith were already in negotiations with Doxford over C210. On page 33 of the notebook, more details are given for the design, including this small sketch. Theodore noted: "Reserve buoyancy better than ordinary open deck vessels and better distribution." The ship would be the SS Sagamore (C218), 2,140 grt, a screw steamer and a general cargo ship, built under licence from MacDougall. McIlwraith later acted as agents for the Sagamore, but the deal took some time, and she was not registered to the Belgian American Maritime Co., S.A., Antwerp until September 1893. She was managed by W. Johnston & Co., Liverpool, who had made the first approaches to WTD. The Sagamore subsequently changed hands four times and her name twice. Finally, under the name of Ilva, and owned by S.A. Ilva, Genoa, she was captured by U-boat UC-69 on 4 May 1917, five miles from Isla Colera on passage from Genoa to Barry Roads. Her captain scuttled her.

Meanwhile, Doxford's Chief Draughtsman, Arthur Haver (1856-1942), having studied the designs for the whale back steamer, noticed a flaw in retaining a watertight hull, and immediately made some improvements to the MacDougall design. Haver produced a sketch outline of the midships section at the end of September 1891. His innovation was to link the small 'turrets' that supported the flying bridge, accommodation and winch platforms into a continuous trunk. This ran along the length of the ship, was about half its width, and rose about five feet above it. The name 'turret' was retained, leading to some confusion over its origin,

37. SS Turret (C217), the first of her kind. Early 1893 on River Wear, prior to delivery at Newcastle.

as the amended design bore little resemblance to a turret. The amendments to the original design resolved the problem of seas washing over the hull, as they were turned back by the turret and no longer reached the hatches and deckhouses. The deadweight in relation to gross tonnage was also improved.

Haver took his redesign to Charles Doxford, as his superior in the Drawing Office. Charles applied for a patent of Haver's sketch that very day, before the Chief Draughtsman had a chance to approach the Patent Office himself. This action led to an ultimate breakdown in Haver's relations with the Company, although Charles Doxford gave him an immediate rise in salary from £125 to £500 a year and promoted him. Charles promised that his fortune would be made along with theirs should the design prove a success, but later reneged on this.

The cross-section drawings were made public in December 1891 and the first ship to this design was set under way. Turret ships became a commercial success that lasted for many years. However, profits were not shared, and Haver took William Doxford & Sons Ltd. to court in 1903 for the loss of his patent rights. He was awarded only £1,250, a paltry sum, considering the profits made by his employer. He left the company and went into partnership with Captain Petersen, who had taken the first turret ships, for whom he later designed a modification that produced a hull with bulges on each side. This became known as the Monitor type, after the prototype Monitoria. The Monitor Shipping Company, directed by Petersen and Haver, ran these vessels into the second decade of the 20th century.

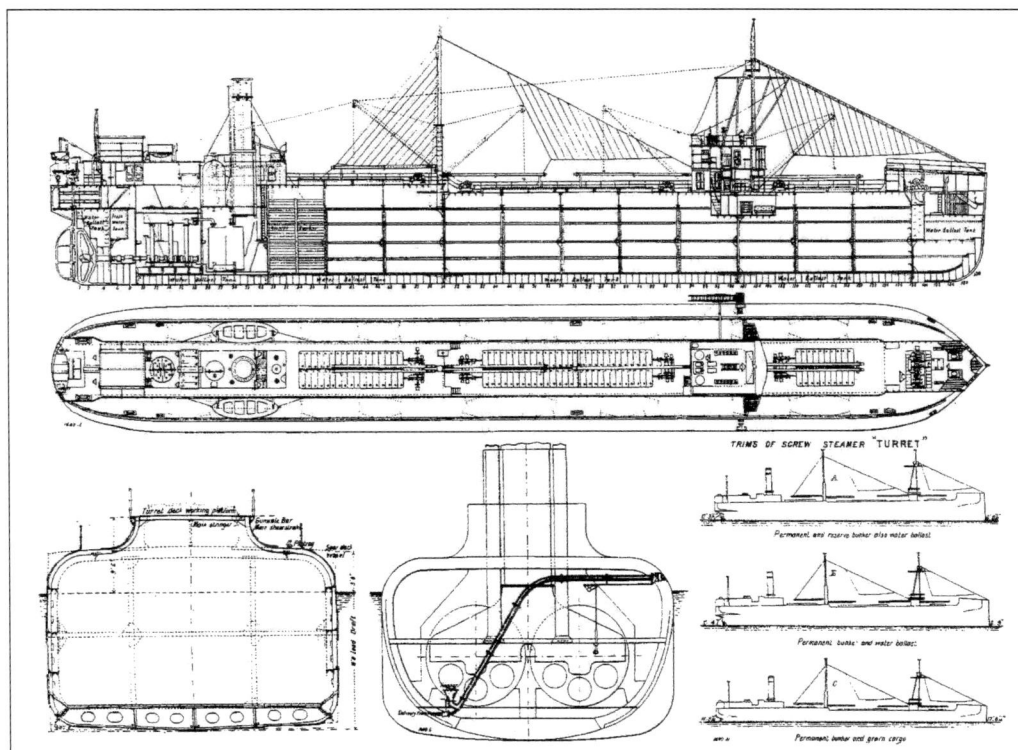

38. Plan showing the configuration of SS. Turret (C217). From The Doxford Turret Ships.
© World Ship Society.

47

The first Doxford turret ship actually left the yard before the whaleback Sagamore. SS Turret (C217), 1,970 grt, was launched on 19 November 1892 and completed in March 1893. She had a deadweight of 3,200 tons. The configuration on page 47 shows the distinctive shape of the prototype, and how the cargo hold became an open space, with all internal supports removed. This meant that 58 cubic feet of cargo per ton could be achieved, rather than 52-54 by earlier designs.

However, finding a buyer for a ship of such a new design proved an uphill struggle. One of the problems was that, as a prototype, she was untested, so Lloyd's Register and the Board of Trade refused to class her. This meant that the first owners would have to take on the insurance risk themselves. Lloyd's had two main objections, the first being the height of the freeboard, as the bulge of the turret deck meant that the deck was considered to be lower than in a conventional vessel. The illustration of SS Turret shows how the deck is virtually dispensed with in a turret ship. The second was over the scantlings, i.e. the collective dimensions of the framing to which planks or plates are attached to form the hull.

39. SS Sagamore, (C218) 1892, whaleback design. Reprinted by George Almond from Doxford archives. Adjusted by Patricia Richardson.

A solution to the lack of buyers was to create a special company, the Turret Steam Shipping Co. Ltd., in which Doxford as a Company had a financial interest. Charles Doxford then set about resolving the problem over insurance. He reported to the Board Meeting held on 15 February 1892 that he had visited Lloyd's Register and the Board of Trade between 15 and 18 December 1891, to discuss their objections to scantlings and freeboard, "but got no satisfactory settlement." He then travelled to Rotterdam and Hamburg, searching for a solution to the lack of an insurance class. At Hamburg he received support from Otto Schlick, a Bureau Veritas surveyor, who introduced him to six German shipowners and, at Bremen, a Mr. Lehman was also interested in the new shape.[15] Between 5 and 9 January Charles returned to London, meeting another potential purchaser, and visited Lloyd's for more discussions with

Mr. B. Martell, their scientific advisor. The Board minutes reported that Charles got:

> "no satisfaction – Mr. Martell objects without giving any distinct reason excepting 'plenty of types can be built under existing rules without introducing new types.' [He] found that Mr. Martell's views on question of Freeboard had been laid before Board of Trade prior to Charles Doxford's interview with Sir Digby Murray."

(Captain Murray had by then been the nautical advisor at the Board of Trade for over twenty years)

In February 1892, Theodore Doxford also travelled down to London. He met firstly with Archibald Denny, of the British Corporation, and reached provisional agreement over the freeboard issue. He then gave particulars of the ship to F. C. Goodall, of Trinity House, who was due to present a paper at the Institution of Naval Architects in April. He was pleased to report that Messrs. Petersen, Tate & Co. of Newcastle had "agreed to have a 'Turret' steamer 280 ft x 38 ft x 22 ft 6 ins, to carry 3,200 tons on 18 ft, Engines 21 inch, 35 inch, 57 + 39 inch stroke, price £22,500, class Bureau Veritas and the British Corporation." To facilitate sales, Doxford established the Turret Steam Shipping Co. Ltd., paying Captain Petersen a commission on orders of one shilling per net ton. They also created a syndicate to offer debentures in the new

40. SS Turret Crown, (C233) 1895, entering No. 2 Lock, Lachine Canal, Montreal, Quebec.

company, attracting investment by Lord Lampton, the local coal magnate. The Turret Steam Shipping Co. retained ownership of The Turret (C217), with Petersen, Tate & Co. acting as managers. She was launched on 19 December 1892 and left Sunderland on 28 January 1893, with Captain Petersen in command. She was loaded at Cardiff with patent fuel and railway plant for Tampico, Mexico. Petersen reported that the new ship had made good progress even in heavy weather, with no damage. He said that:

> "all connected with the vessel (Turret) having satisfied themselves that this type of vessel is superior to any other type afloat for almost all cargo trades, it is contemplated to increase the Capital of the Turret Steam Shipping Co. to £250,000, so as to enable the Company to increase the fleet."[16]

On the strength of his report, Bureau Veritas agreed to class the ship, and Lloyd's underwriters finally abandoned their objections. SS Turret was later sold to Petersen, Tate & Co. for the £22,500 agreed, at a loss of £715. A shipping slump in 1893 did not help, but Petersen, Tate & Co. ordered a second vessel, named Turret Age (C219), slightly larger than SS Turret. The third was Turret Bay (C220), 2,211 grt, for the

41. Grangesberg (C305), 1903, under construction.
Courtesy of the Sunderland Antiquarian Society.

Guildford Steam Shipping Co. Ltd, Newcastle, again managed by Petersen Tate.

By the end of 1894 four turret ships were afloat. Sales were still slow, and Doxford had to offer credit to potential investors in the Turret Company for the first orders, asking only for 25% cash, with the rest as a loan. The contract price for each turret ship was also well below that of earlier ships, at approximately £22-25,500, rather than over £40,000. Despite this, profits for the first half of 1894 were £12,000, allowing a dividend to be paid.

42.43. The first Bureau Veritas classification for insurance for SS. Turret.
Courtesy of the Sunderland Antiquarian Society.

The arguments over fixing the height of the freeboard continued. The Board Minutes of 23 October 1894 record that a conference had been held in Liverpool on 17 July. Present were representatives of the Board of Trade, the British Corporation, Lloyd's Register and Bureau Veritas. The parties had agreed a scheme "which was considered very unsatisfactory by British Corporation and ourselves as it meant a considerable addition to the freeboards already passed & which have proved entirely satisfactory in every case." In fact, the details for the fourth vessel, SS Turret Bell (C231) had only just been agreed, and her freeboard had been raised $4^3/_4$ inches higher than her sister ship. The British Corporation later persuaded the other bodies to agree to reduce this to $2^1/_2$ inches.[18] The Doxford Directors were dismayed that the main argument put forward by Lloyd's at the conference was:

> "that it would be unfair to the older types of vessels to allow the Turrets to load to such a depth as to enable them to carry a greater deadweight cargo than other vessels of a corresponding size, this irrespective of strength or seagoing qualities!"

The Minutes also record:

> "That this argument was used has been practically confirmed by what has passed since at interviews between the directors and Mr. Martell, who still does not think it beneath the dignity of his position as the head of the scientific department of Lloyd's to use his influence to prevent improvements if there should be any danger of such improvements being detrimental to the interest of owners of vessels of older or inferior types."

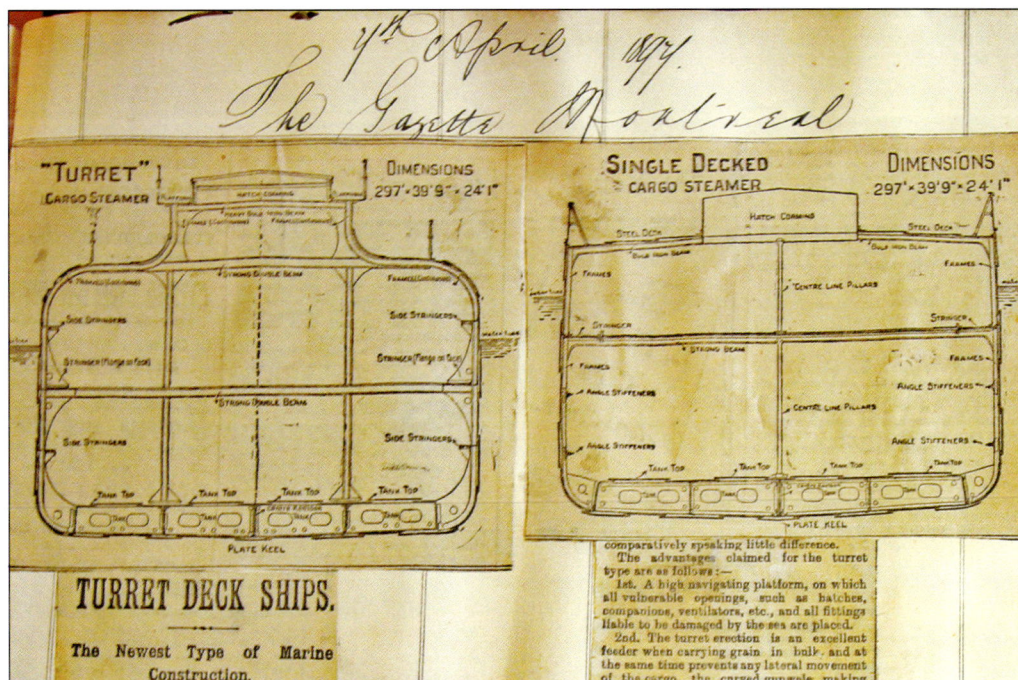

44. *The Gazette, Montreal, of 7 April 1897. Comparison of turret shape over conventional single decked cargo steamer. Courtesy of the Sunderland Antiquarian Society.*

The Board of Trade agreed that the matter could be raised again in two years, "when the Turrets will have fully proved their good qualities." Meanwhile, Bureau Veritas and the Board of Trade both agreed to class the new vessels, as they had been doing in effect over the previous two years.

Lloyd's finally withdrew their objections, and classed later vessels. Petersen, Tate & Co. commissioned four turret ships after the Turret. These were the Turret Age (C219), 2,232 grt (1893), Turret Bay (C220), 2,210 grt (1894), Turret Bell (C231), 2,211 grt (1895) and Turret Crown (C233), 1,827 grt (1895), pictured on page 49 passing through Lachine Canal, Montreal. Turret Cape (C234), 1,827 grt (1895), was purchased by the Guildford Steam Ship Co. Ltd., but managed by Petersen, Tate & Co. These early turret ships were all tramp cargo vessels, of roughly the same capacity. They plied their trade all over the globe, carrying and seeking cargoes, and taking advantage of their superior registered tonnage, vis-a-vis their rivals. Prejudice wore away quickly, and the SS Bencliff (C224) was completed in May 1894 for G. Horsley & Sons, West Hartlepool, though three conventional ships were also built in this period. Four more turrets: two for the Angier Line and one each for Forest Oak Steam Shipping Co. Ltd and Broomhill Coal Co. Ltd. were built before the handover of Turret Bell in 1895. Doxford also received its first commissions from the Admiralty in 1894. Two torpedo boat destroyers (TPD): HMS Haughty (C225) and HMS Hardy (C226) were completed in 1896. The contract price for these was £74,260.

45. SS Scottish Hero (C235) on the West Berths just prior to launch on 26 June 1895.
Courtesy of theSunderland Antiquarian Society.

The turret shape itself underwent modifications as ships grew in size. Cargo space was greatly enlarged over the years. More advantages emerged as Doxford built ships to the new design. In particular, it provided the transverse strength that ships needed once they exceeded 300 feet in length. Formerly the only solution to this weakness had been to insert additional decks and pillars, leading to extra weight, and also to obstructions in the cargo space. Ships of the turret design had a stiff deck structure that increased longitudinal strength. Importantly, turret ships provided shipowners with a lower registered tonnage for their dead weight, and therefore lower Suez Canal dues. However, the construction used a large amount of flanging, so Charles Doxford invented a method of rolling ships' plates with joggled edges. Packing between the plates was rendered unnecessary, as frames butted directly against the plating. He applied for patents for this between June 1894 and August 1896, under the title 'Improvements in apparatus for bending or setting metal plates'.[19]

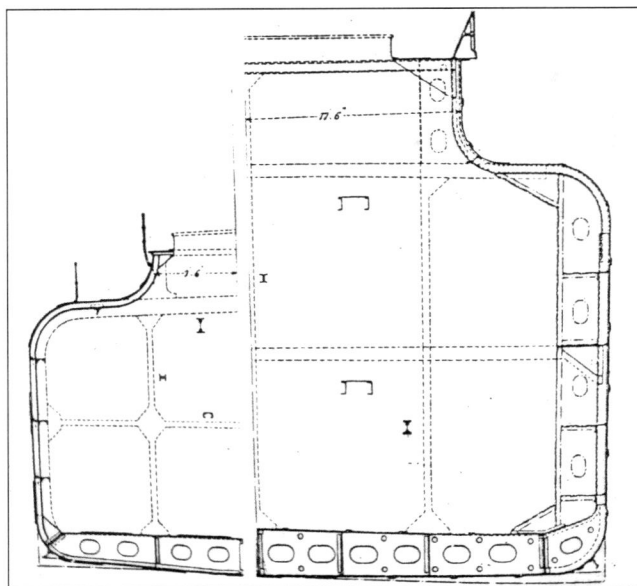

46. Changes to the hold of the turret ship over ten years. Left: SS Turret, 1892 Right: SS Quaeda 1905.
From Building Ships on the North East Coast, Part 1, p 198. © J.F. Clarke, Bewick Press

Doxford were able to sell joggling machines to a significant number of other yards, both in the U.K. and Europe, who paid a royalty of five shillings (25p) per deadweight ton. Six turret ships were also built under licence by other shipbuilders, such as Furness Withy & Co., West Hartlepool, who paid a royalty of 5s per dead weight ton. However, this was rebated at 50% for the first ship and 33.33% thereafter. Swan Hunter of Wallsend jointly built Turret #13 with Doxford.[20] This was SS Forest Brook (Swan Hunter yard no. 198), launched from Wallsend on 6 August 1895. Doxford on their own account launched her sister ship, SS Forest Abbey (C229) that year. Both ships were owned by the Forest Oak Steam Shipping Co. Ltd., Newcastle. In all, 176 turret ships were built by Doxford between 1892 and 1911, plus six more under licence, though Doxford had a 50% stake in these, as mentioned above.

The output grew rapidly. Nine turret ships were built in 1895, and ten the following year. Twenty eight were commissioned by Cayzer, Irvine & Co., Liverpool and Glasgow. These sailed under the Clan Line, the first being Clan MacDonald (C250), launched on 3 March 1897 and completed as quickly as April that year.[21] She was 4,839 grt, and a general cargo ship. The Clan MacDonald was followed that same year by Clan Murray (C251), Clan Monroe (C254) and Clan Robertson (C255) and in 1898 by Clan

47. SS Clan MacDonald (C250), 1897, first turret ship of 21 built for the Clan Line, Glasgow.

MacFarlane (C261). Four Clan ships were built in 1899 as Clan Colquhoun (C269), Clan Farquar (C271), Clan Urquhart (C272) and Clan Alpine (C273), mainly over 5,850 grt, i.e. a quarter larger than the commissions of just three years earlier. Cayzer Irvine purchased six turret ships in 1900, five more in 1902, and seven between 1904 and 1907, making a total of twenty one, all between 3,588 and 5,856 grt.

Two other major purchasers were Walter Runciman & Co., Newcastle (The Moor Line) and Arthur Munro, Sunderland. The Ritson family's Nautilus Steam Shipping Co. took two in 1895. These were the Oak Branch (C236) and the Elm Branch

48. SS Skandia, (C274) 4336 grt. Launched November 1899. Lying at Pallion wharf prior to handover.
Courtesy of the Sunderland Antiquarian Society.

(C239). The gross registered tonnage of the early turret ships measured between 3-4,000, but capacity increased steadily to 6-7,000 grt. The largest was 11,600 deadweight (7,696 grt). This was SS Querimba (C339) built as a coal carrier to India in 1905. The turret ship remained successful for twenty years and the profits from these ships allowed Doxford to restructure their shipyard at the turn of the 20th century. Rules on loading eventually changed, though, favouring ships built with shelter decks. The last turret ship, SS Orangemoor (C423), 4,134 grt, a general cargo ship, was launched from Pallion on 16 May 1911 for the Moor Line. She passed through a number of owners and was eventually named SS Brask by A/S Brask (Nilssen & Sonner), Norway in 1925. She was torpedoed and sunk on 15 January 1941 whilst on passage from Gourock to Durban.

The end of the century

Towards the end of the century, the Wear was hit by a number of workers' strikes, and Doxford was not immune to such walk outs. During 1894, when many turret ships were under construction, the welders and the vital pattern makers came out on strike for an increase in wages, the former staying out for six months and the latter for eight. 2,000 men were refusing to work on Tyneside and the Wear, and causing layoffs in other trades as a result. Doxford were forced to close the yard and engine works for two months, except for work on the Government contracts, and Theodore estimated that the loss of work cost the company £10,000. The last men did not return to work until early January 1895, eventually having been defeated by the availability of a small number of non-unionised operatives and employer solidarity. This was an unusual occurrence, as Doxford are reputed to have had a reasonable relationship with their workforce, but it seems that they must have employed non-union men, as they completed seven ships that year. A further strike by the Amalgamated Society of Engineers for a reduction in the working day from nine to eight hours (a 48 hour week), lasted between July 1897 and January 1898. This delayed work at Pallion, both in the engine works and in the shipyard, though seven turret ships and two destroyers were completed. The employers' association had again been unbending, eventually forcing the men back to work through lack of funds.

Profits had been modest in the new company, but as the century drew to a close they increased. In 1900, the Doxford local accountants and auditors, Henry Rawlings, were examined by W.B. Peat & Co. of London, who gave the following figures, representing a steady, and growing income as the Turret ship design gained in recognition.:

1895:	£36,689.3.5 (The AGM of 1896 gives this as £31,891.6.3)
1896:	£35,322.16.9
1897:	£34,423.1.11
1898:	£42,526.0.11
and 1899:	£52,007.4.2.

Ernest Doxford was elected a Director at the Annual Meeting held on 4 March 1899.[22] One of the final decisions of the dying century was to more than double the capital of the Company. The addition of 300,000 shares at £1, resolved at an Extraordinary General Meeting on 8 May 1899, brought the registered capital of the company to £500,000.[23] Dividends of £30,000 were distributed to the shareholders in the year 1899/1900.

By 1900, the contract price for an average 3,550 grt turret steamer had reached c £50,000. From contracts in hand on 1 January 1900, the cost to the Government for two 30 knot torpedo boat destroyers was £52,751 and £60,620 respectively.[24] A table was given in the minutes for the Annual General Meeting held on 26 March 1900, showing how Doxford had increased its prices over the previous four years. The figures are for cargo ships only, and exclude those for the destroyers.

	1897	1898	1899	1900
per gross registered ton	£9.13.3	£9.14.4	£12.0.0	£13.4.7
per dead weight ton	£6.6.0	£6.6.9	£8.4.3	£8.13.3

Chapter Four

The early 20th Century

In 1900, Doxford were in second position for gross tonnage output on the Wear, producing 34,829 grt, surpassed only by Laings, (40,307 grt), but closely followed by J. L. Thompson (33,649 grt).[1] The rivalry would continue over the coming years. William Doxford & Sons Ltd. had been a private company since 1891. Joseph L. Thompson & Sons Ltd. had followed in 1894, and Sir James Laing & Sons Ltd. in 1898. As a member of parliament serving the interests of the shipbuilding industry, the Doxford Chairman, Theodore, received a knighthood on 2 February 1900. This was a great honour also for the family business.

49. The Pallion Yard in August 1903, showing the open West Berths, with the Plate Yard in the foreground.

Creation of the Public Company

The private company was becoming too restrictive. The need for working capital was intense. The Companies Act of 1900 allowed the creation of debentures, including those backed by a mortgage. Prior to this, under previous acts since 1864, although directors and shareholders had gained limited liability, their ability to mortgage their property was restricted, thereby limiting the amount of extra working capital that could be sought. Doxford became a public company on 8 May 1900, still under the name of William Doxford & Sons Ltd. The Company invited applications from the public for an issue of 5% cumulative Preference Shares and 4% debentures. The share capital issued was £500,000, divided into 25,000 Ordinary Shares of £10 each and 25,000 Cumulative Preference Shares of £10 each. 20,000 of the Ordinary Shares were retained by the Directors and members of their families, fully paid, and 5,000 were available for issue. 1,500 4% First Mortgage Debentures were offered at £100 each. The Company had the right to redeem these from 1910 at £105. (They

50. A Collier turret ship for the Britain to India run. Syren & Shipping 3 Jan 1906 p 46.

would still be on the books into the 1920s.) Mortgage debentures gave the purchaser a mortgage over the fixed assets of the company, both on its present assets, and any that might arise in the future. In addition to their holdings in Ordinary Shares, the Directors were allotted a minimum of 8,000 of the Preference Shares. The remainder of these, and all the debentures were offered to the public. According to a report in the London Times, only just over a month later, the Company invited offers for the remaining 17,000 5% Cumulative Preference Shares, and £150,000 of 4% First Mortgage Debentures. It seems that members of the family acquired the great majority of the preference shares; as at the sale of the company in 1919 they were in possession of 24,543 out of the 25,000 in issue.

Doxford had also by this time acquired the patent rights for the Bell Rockliffe system of plating, which was used by a number of shipyards, mainly in the North East but also abroad. These rights were valued at £58,737 17s 1d, and the works and premises at £202,481 by Thomas F. Hedley & Sons, surveyors in Sunderland.[2] Their report, published in the Times on 7 May 1901, describes the Pallion Yard as freehold, covering around thirty two acres (just under 13 hectares). On it stood:

> "the shipyard, boiler yard, engine works, brass foundry, quay, saw mill, and offices, together with the fixed plant, machinery, engine works' tools and patterns, and sidings, and certain other adjoining property belonging to [the Company] but in various occupations."

Although the company was now publicly quoted, in reality the great majority of the shares were still in family ownership. However, the new structure opened up possibilities for the future needs of the enterprise. In fact, the requirement for more capital presented itself rapidly. Shipyards were always a dangerous environment in which to work. Fire was a particular hazard, and 1901 saw yet another conflagration at the Pallion yard. This time it was the two storied engine works, the fitting, pattern and erecting shops that went up in flames on the night of Wednesday, 11 September 1901. The engine works was a huge building, 130 yards long and 100 yards wide.

By this time, Doxford had their own fire engine and a brigade of thirteen men, led by William Spoors. Even so, it was two hours before they arrived on the scene, by which time the building was well alight. They were assisted by the Sunderland fire boat, but this was hindered by a low tide, rendering the jets of water from the river less effective. Although a stores room was also destroyed and the pattern office

51. The transporting gear over the shipbuilding berths designed by Robert Doxford, son of Robert Pile, 1905. The railway sidings can be seen in the foreground. From: Syren and Shipping, 3 Jan 1906 p 42.

suffered damage at least this last intervention saved the boiler shop. The proximity of each building to each other meant that losses from the disaster were particularly high and even the boiler shop was left with a great hole in its roof. The press recorded that Robert Pile Doxford, together with his son, Robert, and nephew, Ernest, directed the efforts and saved much of the equipment, including one of the boilers under construction. It was estimated that 1,000 men were affected by the damage, losing much needed work, and that the repairs would be in the region of £100,000.[3]

52. & 53. The two entrances to Doxford Shipyard, as they appeared in Syren and Shipping 3 January 1906. Men would enter by the gate on the left; heavy equipment used the East Entrance, seen on the right.

Changes to the shipyard

Perhaps this latest disaster spurred the Board into accelerating plans to reorganise the Pallion Yard, though another driver was that ships were rapidly increasing in size. In 1902 the five berth arrangement in the East Yard was demolished and replaced by three berths. These were larger both in length and breadth, allowing Doxford to build ships up to 540 feet in length. Production continued throughout this work, with launches at the same rate. Robert Doxford Junior designed overhead transporting gear for the extended berths in the restructured yard. These were vertical lattice work columns, 90 feet high (just under 27.5 metres) and 650 feet in length (198.2 metres), supporting nine H-girder tracks above each ship under construction. The tracks carried hoisting trolleys capable of lifting three tons, powered by electricity. They projected beyond the ship at both ends, so that goods arriving by either rail or sea were easy to lift into place. It was an ingenious invention, copied by other shipbuilders.[4] These hoists are very distinctive, and can be seen in the subsequent photographs of the Pallion yard, until demolished in 1973. The reorganisation of the yard meant that output more than doubled over the next five years. Work on the Queen Alexandra Bridge had already begun, and this opened to traffic in 1909 as both a road and rail bridge. The photograph taken in 1906 shows the spans of the bridge, at some distance from the new gantries.

54. Four steam driven crane locomotives and a saddle tank engine. c. 1905.
Courtesy of the Sunderland Antiquarian Society.

The new yard used steam locomotives to shift and lift the heavy materials used in shipbuilding to their destination. This evocative photograph shows five of these locomotives, four crane locomotives and a saddle tank engine, and suggests how difficult it must have been for pedestrians to cross the yard, with its matrix of railway lines.

The workforce

The development of the company, and the success of the turret ship, led to an enlarged workforce. In comparison to the wages of 1883, recorded in Chapter Three, the wage bill for the twenty nine officials and draughtsmen for 28 December 1903 was £98 2s 0d, giving an average pay packet of £3 7s 10d. Robert Haswell, the Secretary to the Engineering Department, was the highest paid, at £5 (rising to £5 10s in 1905). He was assisted by William Rawlings, on £2 5s. Both men would serve Doxford until their deaths. Haswell, having served as Company Secretary, would later become Doxford's Managing Director.[5] William Morris Doxford, son of Alfred, worked at the family firm for all his career. He is noted in the wage books as a draughtsman, on £1 5s 10d, and still gave this as his occupation when a mini census was taken in 1939. He died during the Second World War. He was the last member of the family to serve the firm.

55. The Accounts Department, c. 1905. From Syren and Shipping, January 1906.

It was, of course, a male dominated concern. The only female employees were cleaners, canteen workers or tracers of plans. Apprenticeships took many years, both in manual occupations and as engineers and naval architects. Foremen were admired, feared and obeyed, distinctive in their bowler hats beside the flat capped workers. As life expectancy improved, a significant number of men worked for Doxford for over fifty years.

56. SS Ryall (C368), 4,107 grt, 1906 for Red 'R' SS Co. Ltd., Newcastle. Managed by Stephens, Sutton & Stephens. Author's collection.

The contribution that Robert Doxford Junior gave to the company resulted in his election as a Director at the 1904 AGM. However, it was not until five years later that his two younger brothers, Arthur and William, joined him on the Board. Charles Junior became a Director in 1917, at the age of 29. By this time, Arthur had died, so the number of family members on the Board never exceeded six.

The Blue Riband, 1905 and 1907

Not only related to speed, the Blue Riband was also an unofficial accolade for the highest annual UK shipbuilding output.[6] Doxford won this in 1905, outstripping Harland and Wolf at Belfast and Swan Hunter and Wigham Richardson on the Tyne. (Swan & Hunter had merged with Wigham Richardson in 1903.) That year they built twenty turret ships with a total gross tonnage of 86,632, averaging 4,332 grt.[7] At that time there were sixty shipbuilders in the UK and Northern Ireland, but in reality they produced the greatest output of any shipbuilder in the world that year. In 1906, the Doxford output reached 100,000 grt, but they did not gain the accolade. SS Ryall (C368), a coal carrier, was one of that year's output. She was later sold to Gothenburg and renamed Roland, and later became the Henrik Lund. As such, she was captured by U-151 and sunk off the coast of Carolina on 18 June 1918.

Doxford were awarded the Blue Riband once more in 1907, when they delivered a further twenty ships, at 81,307 grt, all general cargo vessels. This was an average of 4,065 grt, but only four of the ships exceeded 4,000 grt. Addressing the shareholders on 9 March 1908, at their 18th annual meeting, Sir Theodore was proud to announce healthy profits for 1907, and the lack of debt due to the Company, only £36 8s 3d, despite the yard's output. He declared that capital expenditure had been reduced by £10,000, the cost of maintenance for the year was £11,682, and the cash balance in hand was £192,603, against £79,784 at the end of 1906. The net profit had risen to £98,961, against £52,183 the previous year, allowing the company to carry forward £46,058 after paying dividends.[8]

He continued:

"We have completed eight years since the formation of the company upon its present basis, and during that time have spent on:

Extension and improvements	£261,263
Written off for depreciation	£140,358
Spent out of revenue for maintenance	£88,350
Carried to reserve accounts	£120,000
Paid in wages	£1,452,149
Paid in rates and taxes	£47,556
Total expenditure	**£2,109,676**

And built 120 steamers with a gross registered tonnage of 486,691."

However, Sir Theodore warned, correctly, as it turned out:

"The most important is the fact that for the moment there are about as many boats afloat as the trade requires, and the low range of freights, with the heavy cost of running boats, has made the business of ship owning unprofitable, and therefore deterred owners from ordering more steamers at present, except in a few special cases and for special purposes. Of course, the present slackness in building will help a reaction, but what are shipbuilders to do in the meantime? For the few orders about, the keenest competition exists that I have ever known. Not long ago, when slack trade came on we had only to compete with British yards, but now we have foreign competition, which is bad to withstand. Only the other day we quoted a price, and got a reply that the order must pass us as they had a foreign offer 30 per cent lower than any British tender. Now in this there is probably a mistake for we asked very little above cost price, and I don't believe that even a foreign yard can beat us by 30 per cent, but it is a fact that British builders are being cut out by foreign yards; and this position must be faced by reducing our costs."

He went on to say that although the cost of materials was falling, wages remained the same. In earlier days if orders fell, so did wages but that men now argued that they should be kept at the same level, as those in work had to help the less fortunate. He suggested that lower wages would bring in more orders, and that: "It is therefore to the interest of the great mass of workers that lower wages should be accepted." Sir Theodore hoped that a conciliation board would be set up with trusted workers' representatives, so that friction could be avoided. Despite his fears for the future, a dividend of 5% was approved.

The Annual Meetings, now that the company was a public entity, were attended by a wider body of shareholders. At the 1908 meeting, the following were present in addition to family members and officers of the company: B. Sutherland, (Shipowner and client), G.O. Wright, A.E. Usher, J.W. Campbell, Wm. Thackray, Robt. Farrow, (oil merchant), J. Young, P. Lodwidge, Septimus Hedley, a brother of A.O. Hedley, and Rev'd W.M. Teape (the Rector of South Hylton). Even as Sir Theodore spoke, a severe worldwide slump was beginning and production fell sharply. Only eight ships left the yard in 1908, and five in 1909. One reason was that the Tonnage and Load Line Regulations, which had made turret ships so profitable with their single cargo space, had been modified to a more rational standard. Shipowners now demanded the 'open shelter deck' design of a two deck ship, as the between deck space was now exempted from the tonnage measurement for port charges, etc., as long as 'tonnage hatches' were fitted (See end note).[9] Ships with this design were considered more seaworthy than turrets and the shelter deck, whether open or closed, became the standard cargo ship until the 1960s.

The table below was compiled by F. Gray and J. Lingwood for their book on the Doxford turret ships, published in 1975. It details the ultimate demise of the ships and shows vividly how devastating the losses were during the two world wars, in particular in World War I (WWI). But it was not only enemy action that led to a ship's end. Only 29.4% remained in service until the end of their natural lives. 43.8% were destroyed by enemy action, 26.6% met a different unhappy end.

The Fates of the Doxford Turret Ships

Fate	Number of Ships
Casualties of WWI	77
Casualties of WWII	4
Broken up 1921-1930	15
Broken up 1931-1940	30
Broken up 1941-1959	8
Wrecked	25
Collision	10
Foundered	4
Fire	1
Capsized	5
Missing (1907/1908/1909)	3
Total	182

The final turret ship to leave Doxford's yard was the Orangemoor in 1911, built for Moor Line Ltd and managed by W. Runciman & Co., London. She survived WWI and was renamed Bogen, and then Brask, by Norwegian companies. On 15 January 1941, she was torpedoed and sunk by a German submarine on passage from the Clyde to Durban.

The agreement here, dated 1906, is typical of those agreed with ship brokers. It is for six ships. These were firstly given a 'Billiter' prefix, as J. Sunley were based on Billiter Street, in the City of London. They were sold on to different ship owning companies, so were later each renamed. The value of each individual contract was £40,500. The price included the ships, (3,840 grt each) engines and boilers. As can be seen from the terms, the buyer paid £30,500 cash on delivery, unlike in earlier days when instalments were made as construction took place. The remaining £10,000 was repayable over a four year period, with interest, but with provisions for mortgaging. All the vessels were delivered in 1907. This was the second year that Doxford received the accolade.

57. The Agreement to build six ships for J. Sunley & Co. Billiter Street, London.
Courtesy of Francis Budden.

This book has described more than one fire at Pallion, invariably at night. However, over the years the company's response became more effective. As mentioned above, Doxford had owned a fire engine and employed a brigade since the turn of the century. This worked alongside the two from the Borough Brigade when, in the early hours of Wednesday, 2 April 1913, the joiners shop, 130 by 60 yards became ablaze. Unlike earlier fires, this was brought under control efficiently, saving wood in the adjacent timber yard. According to press reports, the blaze was watched by an

58. SS Brask, formerly Orangemoor (C423), the final Turret ship to leave the Doxford yard.
She was launched on 16 May 1911.

excited crowd standing on the Queen Alexandra Bridge. 100 men working as joiners and their mates were reported as potentially losing only a few days' work, though the cost of repairs was likely to reach £10,000. The fire occurred just prior to a major extension to the yard right up to the Queen Alexandra Bridge. Through the indomitable A. O. Hedley, Doxford received permission to relocate the Newcastle Arms beerhouse from its position adjacent to the bridge to a site on New Pallion Road. Doxford had acquired this land in various parcels. That on which the beerhouse stood had been sold to them by Sunderland Corporation Health Committee in 1911. They eventually enlarged their yard by 11,000 square yards (c. 9,200 square metres). This would be of great help in achieving the increased output needed during WWI.

The Great War

WWI brought new challenges to the Pallion yard, but ample work. A series of photographs were taken of the workforce in 1914. The one here is of the blacksmiths and strikers (who did the heavy work of striking the steel). Many of these men would enlist as the war progressed, so Doxford had to encourage men to come out of retirement to replace them. The conflict meant that the order book was buoyant, Doxford received thirty five commissions from the Admiralty for destroyers and, from early 1918, nineteen cargo ships, ranging from 5,171 to 6,701 grt, were built under the directions of the Shipping Controller, given the prefix 'War', but then renamed

59. A patriotic photograph of the Doxford Blacksmiths and Strikers at the outset of WWI. The foreman stands on the left, wearing a bowler hat. Note the flat caps on both men and boys. No protective head gear.

by the manager. The Company's reserve funds had risen from £460, when the company became public in 1900, to £350,000 by the time of the 1915 AGM. One of the difficulties of the War was that the company could not finalise its accounts, due to the uncertainty of what was owed to the Government as Excess Profits Duty.

1916 Change of Leadership at Doxford

The last corporate action led by Sir Theodore Doxford took place towards the end of 1915. The cautious attitude of the directors had meant that not all of the shares in the company had been issued. The reserve fund in November that year stood at £350,000, and a resolution was passed at an Extraordinary General Meeting (EGM) held on 11 November 1916 that the remaining authorised Ordinary Share Capital be issued, reducing the reserves by £50,000. Shares were distributed amongst the existing ordinary shareholders in proportion to their respective holdings. At the same EGM, the rules of the Company were altered. Sir Theodore proposed, with reference solely to preference shareholders:

> "Resolution 2. That Article 72 of the Articles of Association be struck out, and that instead thereof there be inserted an Article as follows:
>
> On a show of hands every member personally present (including the representative of a Corporation) shall be entitled to one vote, but on a poll every member present, either personally or by proxy, shall have one vote for every share held by him."

This resolution to grant votes to the preference shareholders was carried, and may well have sealed the fate of Doxford within a few years.

As 1916 dawned, Sir Theodore suffered from recurring bouts of ill health, though he chaired the AGM of the company in April. Lady Doxford died in August and Sir

Theodore on 1 October. His brother, Robert Pile Doxford was elected Chairman. However, Robert was by then living in Hertfordshire and came up to Pallion less than once a month. His younger brother, Charles David, assumed the role of Managing Director, and took overall control of the business. Charles took the chair at Directors' meetings in Robert's absence.

Visit by King George V and Queen Mary

The Doxford output for the Royal Navy led to a great honour. On Friday, 15 June 1917, their majesties King George V and Queen Mary visited Sunderland as part of their journey to the Mersey and to the three great shipbuilding rivers of the North East. The background to the visit was that, by this stage of the War, British workmen were exhausted and demoralised. Strikes were a distinct possibility, and the King and Queen undertook a series of journeys around industrial areas to show their support.

It was a particularly hot day. The itinerary was arduous, given the weather conditions. Their Majesties left the Royal train at

60. 15 June 1917. Visit by King George V and Queen Mary to Doxford. A.E. Doxford being presented. C.D. Doxford is to the right of her Majesty. From 'Where Ships are Born'.

Southwick and arrived at NEM, South Dock, just after 10 a.m. They next visited the Laing yard at Deptford and Doxford at Pallion, before returning to Southwick. After lunching on the Royal Train, they toured J. L. Thompson's yard at North Sands, John Crown and George Clark Ltd., both at Monkwearmouth and William Pickersgill at North Dock, before returning to London by train. They were greeted at Pallion by Charles Doxford and his nephews, Ernest and William Doxford, whose wives were also presented to their Majesties. This photograph shows the welcome outside the Doxford offices with Charles standing beside Queen Mary who, with her tall hat, appears to tower over him.[10] Ernest is being presented to her.

From the Royal train as it headed back to London, the King's Secretary, Clive Wigram, wrote as follows:

> "Dear Mr. Doxford,
> The King commands me to assure you what a pleasure it was to the Queen and Himself to visit your famous and old established Firm today.

68

His Majesty was struck by the efficient organization and especially by the arrangements for lifting and carrying heavy weights. The spontaneous and hearty welcome in the Yards greatly touched the King and Queen. It was particularly gratifying to His Majesty to hear that so warm a response had been made to his appeal for volunteers, and the King congratulates your establishment on furnishing two Battalions. (Signed yours very truly)"[11]

61. The departure of the Royal Couple, showing the number of the women employed at Pallion during WWI. CDD is seen to the right of the car, with his hat in his hand, with AED behind him. From the Doxford Booklet 1921.

The following week, the King travelled on his own to Scapa Flow in Scotland. James Pope Hennessey, in his biography of Queen Mary, quotes from a letter he wrote to his wife, stressing how much he had appreciated her presence. "It was dear of you coming with me last week, it helps enormously if you come. I only hope you were not too tired, the great heat, of course made it worse, but I know the visit did good. I miss you now abominably..."[12]

The Doxford family also led from the front, as their husbands and sons served in the forces alongside the Doxford workforce. Frank Ritson, the fourth child of Francis and Eveline (Doxford) Ritson, and grandson of William and Hannah, was a married man when he died at Wytschaete (now Wijtschate) in Belgium, on 17 June 1917, during the Battle of Messines. John D. H. Hedley, son of John and Margaret Eveline (Doxford) Hedley, and grandson of Sir Theodore, left Haileybury in June 1917 and was commissioned 2nd Lieutenant, Middlesex Regiment on 25 September. He was killed in Belgium on 8 March 1918, aged only nineteen. Many others in the cousinhood served with the armed forces.

And it was not only the family who suffered losses. Robert Haswell (1866-1941), the secretary to the Engineering Department, who took over as secretary to the company after the retirement of John Holey in 1917, lost two of his three sons in action.

Admiralty orders

The first of thirty five orders was HMS Opal (C483), 1,025 tons displacement, triple screw, the first of twenty five M class destroyers, powered by three turbo engines. She was laid down on 1 February 1915, launched on 11 September and commissioned in April the following year. She reached a speed of 34 knots during her sea trials in early 1916. HMS Opal had a short, but active service. She joined the Twelfth Destroyer Flotilla, based at Scapa Flow and took part in the Battle of

62. The newly launched destroyer, HMS Opal, first Admiralty order, 1915. Lying outside Pallion.

Jutland. She carried out duties of minesweeping and took part in anti-submarine patrols in the North Sea. She foundered on the coast of South Ronaldsea in bad weather when returning to Scapa Flow on the night of 12 January 1918, due possibly to a navigation error of her captain. Her sister ship, HMS Narborough was also lost that night, leaving only one survivor from both vessels. The wrecks were abandoned and quickly broke up in heavy seas. The photograph overleaf is of HMS Orpheus (C489), 1916, 1,025 tons displacement, M class destroyer. She was assigned to the Twelfth Destroyer Flotilla in September, transferred twice, and survived the war. She was scrapped in 1921. Photographs of her in action give her the number H 28.

70

63. *HMS Orpheus, (C489) destroyer with 3 turbines, in the East Berths. She was launched 19 June 1916. Courtesy of the Sunderland Antiquarian Society.*

*64. One of the turbines being winched into a torpedo boat destroyer at Pallion fitting out quay.
From the Doxford brochure of 1921, p 37.*

Chapter Five

Sir William Theodore Doxford (1841-1916)

65. William Theodore Doxford as a young man.
Unknown Immediate source:
'Black -White' Parliamentary Album 1895.

The following chapters are devoted to the biographies of the four brothers. Surprisingly, there is no evidence of rifts between them as they directed their rapidly expanding business. Although Alfred left the business, he used his niece's husband, A.O. Hedley, as his solicitor in his business dealings. The administration of the enterprise seems to have been a successful arrangement, with each taking a different role.

As the lead director of William Doxford & Sons, Theodore was also an active force within the town of Sunderland. He was a Justice of the Peace, a town councillor and a River Wear Commissioner. He served as the Chairman of the Sunderland Conservative Association. In 1878 he was elected to the Institution of Naval Architects, founded in 1860. In 1884, he became a founder member of the North East Coast Institution of Engineers and Shipbuilders (NECIES).[1] He was an active member and served as its second President, from 1886-1888. Theodore remained involved in NECIES affairs until his death in 1916.

Theodore was also a director of business ventures. He was a founding member of the board on the British Maritime Mortgage Trust, which was inaugurated to "make advances upon approved Maritime Securities", according to its prospectus announced in the Times on 1 May 1890. The Trust was backed by the National Provincial Bank and the Bank of Scotland.

On 19 April 1898, he was granted the Freedom of the City of London, in the Company of Shipwrights. He was one of the two Members of Parliament for Sunderland from 1895 to 1906. He was appointed a Deputy Lieutenant for Durham and was knighted by Queen Victoria at Osborne on 9 February 1900.

After leaving school, Theodore joined his father in business, quickly becoming his partner. He encouraged the older man to be forward looking and inventive. It was he who was the driving force in changing to iron in the mid-1860s, leading to a surge in orders. He was 33 in 1874, when the first naval order was received.

Where expertise was missing amongst his brothers, Theodore recruited craftsmen to bring technical skills to the enterprise. In particular, the changeover to iron highlighted the shortages of foremen of the new metal workers on the Wear. Doxford advertised in the Scottish press and the census returns for Pallion show an influx of Scotsmen from the 1860s onwards, their occupations connected with iron and engines. Theodore also ensured that the company devoted resources to research, leading to the success of the turret ships. It was under his leadership that his brother, Robert, recruited Karl Otto Keller in 1905 to undertake the first experiments in the lengthy gestation of the Doxford opposed piston diesel engine.

66. Wm. Theodore Doxford, M.P., photographed by Sir Benjamin Stone outside the House of Commons on 20th March 1899. © National Portrait Gallery, London.

The Doxford family had suffered many setbacks before their eventual success as a major shipbuilder. Theodore was well aware of the hardships suffered by his workmen during recurrent downturns in the economy. Although a firm employer he was judged to be a fair one, who strived to preserve good labour relations. He played a major role in the Conciliation Board established in the town in 1885, when yet another depression hit Sunderland. He understood the need to bring his workforce along with him in decisions. When he gave evidence to the Royal Commission on Labour in 1892, he stated that firms could not enforce decisions, and that "personally I think that position is better than if we had . . . powers to compel compliance." This was at the beginning of unionised labour, of which he was in favour. He believed that unions were essential to both the workforce and employer, and that in many cases they prevented strikes, rather than caused them. He was a member of the Merchant Shipping Advisory Committee, whose meetings were held at the Board of Trade in pre-war years.

Theodore Doxford belonged to the Unionist party, and stood on that ticket when he was elected the first Conservative and Unionist Member of Parliament to represent Sunderland in forty years. Until 1931 the constituency returned two members. At the general election of 1895, Theodore topped the poll with 9,833 votes. Edward Temperley Gourley, one of the standing Liberal members, was re-elected with 8,232 votes, but

67. Margaret, wife of Sir Theodore Doxford. On the occasion of her presentation at Court, 12 May 1900.

Samuel Storey, the other previous Liberal member was defeated, having achieved only 8,185 votes. The turnout was high, with 79.9% of the electorate voting. Five years later, in 1900, he was re-elected, once again topping the poll, with 9,617 votes. However, his fellow Conservative candidate, John Stapylton Grey Pemberton, now joined him in Parliament. A Labour Representative Committee candidate also stood that year. This was Alexander Wilkie, who came bottom of the poll, but received a respectable 8,842 votes.

In Parliament, Theodore acted as a spokesman for the shipbuilding industry, and was knighted whilst a serving member. He did not stand at the 1906 election, at which the two successful candidates were Liberal and Labour.

Personal life

Theodore was educated at Bramham College, near Ilkley, East Yorkshire. The school was founded in 1842, and attracted pupils from Yorkshire and Durham industrial families. The decision to send him to a public school indicates that William Doxford expected his family to rise in social, as well as business terms and that, despite the failure of his second shipbuilding concern, his other business interests were successful. The school was short-lived. A cholera epidemic broke out at Bramham in 1869. Several pupils and their headmaster died, and the school closed in the aftermath. Perhaps it is fortunate that his younger brothers were all educated locally, as Charles might well have been at Bramham during the epidemic.

On 9 April 1863, aged 22, Theodore married Margaret Wilkinson at St Andrews, Deptford, Sunderland. Margaret was 21. She was the only daughter of Richard Wilkinson (1813-1883). Wilkinson was born at South Shields. He had been a minor shipbuilder, with a yard at Pallion during the early 1850s, but was no longer in business by the time of the marriage. The couple settled at the newly built Esplanade West, Ashbrooke, Bishopwearmouth.

Their marriage lasted for fifty three years. There was sadness at its start, as they lost three young sons, but five daughters and a son lived to adulthood.

Their family was:

1. **Margaret Eveline (1864-1960)** who married John Hunt Hedley (1858-1914), a local valuer and arbitrator with Thomas Fenwick Hedley & Sons, one of many sons of its founder. They lived in 1 Elms West, Bishopwearmouth and had six children, but only three sons and one daughter lived to adulthood. John died in early 1914. Their eldest son, Theodore Fenwick Hedley (1886-1929), worked with his father. Theodore served as a Lieutenant with the Durham Light Infantry during World War I, and was awarded an M.B.E. in the King's Birthday Honours List, 1919. The second son, John Doxford Hedley (1898-1918), also served with the Durham Light Infantry, and was killed in action in Belgium. The youngest son, Edwin Ernest Doxford Hedley (1900-1985) was commissioned after the war into the Rifle Brigade. Following his retirement from the regular army, he served in the Territorial Army reserve. He became a Lieutenant Colonel in WWII, working for the Ministry of Supply.[2] Margaret was aged 96 when she died at Kelso, on the Scottish border.

2. William Theodore (1866-1870)

3. **Albert Ernest (1867-1937)** AED became a director of William Doxford & Sons. See below, this Chapter.

4. Harold (b & d. 1869)

5. **Mary Hannah (1876-1948)** married John Hunt Hedley's younger brother, Alfred Octavius Hedley (AOH) (1861-1926) in 1891. She was only sixteen at her marriage, whilst Octavius was thirty. He was, in fact, a contemporary of her uncle Charles, and his lifelong ally.

Octavius Hedley was a Sunderland solicitor, who founded his own firm in 1880, when aged only 19. This still operates under its original name, despite the fact that they had no sons.[3] He later took Edmund Cuthbert Thompson into partnership. AOH concentrated on providing a service to shipowners and shipbuilders based on the River Wear. He and his partner were greatly involved with William Doxford & Sons, as their family solicitor and trustee. He was appointed an executor to his father-in-law's will, and his name appears on numerous occasions in the local press, working diligently for all members of the Doxford family. The couple lived at the Nook, next door to Grindon Hall. Their property had a right of way over its land to reach the Chester-le-Street road (A183). They remained there after the sale of the mansion.

They had a family of eight daughters, most of whom were extremely long lived. Their eldest daughter, Alfreda Mary (1892-1988) married into another shipbuilding family. Her husband was George Anderson Short (1886-1948), grandson of George Short, who founded the Hylton shipyard. His father, John Young Short, died in 1900, leaving three sons, Thomas Smart, George Anderson and Henry Sanderson (Harry) Short (1888-1961). Harry was married to Alfreda's younger sister, Luiela Olga (1894-1990). Short Brothers were known as a 'local' yard, in that their output was purchased by local shipowners. Its management descended through four generations until the yard closed in 1964. In 1946, John Hedley Short, (1918-1988) son of George and Alfreda, was Chairman and, Henry Smart Short, (b, 1929) Harry and Luiela's son, joined the Board of Directors.[4] George and Alfreda Short have living descendants, as do Harry and Luiela. J.H. Short and H.S. Short were the last Doxford family members to run a shipyard on Wearside.

Agnes Vera (1898-1990), the fifth daughter, married her cousin, Charles Doxford Junior, as his second wife, and had two sons. Aline Octavia (1907-1994), the youngest child, married Sir William Graham Esplen, 2nd Baronet, in 1928. He was the son of Sir John Esplen, who was one of the directors of the combine that purchased Doxford in 1919. (Chapter Ten) It is interesting that the two families became allied, despite the upheavals that occurred during the 1920s. Aline's grandson is the present baronet. The other daughters married men with no shipbuilding connections.

68. Park Place East, where Theodore and Margaret lived in the 1870s. No. 8 is the second last at the right of the photograph, taken March 2019.

6. Theodore (1874-1876)

7. **Norah (1876-1965)** Married Andrew Leyland Hillyar Cleland (1868-1943) He was born in Co. Down, and was 'of independent means'. They had five children. They lived at Ripon, but later moved to Northern Ireland, where he died in 1943. Norah then returned to England. She was 89 when she died at Tunbridge Wells, Kent. All their children lived into their eighties or nineties.

8. **Anne Greta (1878-1968)** did not marry. She was 90 at her death in the West Riding of Yorkshire on 16 June 1968.

9. **Wilhemine Vera (1883-1955)** married Stanley Miller Thompson (1880-1948), an accountant, and shipowner. Stanley was a younger son of the Sunderland shipbuilder, Robert Thompson. He and his brother, John Thompson, set up and managed the Silver Line shipping company from 1908, through a merger with the St. Helens Steam Shipping Co., London. Their ships had the prefix Silver, and then the name of a tree. Orders from this company kept the Doxford yard operational during the 1920s. (See Chapter Twelve) They lived at Sockburn Hall, Neasham, near Darlington and had one daughter.

Grindon Hall

During the 1870s Theodore and Margaret lived at 8 Park Place East, one of two terraces that still face each other in a gated enclosure close to Mowbray Park. By the time of William Doxford's death in April 1882, they had moved to 1 Grange Crescent. After taking up residence at the newly renamed Grindon Hall, Theodore's mother, Hannah, moved into this substantial corner building. In 1885, Theodore decided to demolish the original building and build a suitably sized mansion for his now multi-generational family. He commissioned brothers, John and Thomas Tillman, to submit plans, and a solid grey mansion rose on the site. John Tillman (1835-1899) was a

69. Grindon Hall, as rebuilt by Theodore Doxford in the 1880s. Courtesy of Francis H. Doxford Budden.

Scottish architect who established a practice in Sunderland and later took his younger brother into partnership. One of their achievements was the complex that became the Sunderland Museum, Art Gallery, Winter Garden and Library, completed in 1879.

The new Grindon Hall contained 26 rooms,[6] and was surrounded by grounds of about eight acres, with a paddock of five acres to the west. It was approached by a lodged drive. Beside the Hall stood stables, coach-houses, lodges, a cottage and other structures, plus 'vineries', (meaning greenhouses). Further parkland extended over approximately 81 acres, and a second lodge stood to the south east.[7] The family had taken up residence by the time of

70. The drawing room of Grindon Hall. Courtesy of Francis Budden.

the 1891 census, and were at the Hall with their youngest children, Margaret's mother and five house servants. Their coachman was in one of the lodges and the head gardener in the other. The staff grew to six in 1901, and to seven by 1911. Sir Theodore and Lady Doxford had twenty six grandchildren, of whom twenty one lived to maturity. It is clear from surviving family photographs taken at Grindon Hall that he was a proud 'pater familias'.

The photograph overleaf shows the Doxford family at Grindon for Christmas 1911. In the top two rows are Stanley M. Thompson, four Hedley daughters, A. O. Hedley, J. H. Hedley, Sir Theodore, his children, Greta, Ernest and Dorothy, Theo Fenwick Hedley, son of J. H. Hedley, Marjorie, daughter of Ernest Doxford, and Hillyar Cleland. In the lower two rows sit: Vera Thompson, four Doxford girls and two Hedley boys, Mary Hedley, Margaret Hedley, Lady Doxford with Ernest's son on her lap, Mrs. Ernest Doxford, Nora Cleland with her twin sons and six other girl cousins.

Theodore and Margaret celebrated their golden wedding anniversary on 9 April 1913. Unfortunately, by this time their health was failing. Margaret passed away on 8 July 1916 and Theodore survived her for less than three months. In the middle of August, he was recorded as seriously ill in the Court Circular of the Times newspaper.[8] He died at Grindon Hall on 1 October 1916. He and his wife were buried in Bishopwearmouth Cemetery. His obituary was given in a number of publications, including the annual reports of the NECIES known as their Transactions.[9]

71. Sir Theodore and Lady Doxford with their family at Grindon. Christmas 1911.

Sir Theodore and Lady Doxford were sponsors of the new church of St. Mary's, South Hylton, close to Grindon Hall, and one of three churches in Sunderland designed by Charles Hodgson Fowler during the 1890s. Fowler disliked chancel screens, and St. Mary's nave and chancel are light and airy. Lady Doxford gave a great deal of her time to the needs of local people and was a generous supporter of the church. In their memory, their son dedicated the west window by James Eadie Read, and this is the only memorial to the family in Sunderland. Following damage during the Second World War, the broken windows in the church were stored away. They were renovated through fundraising at the turn of the 20th century, but the church was closed for public worship at the end of 2018, so their future conservation is again in doubt.

Sadly, William Doxford & Sons Ltd. left family control within three years of Sir Theodore's death. Family anecdote has it that generosity of share allocation to the next generation weakened the structure of the company, as members of the cousinhood sought to capitalise on their holdings. Theodore's will seems to confirm this. He left his son 2,000 shares in William Doxford & Sons Ltd. His five daughters received 800 shares each, held on trust, with an income fixed at £7 10s per cent.

72. St. Mary's Church, South Hylton. 2018. Photograph by Patricia Richardson.

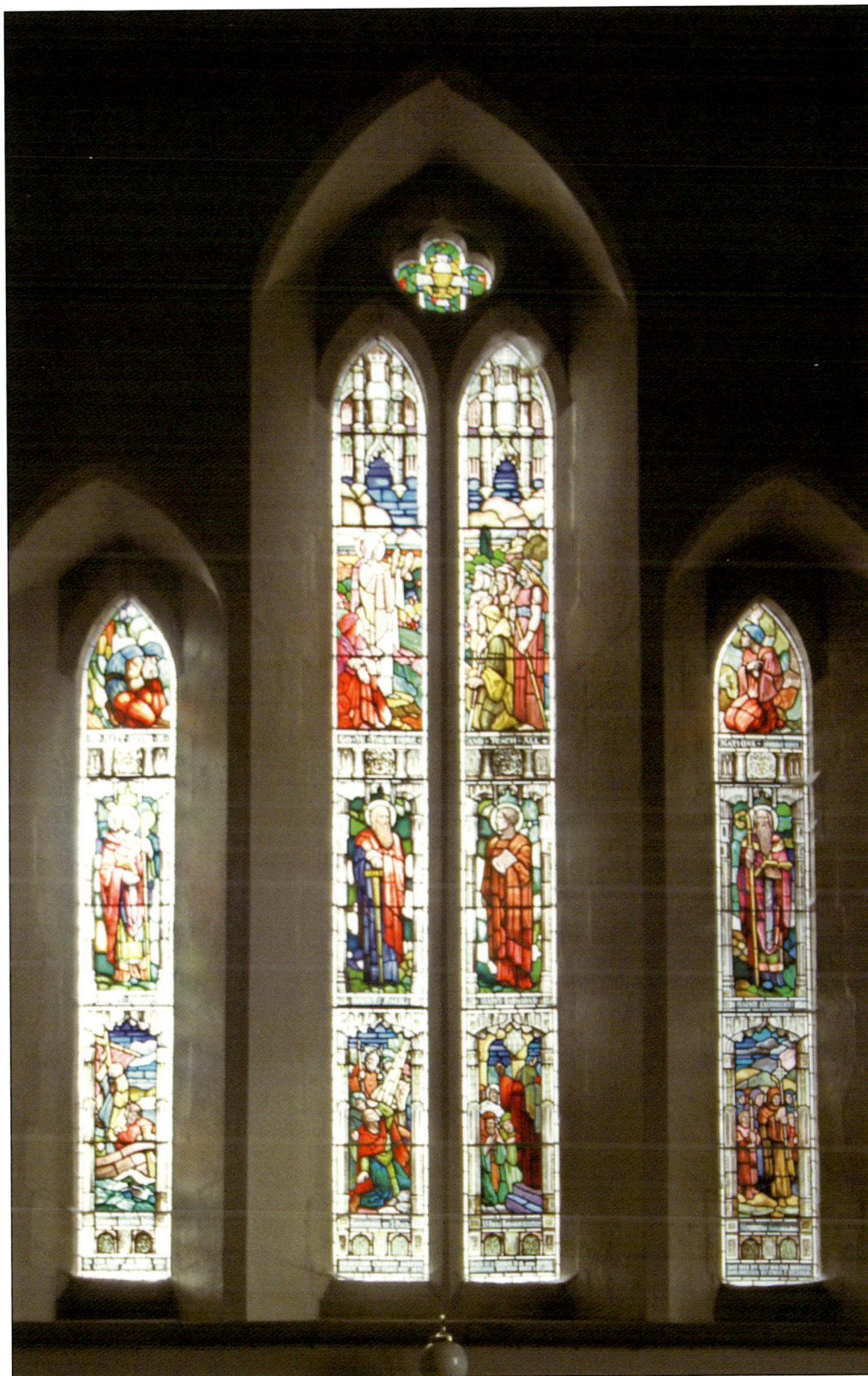

73. *The West Window, St. Mary, South Hylton, built 1890s, designed by James Eadie Read. It represents north eastern saints, and is dedicated to Sir Theodore and Margaret Doxford. Photograph September 2018.*

81

Albert Ernest Doxford (1867-1937)

74. *Albert Ernest Doxford, 1867-1937. Courtesy of Francis Budden.*

75. *Bertha Warner, 1866-1949, Mrs. Ernest Doxford.*

The only surviving son of Sir Theodore Doxford was known by his second name. He was born at Azalea Terrace, Bishopwearmouth on 16 December 1867 and was Theodore and Margaret's third child. At the time of his birth he had an older brother, named after their father, but the child died aged four. Two younger brothers died in infancy. Ernest was therefore the only surviving son, with five sisters. He was educated at Southgate House, Sunderland and then at Durham School. He became the first member of the family to attend university when he was admitted at Caius College, Cambridge on 1 October 1886. He gained a B.A. in mathematics in 1889 and M.A. in 1896. He was nineteen when the NECIES was founded, and became one of its graduate members in 1890, a class of younger men who were 'in study or employment' in the shipbuilding or marine engineering industry on the North East Coast. Ernest joined William Doxford & Sons in the marine engineering department, and took over as manager in 1898. He was made a Director in 1899, and was elected a member of the Institution of Naval Architects in 1900. He was a conscientious worker, and is reputed to have taken his breakfast at the Doxford works each day during the thirty years that he was with the Company. From all reports, he had an exceptionally pleasant personality.

On 17 February 1892 at St. Jude's, South Shields, Ernest married Bertha Eleanor Warner (1866-1949), the eldest daughter of William and Martha Warner. William Warner was a civil engineer with the South Shields Gas Company. They started their married life at Sir Theodore's house, 1 Grange Crescent, Bishopwearmouth. Their family of five children were all born there. They also had a country home at Cleadon Meadows, north of Sunderland, and were there when the 1911 census was taken. Their substantial house held twenty one rooms. The couple were both committed Conservatives. Ernest followed his father as Chairman of the Sunderland Conservative Association, and Bertha was elected Chair of the Women's Conservative

Association. After the war, Ernest was invited to stand as a Parliamentary Candidate, but turned the request down due to their move to Yorkshire.

In 1908 Ernest Doxford was elected a member of the Council of NECIES, and in 1912 became Vice-President. That year he served on the 'Boats and Davits' Commission, which was set up in November by the Board of Trade, following the sinking of the Titanic earlier in the year. Its brief was to look into safety issues connected to lifeboats on passenger liners, but was somewhat controversial. He became President of the NECIES in 1919, the first to follow a father in that position. It was somewhat ironic that 1919 was the year that he and his fellow directors at Doxford sold control of their business to the Northumberland Shipbuilding Company Ltd. The sale is described below, in Chapter Ten. Despite the turmoil in his own firm, Ernest competently oversaw the financial changes needed for the NECIES after the conclusion of war, and the merging of other associations into the Institution. During his presidency, he revived the Graduate Section, which had been suspended during the hostilities, and opened a branch of the Institution on Teesside.

He was also elected to the Council of the Institution of Naval Architects in 1919, the year of his presidency of NECIES. Although retired from business, Ernest continued to serve the INA, and was their vice-president in 1934. Their obituary of him emphasised the gift of friendship that he possessed, and the kindness and encouragement he gave to those younger than himself.

76. 1 Grange Crescent. Home to Ernest and Bertha Doxford up to 1916. Photograph March 2019.

On his father's death in 1916, Ernest inherited both Grindon Hall and 1 Grange Crescent, the latter having been intended as the dower house for his mother. It is probable that he sold Grange Crescent quite quickly, as the couple were then living at West Lawn, near Ashbrooke Park. They took up residence at Grindon Hall. Ernest then contributed to the re-decoration of South Hylton church, and commissioned the west window. It was at St. Mary's that their eldest daughter, Dorothy, married Lieutenant (later Commander) Charles Maurice Stack, on 10 November 1917.[11]

77. Drive and entrance to Grindon Hall. Courtesy of Francis Budden.

In 1920 Ernest Doxford was appointed a Justice of the Peace for Durham. He and Bertha were still resident at Grindon Hall on 15 March 1921, when he was admitted as a Freeman of the City of London. The sale of the house was delayed until after the birth of Charles and Dorothy Stack's second daughter, Althea Fleurette (known as Fleur), who was born at Grindon on 19 January 1922. The mansion, with eleven acres of surrounding land, was then offered for sale at auction by Messrs. Knight, Frank and Rutley on 21 May. During the post war period, many houses failed to find a private buyer, partly because of the attrition of a generation of men, but also because of the post war depression. No private buyer came forward, but Sunderland Corporation successfully bid £14,000 for the house and grounds. Ernest's brother-in-law, A. O. Hedley, purchased other land surrounding The Nook. In September, the decision was taken to convert Grindon Hall into a sanatorium for patients with tuberculosis, and further buildings were added at the end of the 1920s. By 1947 the hospital had 206 beds, many of the patients being

78. Albert Ernest Doxford's photograph that accompanied his obituary in NECIES.

children. Grindon was run as a convalescent home and sanatorium for about fifty years. From 1946 to 1968 it was known as the Grindon Hall Hospital or the Havelock Hospital.[12] Due to successive NHS reforms, the hospital eventually closed, and the property lay vacant until the Government set up free schools in 2010. At the time of writing, the Hall is home to an academy known as Grindon Hall Christian School.[13]

With the proceeds of his shares in William Doxford & Sons Ltd. and the sale of Grindon Hall, AED purchased the historic manor house and 579 acre estate of Newby Wiske, near Northallerton, North Yorkshire, and moved there permanently. He died at Newby Wiske on 30 November 1937, after a long illness, and was buried at nearby South Otterington.

79. Newby Wiske Hall, near Northallerton. Courtesy of Francis Budden.

Ernest and Bertha had five children: four daughters, Dorothy (1893-1992), wife of Charles Stack, Marjorie (1896-1989), Elizabeth (1900-1991), wife of the air ace, Guy Gibson and Joan (1903-1966), wife of Benjamin Chetwynd-Talbot, and one son, Theodore Bertram. All left descendants.

Theodore Bertram Doxford (1906-1976), known as Bertram, trained as an engineer. On 31 July, 1931, he married Beatrice Norah Clark in Belfast. Beatrice was the only granddaughter of Sir George Clark, 1st Baronet, of Workman, Clark, the shipbuilders who had been part of the Sperling Combine. Bertram is noted in the press at the time of their marriage as apprenticed in Northern Ireland, so was probably working at the shipyard though this closed in 1935. They lived in the province, and he stood for election in 1937 as a Unionist in the Belfast City Council, giving his occupation as Company Director. They had a daughter, who has a family. The marriage ended in divorce, and both remarried. Bertram's second wife was Katriona MacLeod, a Canadian. They had two children, a son and a daughter.

Although Bertram inherited the house and estate at Newby Wiske on his father's death in 1937, his mother had a life interest, and remained in residence. That year he joined the Royal Army Ordnance Corps (Supplementary Reserve). At the outbreak of WWII he began service as a Lieutenant, and rose to the rank of Major. After his mother's death on 21 July 1949, Bertram offered the house and its estate for sale by auction (as early as August that year),[13] but the Hall did not become a training centre for the North Riding Constabulary until 1954.[14] It was later the headquarters of the North Yorkshire Police, but they moved to Northallerton in 2017. An application to use the house and site as a holiday activity centre was rejected in mid-2018, but revised plans are still being debated.

Bertram and Katriona Doxford moved to Sowerby, near Thirsk. He served as a Justice of the Peace for Yorkshire. He died on 28 February 1976, aged 75. Katriona returned to Canada, and died in Ottawa in 1983.

Chapter Six

Alfred Doxford (1842-1895)

Alfred seems to have been a talented craftsman, but the least forceful of the four brothers. Both his sons were also technicians. He has a particular distinction, in that his elder son, William Morris Doxford, was the last family member to be employed by the Company. Alfred was born on 10 September 1842, eighteen months after Theodore. He was educated locally and came into the business in 1858 as a sixteen year old carpenter's apprentice. This was shortly after his older brother. He oversaw the shipwright department of the business.

In April 1865, still aged only 22, Alfred married Deborah Morris (1841-1933), the sixth and youngest child of the school teacher at Bamburgh, on the Northumberland coast. On his retirement, Thomas and Dorothy Morris brought the family to Sunderland, and Alfred and Deborah's marriage took place there. Deborah was the only wife of the four brothers who was born outside Sunderland, and also the only wife who come from a family unconnected with the shipping trade. Her brothers became drapers in the rapidly expanding metropolis.

Alfred and Deborah settled close to the Pallion yard. At the 1871 census, they were living in Lucknow House, 2 Peacock Street, Pallion, a road of discreet villas. The

80. & 81. The entrance to Belle Vue Park, early 20th Century. Courtesy of the Sunderland Antiquarian Society, with a photograph of the same houses in September 2018.

homes around them housed skilled men. Next door lived an iron manufacturer and his family. By the 1881 census they had moved to Park Place West, Ashbrooke. Their final home was in Belle Vue Park, a gated development nearby. The homes in Bellevue Park have changed only minimally since Alfred and Deborah settled there, and the development is still accessed by gates.

As recorded in Chapter Four, Alfred Doxford left the partnership with his brothers shortly after their father's death. He then started in business on his own account, building a foundry on St. Luke's Road, Pallion. The site was on the King's House estate, owned by the Fenwick family, and so became known as King's Forge, Pallion. During the recession of 1884, his workmen subscribed to the Sunderland Distress Fund,[1] and at the 1891 census he gave his occupation as Master Forgeman and Smith, though he may have already retired from business. The forge, on a two acre site, was offered for sale or to let in 1888.[2]

During the last years of his life, Alfred suffered from ill health. He was only 53 when he died on 14 October 1895. His death certificate gave his occupation as a former shipbuilder. His widow survived him for 28 years, remaining at their home, 38 Belle Vue Park, with Beatrice, their unmarried daughter. Deborah died there on 24 February 1933, aged 91, survived by five of their children. She and Alfred were buried in Bishopwearmouth Cemetery.

82. A full terrace in Belle Vue Park, Ashbrooke, September 2018. Photograph by Patricia Richardson.

Of their six children, three left descendants. The family was as follows:

1 **Margaret Emily (1865-1950)** married Dr. Andrew Robertson, a general practitioner. They lived in Halifax, Yorkshire and had a son.

2 **Katharine Gertrude (1867-1959)** married John Lofthouse, a flour milling engineer. The couple later moved to Uxbridge, in Middlesex. They left two sons and three daughters.

3 Edith Evelyn (1869-1891) unmarried.

4 **William Morris Doxford (1870-1942),** known as Morris, was born on 3 August 1870 in Pallion. He lived in Sunderland and was taken into the engineering department at Doxford as a draughtsman. His name appears in the wages books of 1903, by which time he had probably been there for some years. (I did not check the years between 1883 and 1903.) He remained with Doxford throughout his working life, as he is recorded as a marine engineer draughtsman in the 1939 England and Wales Register. He was then 69, widowed, and living at 1 Egerton Street.[3] As his uncle, Charles David Doxford, had died in 1935, it was this that made him the last member of the family to work for the Company.

In July 1901, Morris Doxford married Jean Rodie Dalrymple (1873-1929), from Stranraer, Wigtownshire, Scotland, and the daughter of a wine and spirit agent. The marriage took place in Sunderland, where she was living with her widowed father.[4] Morris and Jean Doxford had a son, Alfred Dalrymple Doxford (1902-1991), who left no surviving children, and a daughter, Jean Elizabeth (1906-1978) who married William Ross Henderson, and has descendants.

5 **Beatrice Adelaide (1873-1959)** unmarried. Lived at the family home until her mother's death and then with her brother, Charles Henry.

6 **Charles Henry (1877-1947)** was an electrical engineer. He married Gladys Taylor (1891-1993) in 1914. Their only child died in infancy. His unmarried sister, Beatrice, was living with the couple at 15 Belle Vue Park[5] when the England and Wales Register was recorded in 1939. Gladys Doxford did not remarry. She was over 100 years old when she died at the end of the 20th century. In her widowhood, Gladys worked at a doctor's surgery and moved to Silksworth Lane, Sunderland. Gladys's brother was the stores manager at William Doxford and Sons. As such, he supervised the apprentices in their first weeks and months at Doxford.[6]

The Drawing Office where William Morris Doxford spent his working life. From the Doxford Publicity book, 1921.

Chapter Seven

Robert Pile Doxford (1851-1932)

83. Robert Pile Doxford. Family Photograph.

William and Hannah's tenth child, Robert Pile Doxford, was born on 11 December 1851, when the family were living in Howick Street. This was the year that his father dissolved the partnership with William Crown and began to diversify his business interests. Robert was educated locally. At the 1871 census, he was living at Kensington Esplanade with his parents. He was then nineteen and gave his occupation as 'coal fitter apprentice'. This might sound like a manual job, but a coal fitter was a broker, who arranged sales between the owner of a coal pit and the shipper. Much coal at that time was loaded on to the colliers from 'keels', shallow draft river boats, and had to be manually transhipped. The coal shipper's role disappeared later in the century, as the arrival of the railway meant that coal could be loaded directly on to the colliers at the railhead, and the coal pit owners then dealt directly with the shippers.

However, Robert then joined the North East Marine Engineering Company to train as a marine engineer under William Allan. He remained there until 1878, by which time he was 27. He then joined his father and brothers at William Doxford & Sons, to establish a Marine Engineering department at the family shipyard. His former boss, William Allan, established the Scotia Engineering Works on the Wear in 1888.[1] Allan was the Liberal Member of Parliament for Gateshead, and a noted philanthropist, who received a knighthood in the 1902 Coronation Honours.

On 5 January 1876, at the age of 24, Robert married Ada Barber (1854-1925) at St. Paul's church, Hendon, Sunderland. Ada was the sixth of eight daughters born to William and Elizabeth (Beswick) Barber. Her father was a shipping agent and broker, and the family lived at 39 Villiers Street, in the centre of Sunderland. William Barber was born at Horstead, Norfolk and moved north as a young man. Ada's mother, however, came from Bishopwearmouth. Throughout their lives, the Barber sisters remained in close contact with each other. Ada and her younger sister, Laura, married Doxford brothers and for a while lived next door to each other in Silksworth. Two other sisters married into the Coatsworth family, who were shipbrokers like their father.

Robert and Ada began their married life in 27 Azalea Terrace, Bishopwearmouth, and were living there at the 1881 census, when Robert gave his occupation as Managing Director of the Engineering Department at Doxford. He was elected to the Institution of Mechanical Engineers on 19 October 1880, aged 29, and remained a member until 1923. In 1884, together with his older brother, Theodore, he became a founder member of the NECIES. He was one of only three who were marine engineers.

Robert and Ada had four children: three sons and a daughter. They were Robert (1877-1945), Madoline Mabel (McIlwraith) (1878-1962), Arthur (1882-1914) and William (1884-1953). Their lives are recorded at the end of this chapter.

84. Azalea Terrace, Sunderland. Home to Robert and Ada Doxford. Photograph by Patricia Richardson

Silksworth Hall

Towards the end of the 1880's, Robert purchased Silksworth Hall, Silksworth as his family home. This was probably from the executors of Thomas Edward Chapman (d 1875), of T. E. Chapman & Co., wine and spirits merchants of Sunderland, as at the 1881 census three unmarried Chapman brothers were living at the property. On 1 August 1888 Ada Doxford inserted the following advertisement in the Sunderland Daily Echo and Shipping News: "Wanted, an experienced waiting maid, aged not under 30: Apply Mrs. Doxford, Silksworth Hall." Their new address appears in Kelly's directory of 1890. Silksworth Hall was an eighteenth century house. In 1868, the parish of Silksworth was carved out of Bishopwearmouth, Ryhope and South Hylton parishes. St. Matthew's church was then built. The population of the village at the time was only 400. However Silksworth Colliery was sunk in 1869 and within ten years the population grew tenfold, to about 4,700. Next to the Hall stood Silksworth House, owned then by the Beckwith family. After Henry Beckwith's death in 1891, the property was let. The two properties were then surrounded by farmland, but are now part of greater Sunderland.

The 1891 census shows Robert and Ada in residence at Silksworth Hall, with their four children, three servants, a cook, a housemaid and a waiting maid. Two came from the local area, but the third, Maria Preston, aged 20, was born in Cheshire.

85. Old Silksworth Hall, with the new building under construction next door.
Courtesy of the Sunderland Antiquarian Society.

Their youngest child, William, was nine. Madoline attended the fee paying local grammar school for girls, as her mother donated prizes, according to the local press. This also records Robert and Ada's involvement in local affairs. Robert was the rector's churchwarden for St. Matthew's church, and Ada served as its honorary secretary. He was the founding president of the Silksworth Amateur Cycling Club and was a member of the billiards club.

They also took their responsibilities as an employer seriously. In 1892 they entertained the families of Doxford officials and foremen to a garden party at their home. The group of 350 guests were carried from Chester Road to Silksworth in brakes (flat carts on which were placed chairs for passengers). The group roamed around the grounds and conservatories before having tea in a marquee, entertained by the Silksworth Colliery band. A cricket match between the Doxford officials and the men from the engine works and the foundry was hotly contested and there was dancing before further refreshments and home at 7.30 pm.[2]

At the turn of the 20th century, Robert's younger brother, Charles and his wife, Laura, moved next door. Perhaps this prompted Robert to rebuild Silksworth Hall. The existing building was in very poor condition, with rotting beams. It suffered from having been constructed around an even earlier edifice. He chose the young architect, Clare Arnold Clayton Greene (1875-1949), of Hedley and Clayton Greene, to design a new home for him. Clayton Greene had been born in London, and educated at Lancing College, but had moved with his parents to Newcastle. He established a practice in Sunderland in 1899. Their plans were approved at the

86. Silksworth Hall under construction behind the original building.
Courtesy of the Sunderland Antiquarian Society.

December 1902 planning meeting of the Houghton-le-Spring Rural District Council.[3] A new residence was built in red brick, adjacent to the earlier foundations. The old building was then demolished. Silksworth Hall was completed in about 1904 and, according to the 1911 census, contained 21 rooms, one being a fine billiard room. On 12th April 1905, once in his new home, Robert welcomed members of the Sunderland Antiquarian Society to examine the remains of the two former buildings on the site, in particular the Tudor building which had been enclosed within the walls of the eighteenth century structure.[4]

87. Silksworth Hall 1905, newly completed. Photographed for Robert Doxford. The book was later donated to the Sunderland Antiquarian Society

Robert Doxford commissioned a number of photographic images whilst rebuilding Silksworth Hall. He later donated a book of these photographs to the Sunderland Antiquarian Society.

In 1907 one of William Doxford & Sons' ships was named the Silksworth Hall. She was one of their largest turret ships, of 4,777 grt, registered in London to E. Nicholls

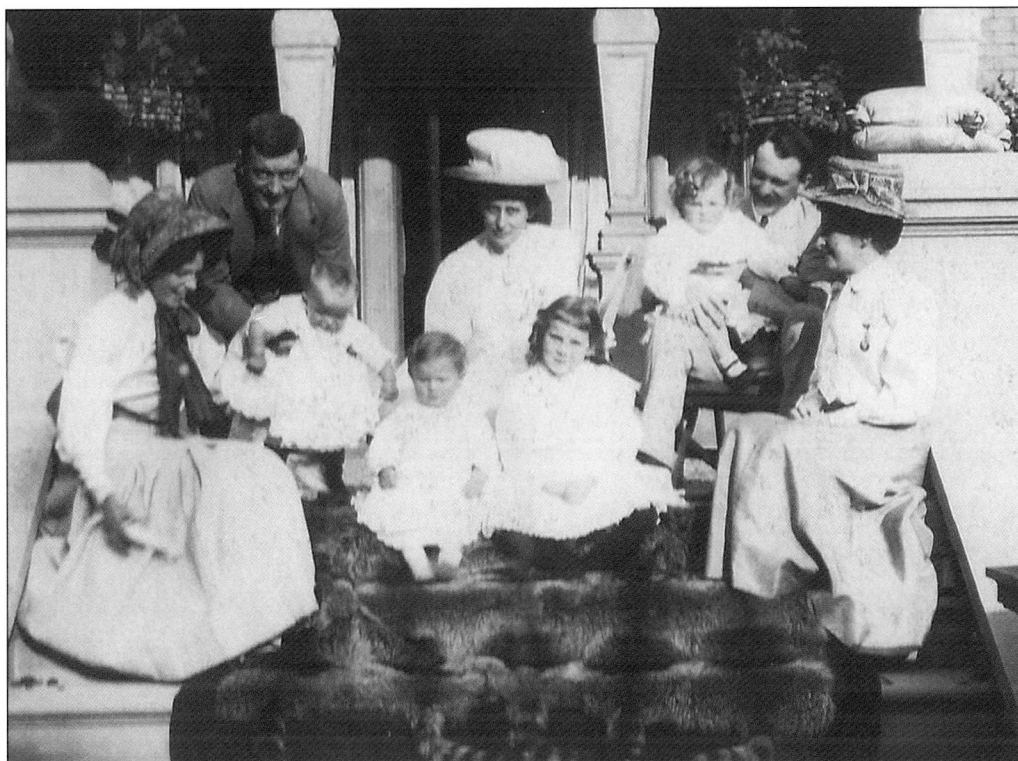

88. The family outside Silksworth Hall, 1908, probably taken by Robert Doxford, Jr. L-R: William and Hilda with William Burton Dallas, b Oct 1907, Madoline McIlwraith with Eric Harold (1907) and Madoline Mabel (1903), Arthur and Kitty with Arthur Dennis (1906). Missing is Alan Doxford McIlwraith, born in 1904. Family photograph.

and Co. of Cardiff. She travelled all around the world, but was sunk by a German U-boat off Lowestoft in April 1916, with the loss of three lives. Captain Ritchie, and thirty of his crew members survived.

The subsequent history of Silksworth Hall

From about 1912 Robert and Ada also had a home at Radlett, Hertfordshire.[5] From this point, the couple lived mainly in the south of England. By 1916, Silksworth Hall was occupied by Bryan Burletson (1866-1949), of the coal exporters Tabb and Burletson, with his wife and daughters.[6] Burletson was born in Sunderland, but the family were living in Newcastle upon Tyne by 1914. They probably first took a lease, and then purchased the property when Robert and Ada settled permanently in Sussex. Burletson had business connections with Sir Arthur Sutherland, the shipowner, who later commissioned the first Doxford Economy Cruise Ship. Their daughter, Hylda Cowans, lived at Silksworth after her parents' death but, in 1969,

89. The front entrance to Silksworth Hall. Taken in 1991, whilst the building was awaiting a new owner. Note the hemispherical domes on each side of the front door. Photograph by Patricia Richardson.

90. Silksworth Hall from the garden, also taken in 1991. With adjacent contemporary housing.

the Hall was sold and converted into a hotel. This had 28 bedrooms, a sauna and solarium, with a ballroom in an extension. The hotel was active throughout the 1980's but the building was later reconverted into a private home.

After the sale of the business in 1919, despite no longer living in Sunderland, Robert was retained as manager by the new owners. His colleague, the engineer K. O. Keller, kept work diaries, now held at Tyne and Wear Archives. From these it can be traced that 'Mr. Robert' only stopped visiting Pallion in 1928, by which time he was in his late seventies. The two men were close friends, and Keller travelled down by train on a regular basis to spend weekends with him in Sussex.

Silverlands

At the end of 1922, Silverlands, Boar's Head, near Eridge, Sussex, was auctioned by Messrs. Giddy and Giddy of Tunbridge Wells on behalf of the executors of a Mr. Robinson. Robert bid successfully for the property and spent the rest of his life there. Ada Doxford died at Silverlands on 13 March 1925. Her body was returned to the North East for burial in Silksworth churchyard. Robert was a widower for seven years. He was clearly still active as, approaching eighty, he travelled with his daughter and son-in-law, Madoline and Christopher McIlwraith, to visit his grandchildren in Melbourne.[7] He died at Silverlands on 25 March 1932, aged 80 and was buried next to his wife. He received only a short obituary in the transactions of the NECIES. This is surprising, considering his contribution to marine engineering in the North East.

After adjustments, Robert Doxford's estate was proved at £204,354. His two surviving sons, Robert and William, were appointed his executors and trustees, together with Edmund Cuthbert Thompson, his solicitor. Having left legacies to his daughter, Madoline McIlwraith, to a number of cousins and to six of his servants, he instructed his executors to sell all his residual estate and property. The proceeds were to be divided equally between his two sons. If one of the sons wished to live at Silverlands, he must buy his brother's half share. Silverlands, with its twenty acres, was offered for sale by auction on 24 June 1932 by Messrs. Brackett and Sons of Tunbridge Wells. Whether the auction took place, or whether the brothers had already agreed a price, is unclear, but the elder son, Robert Doxford Junior, moved into the property.

91. St. Matthew, Silksworth 1999. Photograph by Patricia Richardson.

An assessment of Robert Pile Doxford's contribution to William Doxford & Sons Ltd.

Having joined the family Company in 1878 Robert devoted the rest of his life to the concern. His major achievement was to develop the marine engine and boiler works into a major component of the Company's business. At the turn of the 20th century, he recruited the right engineers to bring Doxford engine production into national dominance. These were Karl Otto Keller and William Hamilton Purdie. From 1914 to 1919, Robert and Keller designed and patented innovations in relation to the marine oil engine that would bring the Company through the lean years of the 1920s and 1930s.

He was Chairman at the time of the sale of William Doxford & Sons. With the rest of the Board, he resigned as a director in January 1919, but was invited by the new management to continue as Manager of the Engineering Works, showing their confidence in his abilities. His enthusiasm and commitment continued virtually until his death in 1932. From the patents he and Keller were granted between 1919 and 1925, it is apparent that his contribution continued to be of enormous value to the development of the opposed piston marine oil engine once it was in general service.

The family of Robert and Ada Doxford

Robert and Ada Doxford had four children, all born in Azalea Terrace, Bishopwearmouth.

1 **Robert (1877-1945)** attended Glenalmond College, Perthshire and then went to Durham College of Science. He joined Doxford in the shipbuilding department, and became Assistant Manager in 1900. It was Robert who designed the overhead transporting gear for the new extension berths for the restructured yard, described in Chapter Four. This led to his appointment as a Director in 1904, the year that the new yard was completed.

92. *Robert Doxford, 1877-1945, as a young man.*

In 1911, Robert was the Managing Director of the shipbuilding department, and visited Germany with K.O. Keller and his younger brother, Arthur, to investigate oil powered engines. (Chapter Nine). He was then still single, and living at Silksworth Hall as its head of household, but moved to Grindon Close, Silksworth by 1914, according to Kelly's Directory. During WWI, Robert served as a temporary Lieutenant in the Durham Light Infantry. He was 38 when he married Muriel Meacock (1890-1965), on 25 November 1915. The wedding took place at St. Andrew by the Wardrobe, London. Muriel's father was a bank manager, and she was born and brought up in Walton-on-Thames.

After the Company was sold in 1919, Robert retired from business. At that time he and Muriel were renting Fyning Foley, Rogate, Sussex.[8] From this point they lived permanently in the South East. During the 1920s, they made their home at Aldenham Cottage, Great Amwell, Hertfordshire,[9] but after his father's death moved into Silverlands. Following a fire, he rebuilt the property in the Arts and Crafts manner. Robert died in London on 11 February 1945, after which Silverlands was sold and his widow retired to London, where she died in 1965.

They had one son, John Knevett Doxford (1919-1992), who was commissioned into the Royal Horse Guards in 1938, and served with them throughout WWII. John had the honour of acting as Silver Stick Adjutant. As such, he stood guard over the body of King George VI, and also attended at the Queen's coronation.[10] This was the year that Her Majesty presented new colours to his Regiment. John married twice, and left children by both wives.

2 **Madoline Mabel (1878-1962)** married Charles McIlwraith (1875-1932), a shipping agent and owner, on 31 October 1901. Charles's father, Andrew McIlwraith, had founded Messrs. McIlwraith McEacharn & Co. in 1875, with fellow Scotsman, Malcolm McEacharn. They shipped frozen meat from Australia to the U.K. and were coal bunkerers and shippers. Charles was in the business, based in Devon, near his father. It was this Company that brokered the order for the Sagamore, the precursor to the Turret, in 1891. (Chapter Three) Two of Charles's brothers, John and James, died of fever during the Boer War, a few months prior to his marriage to Madoline. Charles and Madoline's sons, Alan (1904-1993) and Eric (1907-1993), emigrated to Australia. Only their daughter, Madoline Ransom (1904-1995) remained in England. Madoline McIlwraith was a widow for thirty years. She died in London on 25 March 1962, leaving descendants in both England and Australia.

3 **Arthur (1880-1914).** Like his elder brother, Arthur attended Glenalmond College, Perth. He studied at Durham College of Science between 1899 and 1902, gaining a B.Sc. Meanwhile, from 1898-1903, he was undertaking a five year apprenticeship at Doxford under his father, in the Engineering Works and the Drawing Office.

93. Arthur Doxford, 1880-1914. Family photograph.

Having completed this, he was appointed Assistant Manager of the former.

On 11 May 1905, at St. Peter's, Monkwearmouth, Arthur married Katherine Bertha Featherstonhaugh (1884-1946), a grand-daughter of Sir James Laing, the Sunderland shipbuilder.

Arthur Doxford was elected to the Institute of Mechanical Engineers on 23 April 1909. He joined the board of Doxford at the following (20th) AGM in 1910. His major contribution to Doxford was the research he undertook with his brother and Karl Otto Keller, on the development of the Doxford marine oil engine. Sadly, he died on 5 September 1914, just after the outbreak of war, before the project came to fruition. He suffered from asthma, and was only 34 at his death. His widow moved to Yorkshire and lived through the next world conflict before her death in 1946.

Arthur and Bertha's three children were born at Greenbank, South Hylton and were all known by their second name. Arthur Denis (1906-1974), served with the civil service in India, and later retired to Liss, Hampshire. Denis and his Australian wife, Elizabeth (Lawrance), had twin sons. Katharine Patricia (1909-1991), was married to an insurance executive, Douglas Richardson, and lived in Surrey, and then Hampshire. She and Douglas had two sons, the elder being the author's husband. The third child, Edward Michael (1912-1940), was married, but left no children. Michael died during the evacuation from Dunkirk on 29 May 1940. HMS Wakeful, (1917), captained by Commander R.L. Fisher, R.N., previously part of the reserve fleet, had already made one successful run back to Britain. Michael was one of 640 men who managed to board for her second run. Sadly, the ship was torpedoed by the German motor torpedo boat S-30. She instantly broke in two and sank. The troops had been sent below, and only one survived. Twenty five of the ship's crew, including the Captain, were in the central section, which remained afloat long enough for them to be rescued. Michael's widow, Kathleen (Powell) became a renowned breeder of cocker spaniels at Broomleaf Kennels, Ewhurst, Surrey. She judged at many events, including Crufts and published a textbook on the breed.[11]

*94. William Doxford (1882-1953).
Courtesy of William Warren Davis*

4 **William (1882-1953)** also went to Glenalmond College, but then took a degree in Naval Architecture. He gained his M.Sc. in 1904. Like his two older brothers, William joined the family business, being apprenticed in the shipyard department. He became Manager of the Design Department in 1903, and of the Shipyard in 1905. He was elected a director of Doxford with Arthur in 1910. During WWI he served with the Royal Navy Volunteer Reserve. He was the fourth of the third generation to become a Director of William Doxford & Sons.

On 17 February 1905, William married Hilda Wilson (1881-1915), a daughter of Joshua Stansfield Wilson, a wholesale grocer, of Thornhill Park, Sunderland. They had a son, William Burton Dallas Doxford, born in 1907, but Hilda died in August 1915. Dallas lived for a time in the U.S.A., but later moved to Trinidad, where he died.[12]

William subsequently married Hilda's younger sister, Evelyn, (1883-1972), known as Eva. After the sale of the business, William and Eva moved to Northfields House, Eastergate, near Chichester. The house is now a country hotel. He died at Northfields on 3 August 1953, having returned from visiting Dallas in Trinidad. Eva retained Northfields House, but from then made her main home in Trinidad. She was aged 89, when she died at Brasso in 1972. William and Eva's son, Peter David Doxford, sadly died in a boating accident in 1945, but they have living descendants through their daughter, Evelyn Ann (1918-2002), who married John Warren Davis, the sculptor. John and Ann sold Northfields, but kept a dairy herd on its land.

Chapter Eight

Charles David Doxford (1856 -1935)

95. Charles David Doxford, youngest son of William and Hannah.

Charles Doxford was the twelfth and youngest child of William and Hannah. He was born at 44 Howick Street, Monkwearmouth, on 13 July 1856 and a year later moved with his parents and siblings to Pallion. He was educated locally and joined William Doxford & Sons in 1873, aged seventeen.[1] He was the third brother to join the shipyard and was apprenticed in the Drawing Office. He remained with the Company until his death sixty two years later. His training lasted for five years, after which he became manager of the design and constructional drawing division. In 1882, Charles also became the Managing Partner of the Shipyard.

On 4 June 1883 Charles married Laura Barber (1858-1903) at Christ Church, Sunderland. Laura was his sister-in-law and the seventh daughter of William and Elizabeth Barber. The couple had two children: Aline Sylvia (1884-1968), who remained unmarried, and Charles (1888-1961), who married twice and left children. At the 1891 census the family were living at Bainbridge House, Tunstall Vale, Bishopwearmouth. They moved to Grange House, Stockton Road later in the decade.

As described earlier, as Director in the Drawing Office and Manager of the Shipyard, Charles ruthlessly oversaw the development of the Doxford turret ships, ignoring the contribution and financial interest of Arthur Haver, his Chief Draughtsman. The benefit to the Company in patenting the design was immense, and the rise in output over the next twenty years brought Doxford to national prominence and the Blue Riband for production in both 1905 and 1907. Charles was becoming Theodore's right hand man, and his influence was evident in the development of the marine engineering division as well as his own Shipyard Department. He was also innovative. As also recorded above, it was he who designed the machine that created joggled plates, ensuring a lighter, and more economical ship to build.

Silksworth House

At the turn of the century Charles and Laura moved out of the centre of the borough to Silksworth. Robert and Ada Doxford had been living at Silksworth Hall for fourteen years when John Craven, the tenant at adjacent Silksworth House, died in 1902. Charles took a 99 year lease on the twenty four acre property. Silksworth House was built between 1775 and 1780 for William Johnson, who left the property to his friend, Hendry Hopper, a lawyer. Through marriage, it descended to the Beckwith family. Henry Beckwith (1820-1890) had the main entrance constructed, and the Beckwith arms were carved into stone above the door. After Beckwith's death in 1890, his sons moved away and the property was let by the Hopper/Beckwith family trust, from whom Charles took the lease. He set about improving and extending the formal grounds, laying out pleasure gardens and excavating a lake, which still survives within the modern Doxford Park, adjacent to modern housing.

96. Silksworth House, Silksworth,.home to Charles David Doxford. Later renamed Doxford House. 1996 Photograph by Patricia Richardson.

The families of the two brothers were very close, and their wives are reported to have spent part of each day in each other's company. However, this may have been due to Laura's ill health as on 19 August 1903, barely a year into the tenancy, she died at Silksworth House. She was only 45. Aline, at 19, was expected to assume the role of housekeeper for her father, who remained a widower for 32 years. However, she adapted badly to her new role and remained very much her own person. Her passion was for animals, and was a successful breeder of deerhounds.

Charles, meanwhile, threw all his energies into William Doxford & Sons. He had a lively intelligence. He was reputed to have said that it was his brains and Theodore's

97. Doxford House from the garden, 1996   Photograph by Patricia Richardson.

money that made a success of the shipyard during the years of WWI. However by the end of his life he was a very rich man himself. He was of slight stature, and all the photographs of him show that he dressed modestly, in a light coloured suit and a bowler, even when presented to Royalty, as happened twice during his lifetime. (Though he took his bowler off for them, not surprisingly!) He was respected by both his colleagues and the men at the Shipyard. His workforce at Silksworth House found him a benevolent employer, and he seems to have made few enemies.

Charles and Laura inherited their head gardener from the Beckwith family. He was Henry Whiteley (1874-1939), who had lived at Silksworth in his childhood, as his father, also named Henry, held the position before him. After his apprenticeship, H.S. Whiteley left to develop his career before returning to become head gardener in 1900. The two men became old friends, and frequently strolled around the gardens arm in arm. He served as factor to Charles, and then to Aline Doxford until his retirement in 1938, shortly before his death.

98. Henry S. Whiteley (1878-1939). Head gardener at Silksworth House. Courtesy of Douglas Smith.

In 1915 Charles founded National Galvanizers Ltd. on Pallion New Road, as part of the war effort. This made galvanised steel plates for destroyers. It was a private company and was still in operation in 1961, according to Dun & Bradstreet's guide. The business had closed by 1980 and the site became a builders' merchant.[2] Charles played another role during WWI, as adviser to the government over underwater barriers within Scapa Flow. This was intensely secret work, that demonstrates the respect that he had gained on a national level. When Sir Theodore died at the end of 1916, Charles assumed the role of Managing Director of the Company, which was then in full production, launching twenty one destroyers and an almost equal number of merchant ships during the conflict. However, towards the end of the war, Robert and he called a meeting of the shareholders of Doxford to discuss the future of the Company in peacetime. This led to the eventual sale of the business in 1919, described in Chapter Ten.

Charles was invited by the new owners to remain as General Manager, and was later referred to as the Managing Director, though he was not reappointed to the Board until 1930. It was his determination in finding orders that kept the Company afloat during the long years of the depression during the 1920s. He used his own money to support the Company. In 1924 Charles Doxford personally underwrote the shortfall in financing three ships built for the Silver Line, run by the Thompson brothers (See Chapter Twelve). Ten years later his will dealt with the outstanding bills of exchange still in existence with regard to the Silver Line.

He remained in post through the bankruptcy of the new owners in 1923 and the disastrous years between 1925 and 1927, when not one ship left the Pallion yard.

99. The launch party for MV Silvercedar. 1924. Charles Doxford is holding the car door.
Courtesy of the Sunderland Antiquarian Society.

He lost his close friend and ally, A.O. Hedley, in 1926, leaving a huge gap in his personal life. Once he became a Director in 1930, he made a key decision and recruited John Ramsay Gebbie to manage the Shipyard. This led to the successful design of the Doxford Economy Cargo Ship. The early 1930s were further years of dearth, and it was only in his last year of life that the yard reopened.

Charles regularly attended the meetings of the Baltic Exchange in London. He stayed at the Savoy Hotel mid-week. The Company Secretary, Robert Haswell, reported to him by post each day. He took the overnight train home and visited the Pallion office to take breakfast before reaching Silksworth for lunch. According to Douglas Smith, President of the Sunderland Antiquarian Society, Charles often dismissed the chauffeur, took the train from Pallion to Coxgreen and then walked home via the Grindstone banks to Offerton, along Hasting Hill Road to Herrington and thence to Silksworth House. It was only in his last few months that his health failed.

Charles Doxford was a Justice of the Peace but, as he grew older, he sat very rarely because of increasing deafness. According to his obituary in the Sunderland Echo, this also prevented him from taking part in shipping councils. However, he was trusted and respected by both his friends and commercial rivals. After his death on 21 January 1935, his funeral at St. Matthews, Silksworth was attended by a large number of his shipbuilding competitors from throughout the north.

Despite the difficulties of the 1920s and early 1930s, Charles left an estate of £643,988 19s 3d, a considerable fortune for the time. His executors were Clement Davies, K.C., M.P., and Edmund Cuthbert Thompson, the late Octavius Hedley's partner. They negotiated successfully with Doxford to recover most of the advances he had made to the Company during the lean years. By his will, Charles confirmed that the furnishings in Aline's bedroom and in the drawing room and the dog kennels within the house were, and always had been, her personal property. He left his residual estate under trust to his children, with two thirds to Charles Junior and one third to Aline. He then directed that his trustees could not be forced to sell any property, and were to maintain the same in good order, ensuring that Aline could remain at Silksworth House.

Charles David Doxford – an assessment

Charles Doxford's contribution to William Doxford & Sons was massive and complemented that of his two older brothers. He was a ruthless businessman who, under a mild manner, not only grabbed the initiative over the development of the turret ship design, but ensured that Doxford won orders throughout periods of uncertainty and outright depression. He kept the Company from liquidation. He was prepared to defend any court cases brought against Doxford.

He was a man who saw things through, whether as a member of the Bureau Veritas classification society, the Baltic Exchange or his long years as a Justice of the Peace.

As regards to the sale of his beloved business, Charles may have been prescient enough to see the oversupply of ships as the war reached its conclusion, and decided to act in the best interests of the family shareholders. He fought for a guarantee from Kleinworts, to safeguard the family against default by the buyers, the full story being recounted in Chapter Ten. It was his strength of character, as well as his money, that ultimately saved the Company from closure. Many other shipbuilding firms in the North East went to the wall in either the late 1920s or the 1930s. He was, sadly, not to see the resurgence of Doxford that took place during World War II and the peace that followed. His most observant obituarist, a colleague at Doxford, writing in the Motor Ship,[3] stressed not only his achievements, but his continuing determination into old age. 'A. P. C.' stated:

> "He was one of those rare men who knew how to look ahead, even beyond his own lifetime. Only a few months before he died, in describing some development he was making at this yard, he remarked to the writer that he did not suppose he would live to see the results. He did not say this in any sort of melancholy way, but as a simple fact which would not affect his plans."

Aline Doxford and Charles Doxford Junior

100. Miss Aline Doxford, daughter of Charles David, with seven of her prize deerhounds. Press photograph.

Aline Sylvia Doxford (1884-1968) and her brother seem to have come to an arrangement, as she later bought the freehold of Silksworth House and its land. She remained there until her death, surrounded by her deerhounds, her kennels being named Ruritania. She had a successful career showing her dogs, though she refused to be drawn into the role of judge. She served as Hon. Secretary to the Scottish Deerhound Society and, when she was elected a committee member of the Ladies' Kennel Association in 1918, this was recorded in The Tatler.[4] It seems that, as she grew older, she withdrew from people and became a solitary figure. She stopped showing her dogs in the late 1920s, even before her father's death. Once alone, she closed off the Silksworth House grounds to visitors and was rarely seen in the community. She kept only a minimum of staff and lived very simply, despite being a wealthy woman. After her death on 1 June 1968, her estate was valued at £292,231. Aline Doxford bequeathed Silksworth House to Sunderland Corporation, for educational purposes. At the recommendation of the Housing Committee, the property was renamed Doxford House in her memory, and the grounds were opened as Doxford Park. It was used as student accommodation by Sunderland Polytechnic (later Sunderland University). A large red brick extension, partly one storey high, and partly of three storeys, was added on the north side of the property.

The University had vacated by 1994, as the property was no longer considered fit for this purpose. Doxford House was advertised for sale that year by Chesterton & Co. as having planning potential for residential, social or commercial use, but no buyer came forward. The Lazarus Foundation, who cared for people recovering from addiction, took a short lease on the property in 1997 but, a year later, the University again offered the property for sale for any purpose, this time giving a figure of £880,000. This provoked a storm of indignation from the local community and surviving members of the Doxford family, because of Aline's wishes. The Silksworth Heritage Trust undertook a photographic survey to record its architecture because of its sorry state. English Heritage had given the building a Grade II* listing, but this did not prevent it from falling into disrepair, and being listed as 'at risk'. The property failed to achieve the sale figure and subsequently passed through a number of owners' hands, becoming more derelict with each of these. Some repair work has been effected, but the property is still vacant.

101. Charles Doxford Junior (1888-1961). Courtesy of the Sunderland Antiquarian Society.

Charles Doxford's son, always referred to as Charles Junior (1888-1961), was the younger child. He was educated at Durham School and then joined Doxford, becoming a Director in 1917. He suffered even more than his father from debilitating deafness. He accompanied his father to London in January 1919 to hand over the family firm to its new proprietors, but left the business shortly afterwards. Charles Junior married twice. His first wife was Kathleen Vasey Storey, the daughter of a Sunderland solicitor. They were married in January 1912 and lived at Burdon Hall, a few miles to the south of Silksworth[5], but the marriage ended in divorce. Their only daughter, Aline Sylvia (Greenwell), left three children. In 1929 Charles married his cousin, Agnes Vera Hedley (1898-1990), grand-daughter of Sir Theodore. Although a near contemporary in age, Agnes Vera was of the next generation. Charles and his second wife left Sunderland and moved to Bowness, in the Lake District. They had two sons, Antony Charles (1930-2013) and David Iain Doxford (1932-2006), both of whom have also left descendants. Iain was a keen family historian and became the inaugural President of the Doxford Engine Friends Association. (Chapter Sixteen)

Chapter Nine

The Doxford Opposed Piston Marine Oil Engine

I would like to acknowledge the research undertaken by J. F. Clarke into the development of marine propulsion that he included in Part 2 of 'Building Ships on the North East Coast'[1]. My thanks also go Alfons Verjheidhen, host of the Diesel Duck website on marine engines, who led me to Tom Scott and John (Jack) Jordan, co-members of the Doxford Engine Friends Association. Jack, formerly the Assistant Drawing Office Manager at the Doxford Engine Works, recently published: 'Notable Points in the Design History of the Doxford Opposed Piston Marine Oil Engine'[2] in collaboration with the late Rodney Cartridge. I have drawn on this and Jack has also allowed me to use his images. Tom Scott salvaged many Doxford papers when the Engine Works closed and also provided me with material and advice.

At the end of the 19th and beginning of the 20th century, shipbuilding and marine engineering companies, both on the Clyde and in the North East, were exploring different methods of propulsion for vessels. Although, coal-fuelled steam power continued to be the favourite for shipowners until well into the 20th century, as early as 1889 Doxford had used petroleum to fuel the boilers in their first torpedo boat. The North East coast pioneered steam turbine driven warships, though it was shipbuilders on the Clyde who installed the first turbines in merchant ships. The move to oil was resisted by many shipowners because of its cost, even though this fuel weighed far less than coal and took up less space, thus potentially giving more cargo capacity. The North East in particular had a plentiful supply of cheap, high quality coal which was shipped by rail directly from the mines to the loading staithes. In addition, there were few storage facilities available for oil at that period. Even so, ships and cargoes were getting larger, and companies needed extra capacity in their tramp ships, which oil could provide.

In the first decade of the 20th century, Doxford explored oil-fuelled internal combustion engines for marine vessels in the U.K., though their first experimental engine was gas driven. The gas used was the same town gas (from coal) as that which lit homes,[3] and had been used for static engines since the mid-19th century. However, industry was turning to electricity and, by 1905, Doxford had abandoned using gas for the static engines in their yards. Despite this, that year they began to explore the possibility of a marine engine fuelled by gas. Robert Pile Doxford, as head of the Marine Engineering Department, recruited Karl Otto Keller (1877-1942), a twenty-eight year old Zurich born engineer. Keller was already in Britain, having arrived in 1903 to develop a large static gas engine in Birmingham. He then moved to Napiers, shipbuilders on the Clyde, where he worked on a motor car engine, and afterwards to Thornycrofts at Southampton for the development of a submarine engine.[4] Keller joined Doxford on a three year contract, specifically to undertake experimental work on a gas powered marine engine. The Doxford wage book for officials and draughtsmen confirms Robert Doxford's role in Keller's recruitment.[5] Page No. 1411, for the week ending 12 July 1905, has an insert added. This reads:

"Otto Keller appointed Gas Engineering Expert at upstanding wage of £4 £5 per week commencing 6th July 1905. – see special agreement. – (Signed R.P. Doxford) and noted: 14/7/05 should read £5 per week, see next week.

WILLIAM DOXFORD 7 SONS LTD.
R.P. Doxford (signed) Director"

The only higher paid 'official' at the time was Robert Haswell, the Secretary to the Engineering Department, who was on £5 10s per week. A. Bain, in the next section as the Chief Draughtsman, was, however, paid £6 per week. Keller's salary later increased to this.

At Pallion, however, despite Keller's expertise and experience, the work did not go to plan, and was abandoned in 1908. Keller's contract was not renewed, and he worked elsewhere in Britain during the next three years. After this set back, in 1909 Robert Doxford's sons, Robert Junior and Arthur, visited Germany to investigate engines powered by oil. Rudolf Diesel began development on what he called a 'Rational Heat Engine' in 1890, as a compression ignition engine, and eventually produced a working prototype in 1897. Over the next ten years, although designs were worked up by other manufacturers, including Swan, Hunter & Wigham Richardson on the Tyne, no effective marine oil engine was developed. The advantage of oil over gas was that, whilst the latter needs an electric spark to generate ignition, the grade of oil used by Rudolf Diesel, and given his name, ignites by the heat of compression. Robert and Arthur Doxford reported back that they considered that none of the prototypes that they had seen in Germany were viable for marine conditions. They recommended to the Board in September 1910 that Doxford should develop their own marine oil engine, because of their long experience of ship behaviour at sea.

Doxford's decision to pursue an oil-fuelled engine attracted attention. In October 1910 Sir Theodore was approached by James Knott,[6] a shipowner from Howdon-on-Tyne, who had founded the Prince Steam Ship Company in 1887. Knott wanted to order two tankers using the fuel immediately, and other shipowners were also in contact with him at this period. Sir Theodore had to make clear that development was at a preliminary stage. A potential disaster had occurred earlier that year, when the Doxford engine works suffered a major fire, but this turned out to be a spur to the development of the marine oil engine. A new engine works was built, and experiments were then conducted in a modernised environment.

The decision was taken to work up an experimental single-piston single-cylinder Diesel engine. This was the first example on the North East Coast, but not a new design. Robert Pile Doxford invited Otto Keller to return to Pallion as head of the design department. Keller started on 1 February 1911, at a salary of £7 per week, only £1 more than he had been paid three years earlier.[7] He in turn recruited William Hamilton Purdie (1888-1971), then aged only 23, as his senior draughtsman and designer. Both men remained with the Company for the rest of their working lives. After Keller's death, Purdie became Director of Engineering.

When Robert and Arthur Doxford visited Europe once again in 1911 for further

102. First Doxford test engine 1912. Single cylinder, 2 stroke, Diesel cycle.

investigations, they were accompanied by K. O. Keller. The experimental engine was up and running by June 1912. To quote J. F. Clarke:

> "It was of the Diesel Cycle, operating on the Blast Fuel Injection system, as was the norm for the time. It was not an opposed system engine."

Dr. William Ker Wilson, who worked with Keller and Purdie at Doxford during the 1920s and 1930s, wrote a number of technical books on engines. He was of the opinion that "the mechanical design was based as far as possible on characteristically rugged construction of established marine steam reciprocating-engine practice." However, the test engine quickly ran into problems. Doxford Board Minutes of October 1912 state: "We abandoned the Diesel type of engine as being unsuitable for Marine work, owing to the unreliability of cylinder covers, scavenge valves, exhaust valves head etc. as ascertained by our experiments, and reports which we had of other marine Diesel Engines, and we decided to adopt the Junkers type."[8]

In 1912 Doxford obtained the sole U.K. licence to build an opposed piston engine to the design of Wilhelm von Oechelhäuser and Professor Hugo Junkers. The opposed piston design does away with cylinder heads. Instead the pistons work against each other. Junkers came to England from Dessau, East Germany, with members of his staff, to work at Pallion. In 1913/14 a single cylinder unit was built generating 450 bhp (brake horse power). This was erected in an extended test house in the yard, and proved to have great possibilities. The second Doxford test engine was 500 mm bore with equal upper and lower piston strokes of 750 mm giving a total stroke of 1,500 mm. It was designed to produce 450 bhp at 130 rpm, enabling a 4-cylinder unit to develop 1,800 bhp. The engine was a blast fuel injection engine and operated on the Diesel Cycle, using compression for ignition.

103. Second Doxford test engine 1914.
Junkers/Oechelhäuser type, vertical opposed piston,
single cylinder
Courtesy of the Doxford Engine Friends Association

The Board decided to commence work on a 4-cylinder engine of 3,000 bhp. The Junkers/Oechelhäuser engine was horizontal, but Doxford version was vertical. The intention at that stage was to build a 420 foot ship in which to install the engine. By January 1914 Doxford had spent about £30,000 on the development of an oil-fuelled engine, firstly to their own design of a single piston engine and secondly on the adaptation of the Junkers type of opposed piston. This expense, as reported to the Board in January 1914, was for the first experimental engine, followed by work on the Junkers type; building an engine shop that was suitable for the production of internal combustion engines; the time taken for the experimental work, and for the licence. Robert Pile Doxford was by now in his early sixties, but it seems that his enthusiasm, drive and commitment to this new product was undimmed. He presented a number of papers on the engine's development to the Board.

Innovation at Doxford was intense in the immediate pre-war period. As well as developing an internal combustion engine, on 26 November 1912 Doxford launched SS Cairnross (C452), a steel cargo ship of 4,016 grt, with steam turbines built by Parsons Marine Steam Turbine Co. at Wallsend. The ship was completed in January 1913, and registered to the Cairn Line of Newcastle. Doxford now advertised themselves as: "Builders of all types of Steamers up to 20,000 grt, Torpedo and other High-speed Vessels either with Reciprocating or Turbine Engines, Patent Belt-Discharging Vessels for Coal or Ore, Internal Combustion Engines and Floating Oil Storage."[9]

Sadly, Robert Pile Doxford's second son, Arthur, died on 5 September 1914, aged only thirty four. His elder brother, Robert, was also a skilled engineer, but Arthur's loss would have been a particular setback for the firm. In addition, WWI had just begun, ending the association between Doxford and Professor Junkers, who returned to Germany even before engine trials commenced in November. However, Doxford continued to have a relationship with Junkers over the licence and patents, until these were formally terminated in February 1926.[10]

As has been recorded in Chapter Four, WWI generated an enormous demand for ships, and this impacted on experimental time. It also delayed the building of an experimental motor oil driven vessel. In 1913 and 1914, Doxford launched ten and nine ships respectively, all for commercial shipowners, including two for the Hamburg Amerika Line. In line with the developing need for liquid fuel, two were oil tankers for the Eagle Oil Transport Company of London: SS San Jeronimo (C457) and SS San Nazario (C459), each with 15,000 grt capacity. At the end of 1914, Admiralty work took priority at the Pallion Shipyard and Engine Works, as destroyers were commissioned. Twenty one of these were built by Doxford over the next four years, each with 25-27,000 bhp, in addition to merchant ships. In 1915 of the twenty ships left the yard,

104. The experimental submarine engine ordered by the Admiralty.
Courtesy of the Doxford Engine Friends Association.

fifteen were landing craft for the Navy. Additionally, the Admiralty asked Doxford to build an engine suitable for submarines. They developed a single-cylinder high speed experimental engine that could provide 400 bhp at 360 rpm (i.e. medium speed). According to J. F. Clarke (p. 98), this was the only oil engine to be constructed during WWI. Despite the urgency of this project, delays occurred because of the general demands on the yard. The submarine engine was not ready until the end of 1917, when it was sent to the Admiralty's Engineering Laboratory at the City & Guilds College, in south London. It did not come into service.

The surge in orders placed the Doxford workforce under strain. There were no reserved occupations as in WWII; men were actively encouraged to volunteer, and later conscripted. Doxford placed advertisements in the press urging past employees to return to their yard but, not surprisingly, the development of the experimental internal combustion engine was frequently interrupted. In addition, despite interest from shipowners prior to the War, during the conflict no firm orders for installing a marine oil engine in a ship came forward until 1917, when there was at last a glimmer of hope for peace. The first three ships fitted with a marine oil engine did not come into service until 1921/22.

However, trials went ahead. In early 1916, Doxford took out a patent on a fuel oil injection valve, with R. P. Doxford, K. O. Keller, and Commander Charles J. Hawkes as joint patentees.[11] Hawkes (1888-1953) was a university lecturer who was appointed the first superintendent of the Admiralty Engineering Laboratory in 1917. He was always a practical engineer. The test team subjected the Doxford experimental marine oil opposed piston engine to an overload at 165 rpm. The high pressure stage air-compressor piston seized in the cylinder, and the engine stopped almost immediately. Luckily it suffered no damage. The test team then tried using solid fuel injection, without blast air, and eventually achieved success by reducing the compression pressure from 600 psi (pounds per square inch) to 300 psi to allow fuel a longer period to burn, and then gradually increasing the pressure back up to 600 psi. This became known as the 'Dual Combustion Cycle'. The process produced a cycle diagram that was quite different to that which Rudolf Diesel had patented, as it dispensed with the need for the high pressure blast injection air compressor. It also eliminated the need for a highly complex scavenge pump system and increased the engine power by 7%. The Doxford engine now became known as an 'Opposed Piston Marine Oil Engine', rather than a 'Diesel Engine' because Diesel's patent specifically stated: "Combustion of the charge proceeds at or approximately at constant pressure." During this period, Robert Doxford, as Director of the Engineering Department, kept the Board up to date on the progress and possibilities for the new engine.

The end of 1916 saw changes at Doxford. Sir Theodore died in October, so Robert became Chairman whilst Charles took the role of Managing Director. It seems that Charles set his first priority as finding a commission for a ship to be fitted with one of the new engines. This was not an easy task, and one option considered was to build a ship for an associated shipping Company, the Grindon Hall Steamship Company Ltd., Cardiff (managed by E. Nicoll), under whose name two ships named SS Grindon Hall (C346 and C398) had been registered, in 1905 and 1908 respectively. (The second followed the loss at sea of the first.) This had been the approach used when launching the first turret ship. I have been able to find little more about this registered Company, though in 1920 Doxford built SS Kincardine (C519) under its name, managed by B. J. Sutherland of Glasgow. (She was later renamed Antar, and eventually became Artemisia.) It was, perhaps, a holding device for private investors. The shipowners who eventually came forward in 1917 were:

* the Norfolk & North American Steam Shipping Company Ltd., London, who ordered MV Dominion Miller (C521), 5,089 grt, and
* Transatlantic Rederi A/B of Gothenburg, Sweden, (then called Göteborg), managed by Gunnar Carlsson, whose contracts were MV Yngaren (C549), 5,247 grt and MV Ektaren (C556), 5,243 grt.

The Yngaren was the first to go into service. The prototype engine, type 58L4[12], had four cylinders developing 3,000 ihp[13] at 77 rpm (i.e. low speed). The designation comes from 580mm bore/Long Stroke/4-cylinders. The upper and lower piston strokes were identical (1,160 + 1,160 mm). The three ships were each propelled by a single screw. The cost of developing this engine had been a staggering £100,000, demonstrating the profitability of the yard during the war years. However, it was not until after the end of hostilities that work began and, as this started, Doxford came under new ownership (Chapter Ten). Despite the upheaval, continuity was maintained at Pallion. Steam powered ships continued to leave the East Yard under contracts supervised by the Shipping Controller, whilst the three oil powered ships were built in the West Yard, next to the Engine Works. The Dominion Miller was launched first, on 20 March 1920. The Yngaren followed, on 28 September.

However, on Friday, 1 October, K.O. Keller wrote in his diary:

"Decided to put 521 engine into 549 and hurry on 549 auxiliary incl. oil engine driven generators."

105. *The prototype Opposed Piston Marine Oil Engine 58L4 fitted to MV Yngaren (C549) 1921. Courtesy of the Doxford Engine Friends Association.*

Keller had a good relationship with the Transatlantic engineer, Tage Madsen.[14] Transatlantic had requested Doxford to build the auxiliary engines to drive the generators for C549 as oil engines, rather than powered by steam. This extra factor might explain why the Yngaren was completed before the Dominion Miller.

MV Yngaren was a steel general cargo ship, registered in Belgium under the Swedish flag in March 1921. The builders' sea trial went ahead on Thursday, 9 June. Keller noted that the check nut on the front cam shaft came loose, bursting the gear case, and that the two inner bearings of the main fuel pump became red hot, and had to be lifted out of gear. A further casing was put around the main exhaust pipe to solve this problem.

MV Yngaren was then moved to the Tyne and its maiden voyage via Gothenburg to Australia. Public sea trials started on 14 June 1921.[15] K.O. Keller's exact words including his punctuation, (or lack of it) read:

"C549 Yngaren – Official sea trial about 200 visitors present
         including Board of Directors.
Very successful trial, though No 2 back fuel valve seized without observation by visitors.
At 7 pm we left the Tyne for Göteborg.
At 1 am centre legs and bearing run dry due to defect in lubrication.
At 3 am stop engine to open all bearings, found in good order
    muslin cloth on lubr. filters removed.
at 1 pm started engine again both lubr. pumps working
    and all went well."

To interpret the diary entry, I consulted Jack Jordan, who told me that the exhaust pipe ran directly over the heads of engineers when working on the camshaft platform, and the exhaust temperature could reach the temperature of red hot steel, so robust insulation was needed to keep the heat within the pipe.

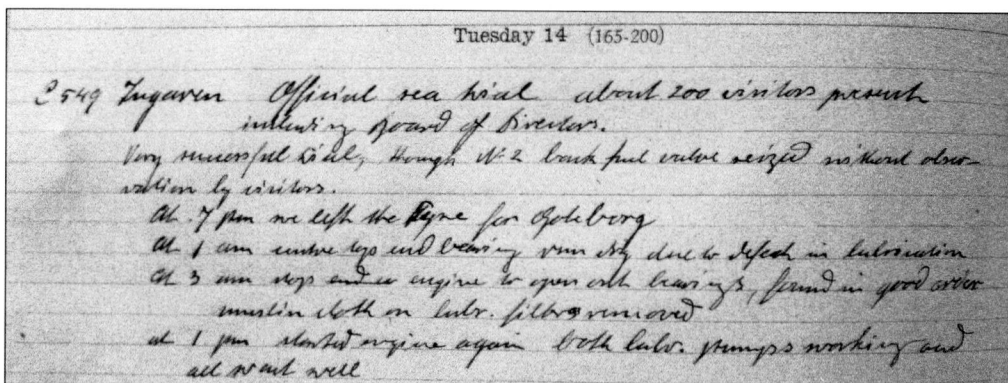

106. Karl Otto Keller's diary for Tuesday, 14th June 1921. © Tyne and Wear Archive Service. DS.DOX/2/2/27.

Jordan advised that the 'legs' referred to were probably the centre connecting rods. He continued that it is quite normal, when a ship is new, that the pipe lines feeding the oil to the bearings are not 100 per cent clean. Engineers used to insert fine muslin between the ranges of the oil supply pipe, to hold back heavy particulates, such as rust or steel filings. However, as the muslin itself became clogged, the oil pressure reduced. Keller's diary indicates that he found the bearings to be in good condition, so removed the muslin, to allow the oil to flow at full pressure. On later engines fine mesh gauze was used and, later still, large oil filters were relied on. This cleaning process began on the test bed and continued on sea trials throughout the life of Doxford and its later incarnations, until a ship was signed off as fit for service.

107. MV Yngaren (C549), the first ship fitted with the Doxford opposed piston oil engine
From 'Where ships are Born'.

The Doxford directors on the ship for the official trial were R.A. Workman, Sir John Esplen and W.O. Workman. Sir Alexander Kennedy represented the Northumberland Ship Building Company (the NSBC) and Tage Madsen represented the new owners, the Transatlantic Steam Ship Co. of Gothenburg. Robert Pile and Charles David Doxford were also on board, together with representatives of the Cunard Line,

Three photographs taken on board. Mr. T. Madsen, on the left, looks distinctly pleased. Capt. Huldtgren is in the centre. On the right is Mr. K. O. Keller, the engine designer.

108. Cameos of the owner, captain and engine designer for M.V. Yngaren. From The Motor Ship July 1921.

B.J. Sutherland, the Fairfield Shipbuilding Co., the Cairn Line, the Anglo-American Oil Co., and the Monmouth Shipbuilding Co. Some were long term clients; others were already part of the NSBC, the new owners of Doxford. Mr. Wesselman represented Rotterdam Lloyd's, and Mr. R. Haig of the Sun Shipbuilding Co. of Chester, Pennsylvania, was on board. Shortly afterward, his Company took out a licence to produce the new engine. Jordan told me that Keller was lucky that such visitors failed to notice the No. 2 back fuel valve seizure, as most were themselves

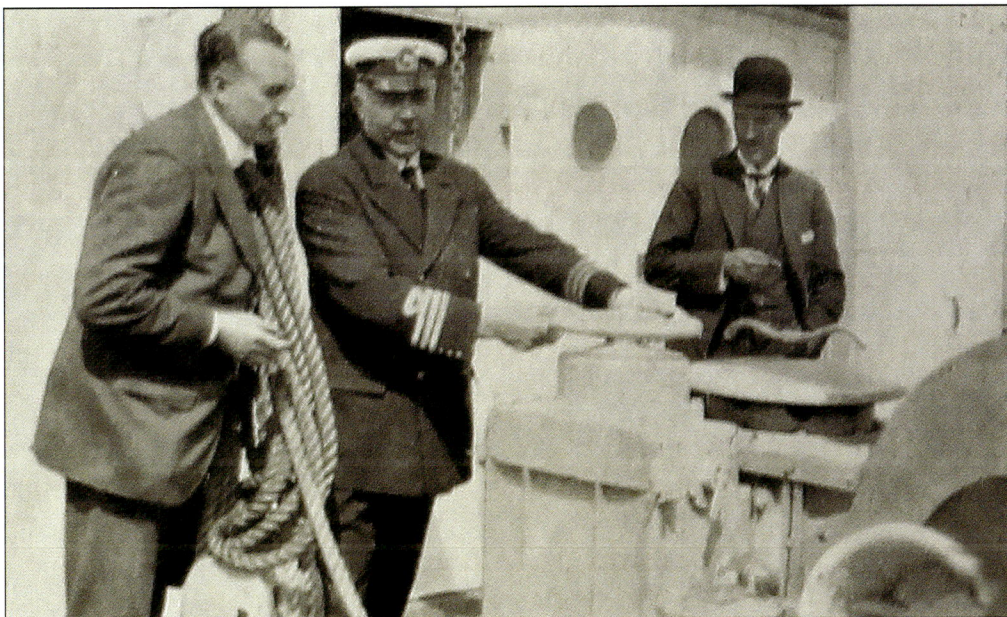

109. Captain Hultgren at the helm of MV Yngaren on her sea trial, with Tage Madesen, representing the owners, in the bowler hat. I believe the man on the left is R. A. Workman. From The Motor Ship July 1921.

sea going engineers. He suggested that either Keller placed himself in a strategic position to prevent this or that, because the ship was not fully loaded, she may not have needed full power.

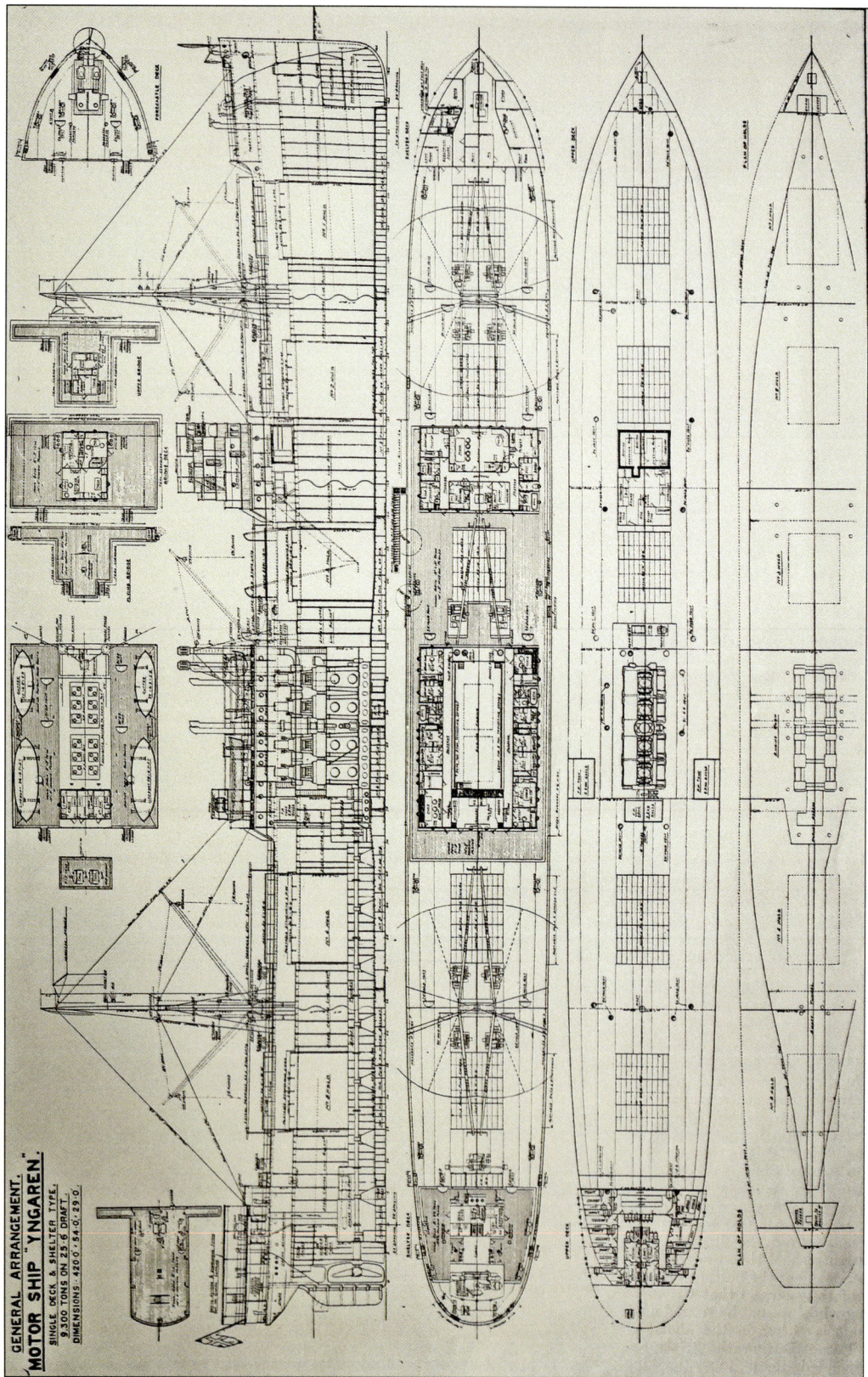

110. "Plans for the Motor Ship, Yngaren." From The Motor Ship July 1921.

120

The Yngaren's first voyage to and from Australia, including a 10% overload, required no adjustments to the engine, whose condition was "entirely satisfactory after the full six months' work under the usual machinery guarantee", according to the publicity leaflet produced by the Sperling Combine that year.

Auxiliary power

The Yngaren had three 2-cylinder auxiliary opposed piston engines installed beside the main engine. The original idea had been that steam would be used to generate auxiliary power, but in October 1920, Transatlantic asked that Doxford manufacture oil fuelled engines for the tasks required. They were based on the earlier submarine engine, but this request led to a frantic rush to complete three such engines in the time frame. The Yngaren actually completed her

111. 2-Cylinder Doxford Auxiliary Engine, 1921.

first trials with only two in place, and although three were installed, only two were operated at any one time. The engines had two cylinders of 180 mm bore, with a total stroke of 500 mm (upper stroke 220 mm, lower stroke 280 mm) at 320 rpm, producing 65/70 KW of power.[16] They operated by solid fuel injection. They were used to generate electricity for shipboard lighting and to service the lubrication, cooling water and fuel oil transfer pumps etc. The first three motor vessels, Yngaren, Dominion Miller and Ektaren, were all fitted with these engines. However, the decision was then taken to cease development on auxiliary engines, for cost reasons, it seems. From this point, such engines were purchased from other manufacturers. The main engines were considered to be more cost effective in terms of Doxford engineering staff time, though work was undertaken on a single cylinder opposed piston oil engine for auxiliary power between 1922 and 1926 by Keller, W. H. Purdie and W. Ker Wilson. It seems that this last engine was never subjected to trial on a vessel.

The Yngaren remained in service for 31 years, until 12 January 1942, when she was sunk within a minute by two torpedoes from the German submarine U-43, en route from Bombay to Hull. Her crew of 34 and 6 passengers were lost, plus a cargo of copra, manganese ore, 80 tonnes of trucks and 8 aircraft.

3 auxiliary engines

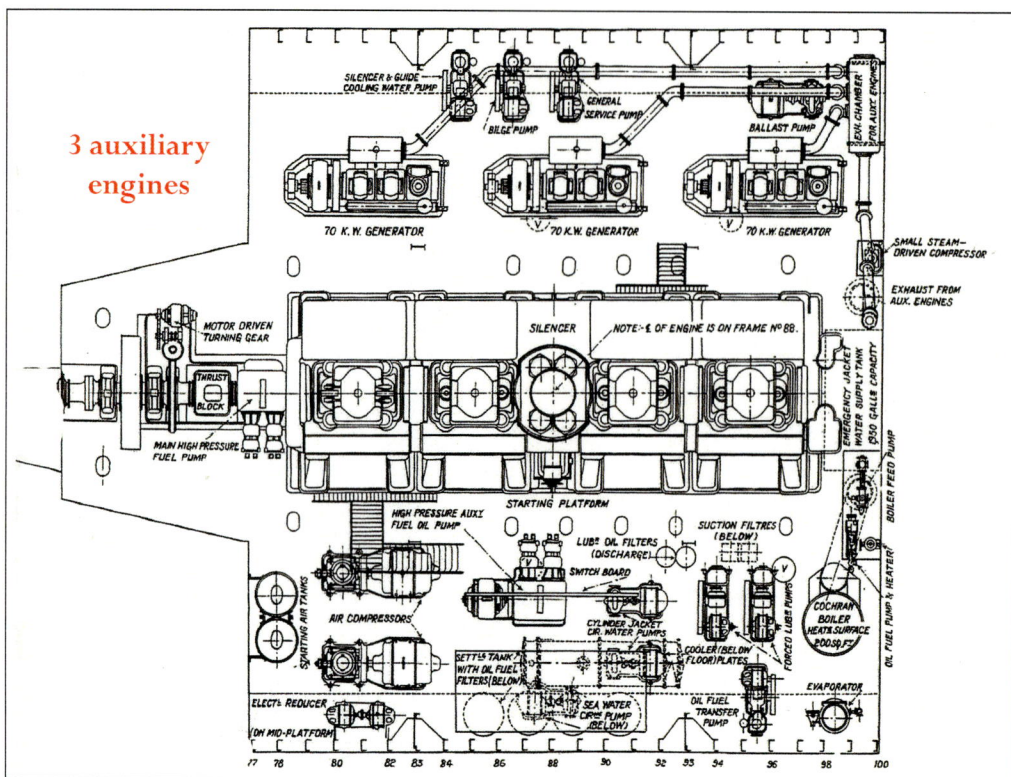

112. A plan of the layout of the engine room of MV Yngaren, showing the main engine and the 3 auxiliary engines.
Courtesy of the Doxford Engine Friends Association.

Her sister ship, MV Eknaren (C556), 5,243 grt, was completed in September 1922, but the second ship to go into service fitted with the opposed piston oil engine was MV Dominion Miller (C521), 5,089 grt, as she was handed over in February 1922 to the Norfolk & North American Steam Shipping Company. Dominion Miller was renamed Pacific Commerce in 1925, and was sold to the Brynmoor Shipping Co. London in 1936. A year later she joined the fleet of A/S Viking Lundegaard & Sonner, Farsund and took her third and final name, the Norbryn. She was in service until January 1959, when she was broken up at Grimstad.[17]

Despite the difficulties of the 1920s, both the Doxford brothers, Keller and Purdie remained in post. By the end of 1931 Doxford had fitted 58 opposed piston marine engines on their own account and their licensees had built a further 51 units.[18]

Karl Otto Keller (1877-1942)

K. O. Keller was one of the pivotal employees of Doxford. With 'Mr. Robert', he registered five patents in relation to oil engine development prior to the sale of Doxford and before the launch of MV Yngaren. The first has already been mentioned, the other four were: Patent no. 113301 for 'Improvements in valve-gear for internal combustion engines' (11 February 1918), no. 124534 for 'Improvements in or relating to pistons for internal combustion engines' (16 Nov. 1917 - 18 March

1919), no. 1276980 for 'Improvements in or relating to fuel-injection valves for oil engines' (11 June 1919), and no. 21643/20 for 'Improvements in or relating to diesel and similar combustion engines'. The last two were granted after the sale of the Company.[19] These show the painstaking work that the men were undertaking to achieve a viable and economic internal combustion engine.

Keller registered three more patents in 1922-23 and another in October-November 1925, again in partnership with Robert Doxford. After Robert Doxford's death in 1932, Keller's last six patents were applied for in partnership with the Doxford Company. The final two were granted in January 1943, after Keller's own death.[20] These brought the efficiency of the Doxford engine forward by steps. In 1923 he was appointed the General Manager of the Engineering Department. He rearranged and later extended the Engine Works and installed new machine tools to modernise production. Sadly, during his first year in post, the only ship launched from Pallion was MV Pacific Shipper (C577), 6,304 grt, for Furness Withy & Co. London, on 22 December 1923. She was completed in March 1924.

113. Karl Otto Keller. From Shipbuilding and Shipping Record 1942.

During the 1920s and 1930s Keller wrote technical papers on aspects of marine oil engine development, such as 'Combustion and its Difficulties in Marine Oil Engines', 1929, 'Torsional O scillations in Marine Shafting', 1934 and 'Diesel Engines for Cargo Ships' in collaboration with H. Hunter and B.J.O . Stromberg, 1939.[21] The depression years of the twenties eased but then deepened during the even grimmer times of the 1930s. However, K.O . Keller changed engine frame production from castings to welded steel plate in 1930. This ensured a saving about a quarter in the weight of the engine. He also opened a department for flame cutting and electric welding of engine parts. These measures ensured that Doxford remained competitive for engine production, as they were more economical than their rivals. It was not until 1937 that Keller finally became a Director. And, sadly, although born in Switzerland, and despite his sterling work for Britain during WWI and the inter-war years, Keller was persecuted when WWII broke out. However, he was still in service when he died on 22 July 1942, aged 65.

The story of Doxford marine oil engines in operation continues in Chapter Twelve.

The First Doxford Opposed Piston Oil Engine on Test Bed with Water Brake, 3,000 I.H.P.   1920

Chapter Ten

1918-1923
The Sale of William Doxford & Sons Ltd.

There was and still is controversy over the apparently sudden decision at the beginning of 1919 to dispose of the overwhelming majority of the shares in the family run Company. Perhaps it was a shrewd move, considering that within a year all Wear shipyards faced a severe downturn in orders, but this was not apparent at the time. The financial beneficiaries were the two surviving Doxford brothers and the extensive cousinhood of the next generation, a number of whom bought country homes away from the smoke of Sunderland with the proceeds. The Company itself was the loser, together with its employees. Almost immediately its reserves were sequestrated to support the other members of a fast expanding conglomerate, known as the Sperling Combine and Doxford faced an uncertain future.

The background to the sale is that towards the end of the war shipbuilding yards had full order books, and this attracted attention from investors. In 1915, even Doxford themselves had created an associated private Company, called Collective Industries Ltd. (CIL), with a capital of £25,000 "to carry on the business of bankers, financiers, capitalists, Company promotors, underwriters, etc.", the first subscribers being A.O. Hedley and his daughter Alfreda Short.[1] CIL took shares in Doxford, and were represented at their AGMs by Charles and Ernest. The extension of voters' rights in 1918 to the numerous cousins who held Preference Shares also stimulated family interest in the Company's affairs.

114. Alfred Octavius Hedley, son-in-law of Sir Theodore Doxford and Solicitor to William Doxford & Sons Ltd.

Robert Pile Doxford, as Chairman, convened an Extraordinary General Meeting on 11 February 1918, to put forward the Directors' proposal to alter Article 72 of the Company's regulations, by limiting the subjects on which preference shareholders were permitted to vote. From henceforth these were to be (a) winding up the Company, (b) sanctioning a sale of the undertaking and (c) altering the regulations of the Company. It is probable that the two brothers and their nephew, Ernest, had been approached by potential buyers, and that absolute secrecy was required, as the second proposal was to strike out the text of Article 131 and insert "No copy of such Account Balance Sheet and Report shall unless with the sanction of the Directors be circulated nor shall any extract from same be taken or made." Both resolutions were ratified at a second EGM that month.

A meeting of the Directors took place on 25 March 1918 chaired by Robert, with Charles, Ernest, Robert Junior and William Doxford present. The only Director absent was Charles Junior. The Directors resolved to issue from reserves 50,000 as new £10 shares. 25,000 were Ordinary Shares and 25,000 were 6% 'B' Cumulative Preference shares. This led to yet a third EGM within eight weeks, held on 8 April. At this meeting, Article 126a was altered to read that a general meeting could authorise the Directors to capitalise "all or any part of the undivided profits of the Company", whether from trading profits or the appreciation of capital assets, and to allot such monies to the ordinary shareholders in proportion to their existing shareholding as fully paid shares. Article 126b was altered to allow dividends to be paid as fully paid shares or debenture stock, rather than as cash. The fourth EGM of the year was held at 10 am on 24 April. Having ratified the changes to the above articles, the Directors' resolution of 25 March to issue shares from reserves was carried unanimously. This led to the increase of the Company's issued capital to £1,000,000. In the case of a sale or voluntary winding up of the Company, the price of the 'B' Preference Shares was to be the average selling price over the previous six months. The EGM was followed immediately by the 28th Annual General Meeting of the Company, which simply appointed Directors and auditors.

In 1891 the Private Limited Company was inaugurated with capital of £200,000, and in 1899 this was increased by £300,000. In 1900 the new Public Company confirmed the capital as 25,000 £10 Ordinary Shares and 25,000 £10 Preference Shares. Between 24 April and 6 May 1918 the authorised capital was increased by £500,000 to £1,000,000: 50,000 Ordinary shares, 25,000 Preference Shares and 25,000 'B' Preference shares, all at £10 each. However, over £250,000 of these shares were not issued.

The fifth EGM of 1918, held on Monday, 6 May, authorised the capitalisation of a further £250,000 of reserves, so that the 25,000 6% 'B' Preference Shares of £10, could be issued to those on the share register, pro rata as to their existing holdings. Charles Doxford took the chair, the other Directors present were Ernest (who was also noted as representative for the trustees of his late cousin, Arthur, and for Collective Industries Ltd.), William and Charles Junior. A.O. Hedley was in attendance, as the Company solicitor. 23 shareholders, descendants of William and Hannah Doxford and their spouses, gave their proxies.

They were:
* Mr. Robert Pile Doxford,
* Mrs. Ada Doxford (Robert Pile's wife),
* Mr. Robert Doxford Junior (Robert's son),
* Mrs. Muriel Agnes Doxford (Robert Junior's wife),
* Mrs. Eveline Mary Doxford (William's wife),
* Mrs. Margaret Evelyn Hedley, Miss Annie Greta Doxford and Mrs. Wilhelmina Vera Thompson (Theodore's daughters),
* Mrs. Norah Cleland (Theodore's daughter),

* Miss Margaret Cleland (Norah Cleland's daughter),
* Mrs. Mary Hannah Hedley (Theodore's daughter),
* Mrs. Alfreda May Short, Mrs. Eveline Doxford Short, Miss Mary Greta Hedley and Miss Theodora Brenda Hedley (Mary Hannah Hedley's daughters),
* Mrs. Bertha Eleanor Doxford (Ernest's wife),
* Mr. Theodore Bertram Doxford (Ernest's son),
* Mrs. Dorothy Bertha Stack. Miss Marjorie Doxford, Miss Betty Doxford and Miss Joan Doxford (Ernest's daughters),
* Miss Aline Doxford (Charles's daughter),
* Mrs. Kathleen Vasey Doxford (Charles Junior's wife).

When a full list was later recorded for the distribution of the 'B' Preference Shares, a further seven cousins were included:

* Mrs Madoline McIlwraith, (Robert's daughter),
* Theodore Fenwick Hedley, (Margaret Evelyn Hedley's son),
* Luielia Olga Short, Agnes Vera Hedley, Margaret Norah Vereker Hedley, Doreen Sheila Hedley and Aline Octavia Hedley, (all five being daughters of Mary Hannah Hedley).

The long list of names may suggest a reason for the sale of the Company within a year. The number of family shareholders may have made it hard for the Directors to resist a determined bid when it came. Patricia, Arthur Doxford's daughter, and her brother, Denis, always maintained this.

This was the last general meeting of Doxford to be chaired by a family member. The minutes of 6 May 1918 were signed at the 29th Annual General Meeting held on 27 May 1919 by the new Chairman, Robert Alfred Workman.

The Directors held a meeting directly after the EGM on 6 May 1918, at which general business was conducted. It was reported that Torpedo Boat Destroyer (TBD) Velox (C516) had been handed over to the Admiralty and TBD Whitley (C520) had been launched on 13 April.[2] The first Standard Vessel contract. SS War Gazelle (C523) had been handed over to Messrs. Watts, Watts & Co. three days earlier, "the Builders Certificate having been delivered to the Ministry of Shipping by post on 29th April 1918." The order book was very healthy, with fifty four contracts in hand on 1 April 1918. One of these, C521, in due course became MV Dominion Miller and held the second Doxford opposed piston marine oil engine, as described in Chapter Nine. Fourteen vessels were standard vessels, three of type B, seven of type A and four of type F. Thirty three were deemed post war vessels. This suggests that the Board, and the country, were expecting the conflict to cease fairly quickly, as the German offensive in the spring of 1918 had been successfully resisted. Sadly, many of these ordered in 1917 from Norway were subsequently cancelled, but this was not anticipated at the time.

The Directors' meeting of 6 May also reported on the Company's financial position. The wages for the year to date were given as £188,202 15s 11d for the seventeen weeks, making the average weekly wage bill £11,070 15s 1d. During April, they started at £7,829 in Week 1 (of which the Monday was the Easter Bank Holiday) and rose to £13,017 in Week 4, averaging £11,368. Wages were around £12,019 per week by the year end.[3] This confirms that work in hand had been reasonably consistent, but had grown since the start of the year. There was a significant disparity between skilled and unskilled wages. The comparative wages on Tyneside achieved by platers and labourers during WWI have been studied by Dr. Buxton. In May 1914, before the start of the conflict, a labourer received 24 shillings per week (£1.20): 61% that of a plater, whose wage packet contained 39 shillings (£1.95). The sheer volume of work ensured that by mid-1919 the unskilled man received 77% of a plater's wage. His wages had grown to 57 shillings (£2.65) per week, as opposed to 74 shillings (£3.70). This suggests that although the wage bills more than doubled over four years, Doxford were not employing that many more men.

The minutes continued that the Company borrowings amounted to only £12,409, and £3,327 was held on deposit. £1,710,550 was held in government bonds representing a net cash and near cash position, £1.5 m higher than the £279,000 on the books in 1914. This rose to £1.984 million by the end of the war, of which £1,860,550 was in war loans or bonds.

However, some due debts were difficult to collect. Doxford had been owed £24,000 (over £2m in modern terms) since 1914 on Austro-Hungarian bills drawn by Natale Banaz Senior and Junior, M.U. Martinolich and Giovanni Racich. They had been secured on SS Izgled (C426) completed in July 1911 for the Nav. Libera, Ragusa, Sicily. (Giovanni Racich & Co.) This situation was not resolved until the 1920s. Banaz junior managed to recover £22,000 for Doxford in 1921. The remaining £2,000 was written off on 7 April 1925.

The Board of Directors convened a week later, on 14 May, to ratify the decisions taken by the shareholders, and to authorise the distribution of the 'B' Preference Shares. Two shareholders wished to nominate family members to receive some of their personal allocation. Charles relinquished 1,500 of his shares in favour of his son (600), his son's wife (350) and his daughter (550). Ernest Doxford relinquished 1,750 of his shares in favour of his wife (550), and his five children (200 each). The nominations point to the particular pressures on Ernest Doxford. His children were now young adults, so needed independent security.

Charles remained the largest personal shareholder in the Company, with 4,500 shares. He also held 125 shares jointly with A.O. Hedley. However, Ernest had the largest holding overall: 2,018 shares held personally, 2,125 held jointly with A.F. (Arthur Freville) Maling, and 4,000 held jointly with A.O. Hedley, making 8,143 in total. It is likely that, as Maling and Hedley were both solicitors, the joint holdings were for associated business concerns.

The lead up to the sale

As the details and aftermath of this takeover are somewhat notorious, I have studied

* J.F. Clarke, Part 2, pp 218-221,
* the essay by Stefanie Diaper on the Sperling Combine in 'Capitalism in a Mature Economy',
* 'An anatomy of speculative failure: Wm. Doxford & Sons Ltd., Sunderland and the Northumberland Shipbuilding Company of Howdon on Tyne, 1919-1945', by Professor Hugh Murphy, Hon. Professor at Glasgow University, published in the Mariner's Mirror in November 2017,
* the Northumberland Shipbuilding Company (the NSBC) section of the Kleinwort Benson papers lodged at the London Metropolitan Archives
* and the Doxford Board Minutes, held at Tyne and Wear Archives, Newcastle.[4]

The transaction attracted great public interest, and was reported in the national press.

115. The Canadian financier, Edward Mackay Edgar, driving force at Sperling & Co.

The Great War had attracted speculators, one of which was Sperling & Co., a London stockbroking partnership, based in Moorgate, who operated outside the London Stock Exchange. They had specialised in company share issues and promotions since the early 20th century. They were described by the Bank of England as "not strong", following some poor underwriting, and the Bank recommended caution in dealing with them. E.C. Grenfell of Morgan Grenfell was more scathing, referring to them in 1914 as "very second rate".[5] At the outbreak of war, such activities were banned to stockbrokers, so Sperling then referred to themselves as bankers, and later as merchant bankers. By 1918 only one family member was a partner: Eric Stephen Astley Sperling (1878-1962).

The other partners were

* Edward Mackay Edgar (1876-1934), a Canadian, who became the firm's driving force,
* Sir Edward Paulet Stracey, 7th Baronet (1871-1949),
* James Walter Strange (1873-1951), and
* Edward Welton (1875-1942).[6]

As can be seen, these men were contemporary in age, in their forties, and eager to diversify their business. MacKay Edgar had been involved in company acquisitions in Canada and came to Britain with the intention of capitalising on his expertise. He was made a partner of Sperling & Co. in 1908. In 1918, Sperling were approached by one of MacKay Edgar's business acquaintances, Robert Alfred Workman (1873-1948), a ship broker in the City of London,[7] and a junior member of the Belfast shipbuilding family, Workman, Clark & Co.[8] He was a nephew of its chairman, Frank Workman. Workman's wife, Elizabeth, was a member of the shipping family that owned the Allan Line.

Workman had been negotiating a deal to acquire a North East coast shipyard, and put a proposition to Sperling. The Northumberland Shipbuilding Company Ltd. (the NSBC) at Howdon, on the Tyne, was seeking a purchaser. The yard had been established in 1883, and was acquired in 1898 by Rowland Hodge (1859-1950), who renamed it. In 1901, needing more capital, Hodge sold his controlling interest to the Furness Withy Group, shipowners and shipbuilders at Hartlepool, who were looking to expand. The yard prospered, building mainly general cargo ships. Their reputation meant that the Shipping Controller allowed them to design their own variety of standard cargo ship during WWI. Hodge continued to manage the yard, though he was later found guilty of breaking rationing rules by hoarding.

When Christopher, 1st Baron Furness, died in 1912, his son, Marmaduke (1883-1940), succeeded him in running the business. The second baron sold a number of his father's yards, in order to construct a modern shipyard on virgin ground at Haverton, on the Tees. By 1916, this was proving a costly mistake, due to the low lying ground, and he was forced to split the two sides of the business. His father's advisor, F.W. Lewis, bought out the Furness family's interests in the shipping concern, whilst Furness Withy retained the shipyards. At this point Lord Furness decided to sell the NSBC to finance the Haverton Hill site.

R. A. Workman heard of his intentions and began negotiations with Lord Furness. As he did not have sufficient funds to act independently, Workman approached Sperling through Edward MacKay Edgar, who brought in the London bankers, Kleinwort, Sons and Co.[9] Edgar was a friend of the junior partner, Herman A. Andreae, a grandson of Herman Kleinwort, the German founder. Both Sperling and Kleinwort at that time had a relationship with Clarence Hatry (1888-1865),[10] a charismatic entrepreneur and asset stripper of companies, who used his Amalgamated Industrials as a parent Company. Hatry later became notorious and was eventually jailed for fraud, but at this period he was a sought after advisor and/or partner, though treated with some caution by most of the long established City firms. MacKay Edgar had introduced Hatry to Sperling in 1918, when they acquired shares in Irvine's Shipbuilding and Dry Dock Company at West Hartlepool, also previously owned by Furness Withy. Hatry was one of the Directors at Irvine's, as was R.A. Workman.

At the time, the NSBC had a healthy order book, promising an income of £1.1m in the following three years. Its credit balance (retained earnings) had grown over the war years from £84,000 to nearly £163,500. Order books for most shipbuilders were then buoyant. The 'Estimated Margin of Profit' for the twenty one ships on its order books to be built post war for Norwegian and Italian shipowners was presented to Sperling and Kleinwort during negotiations in 1917 as £1,325,730, i.e. an average of around £65,000. This sheet is amongst the Kleinwort papers at the London Metropolitan Archive. When shown these figures, Dr. Buxton considered that they may have been over-optimistically estimated by Rowland Hodge to secure the sale of the NSBC, in which he still had an interest. However, purchasers of NSBC yard nos. 241, 242, 246, and 253-270 put down non-returnable deposits.

241, 242 and 253-264 were eventually completed and handed over, but only six were delivered to the original Italian purchasers (five to Lloyd Adriatico Soc. Di Nav. Venice). British shipowners took up the remaining contracts, and some were delayed until 1924, and no doubt delivered at a lower price. For instance, SS Peruviana (C242), was launched on 3 May 1920, but Furness Withy did not take possession of her until October 1923.[11] 265-270, for six cargo ships ordered by Norwegian owners, were cancelled in 1920.[12]

The future was expected to be bright, and this was the sort of asset rich company that Hatry specialised in acquiring, in order to extract the most profit from its component parts. The deal proved successful. In July 1918, Furness Withy sold the NSBC to R.A. Workman for £830,000. This was financed mainly by Sperling, but Kleinwort paid £50,000 outright and took out a further £350,000 in debentures. The conglomerate was placed under the trusteeship of the Canadian and General Trust Company, an associate of Sperling through Mackay Edgar. The two banks were to be repaid through the sale of shares in the new Company, and the promise of income through the order book. Because of wartime restrictions, rather than going to the London Stock Exchange, the shares were offered privately, under a trust deed. They were quickly taken up. This was despite the lack of a public prospectus, something that attracted criticism in both the City and the press. Amongst the Kleinwort papers is the prospectus, marked 'For Private Circulation Only', offering 400,000 10% Cumulative participating Preference Shares of £1 each and 2 million Ordinary Shares of 1 shilling each.[13] The NSBC then had seven shipbuilding berths, held on a lease of which forty years were still to run. No specific guarantee of future work is in the document, but it was widely reported to be in the region of £1.3 million. R.A. Workman took the chair of the NSBC, which continued to trade under its old name. The other Directors were his brother, William Orr Workman, Managing Director of James Allan Senior & Sons, Sir John Esplen, of Esplen, Sons & Swainston, Liverpool, E. Mackay Edgar, representing Sperling, and the previous owner, Rowland Hodge, the great survivor, who remained as Managing Director. However, the NSBC under its new ownership was not only expected to build ships, but also to act as a parent company. The Directors quickly looked for other shipbuilding yards to acquire, even though Sperling & Co., as backers, had little knowledge of shipyards or the international shipbuilding market. They saw the acquisitions simply from a financial viewpoint, and took no interest in the running or output of any of their yards, except as a source of funds to the parent company to fund further purchases.

Workman had intimated that he did not intend to remain at the NSBC as a long term measure. He planned to sell his interest quickly, either to Hatry or to others.

However, he formed a close relationship with Sperling, and remained as a co-proprietor. He also quickly revealed his modus operandi over his involvement in shipbuilding companies. The Daily Mail of 12 February 1919 reported:

"A Strange Shipping Deal

Shareholders of a concern called the Northumberland Shipping [sic] Company Limited, will be asked at its meeting today to confirm two most remarkable agreements which the Directors have made with their chairman, Robert Alfred Workman. The Company has nineteen contracts to build ships for foreign owners and the Directors have agreed to pay Mr. Workman half the net profits of such contracts because he has procured Messrs. Furness, Withy and Company to guarantee the Company against loss in their execution.

That is the first of the two agreements. Under the other they have lent to Mr. Workman the sum of £566,000 which the foreign owners have paid in respect of the nineteen contracts. The huge cash loan bears no interest and in complete discharge of it the Directors have undertaken to accept from Mr. Workman the return of his half of the profits on the contracts, less the one-third of that half which is to be retained by Messrs. Furness, Withy and Company.

The circular asking the shareholders to confirm these agreements says nothing more about them. It seems to us that agreements of so remarkable a nature should be accompanied by a full explanation of their reason."

This is mild comment on arrangements unacceptable today. Admittedly, as has been noted above, the £566,000 was non-refundable, but six of these contracts were later cancelled.

However, at the start, it was all very promising. R. A. Workman and MacKay Edgar set about expanding the NSBC's investments. Their first purchases, at the start of 1919, were of William Doxford & Sons Ltd., and of a large number of shares in Fairfield Shipbuilding and Engineering Company, at Govan, on the Clyde, another Furness Withy shipyard.

The End of Doxford Family Control

The sale of Doxford to the NSBC was agreed at the beginning of 1919, following discussions between the two remaining Doxford brothers and their nephew with Kleinworts, who gave the family a specific guarantee, noted below.

The Directors met on 9 January 1919. All six were present: Robert, Charles, Ernest, Robert Junior, William and Charles Junior, with Robert Haswell in attendance. These minutes began quite calmly, noting that a ship named 'War Beryl' had been launched, and that:

> "In accordance with instructions received from the Employers' Associations one half week's wages were paid to our workpeople on the 20th December 1918 in connection with Armistice Celebrations, it being understood that for the present the payment will be regarded by the Board of Inland Revenue as allowable working expense for the purpose of assessment to Excess Profits Duty."

The last sentence was important as shipbuilding companies were particularly concerned about Excess Profits Duty. EPD was introduced in 1915, to tax the large profits achievable through restricted supply of commodities and goods in wartime conditions. The duty, levied on what the Government deemed excess profit, ranged from 40-80% and was not repealed until 1921. Companies were broadly compliant, and the tax raised significant amounts for the war effort. However, individual assessments were contested, and at times this prevented the closure of books at year end. Clearly, Doxford had been very successful during the war. The next item on these minutes showed a financial position at 31 December 1918 of cash and near cash standing at £1,960,401, (as opposed to just over £270,000 at the end of 1914). On 14 December 1918, the Company Seal had been fixed to three leases of land to their subsidiary, National Galvanizers Ltd. These leases were for the land on which their main buildings stood adjoining Queen Alexandra Bridge and further land under its arches. This, it seems, was to protect the position of National Galvanizers after the impending sale.

The following day, 10 January 1919, an agreement was made in the form of an indenture (later called the Principal Indenture) between the NSBC and the Directors of William Doxford & Sons Ltd on behalf of the shareholders to sell their shares to the NSBC.[14] These amounted to 24,543 5% Preference Shares of £10 each, 25,000 6% 'B' Preference Shares of £10 each, 25,000 Ordinary Shares of £10 each and 596 certificates of 4% debenture stock at £100. The remaining 457 Preference Shares, issued in 1900, with a nominal value of £4,570, represented the amount of capital held outside the family. Clause 4 was an agreement to pay to the previous shareholders in Doxford a quarter of the profits from the manufacture and sale of internal combustion engines, oil storage facilities and electrical oil fuel indicators.[15]

The nominal amount of the family held shares and debentures was £805,030, though of course their market value at that date was considerably higher. The articles of association of the Company stated that if the Company were to be wound up voluntarily, the price of each Preference Share should be calculated as the average selling price over the previous six months. This is where I diverge from Professor Murphy's paper, as he states that the Company was actually sold for £805,030, whereas the true figure was £3,000,000 as reported by the Stock Exchange. The Doxford family received cash, except for £500,000 in NSBC mortgage debentures. It seems that they had strong reservations about accepting debentures from the NSBC as part of the purchase price, and that Kleinwort gave them a guarantee to honour the debentures in the event of the dissolution of the NSBC. At present, I have been unable to locate the guarantee, as it is missing from the Kleinwort papers at the London Metropolitan Archives, but notes made by the Kleinwort secretary in 1923 make clear that this was the wording.[16]

An indenture was signed on 1 May 1919, clarifying that all the original shareholder members of the Doxford family (the Vendors) were eligible for royalties in the future by the NSBC (the Company), under Clause 4, above.

The Company agreed:

> "to pay to the Vendors [or agents etc.] such sum of money as shall be equal to
>
> (1) one equal fourth part of the net profits of William Doxford and Sons Limited (hereinafter called 'the Doxford Company') or its successors in business arising in each year from the manufacture and sale by the Doxford Company of (a) Internal Combustion Engines (b) Floating Oil Storage and (c) Electrical Oil Fuel Indicators and of fittings or auxiliary appliances in connection with any such engines oil storage and indicators and
>
> (2) One equal half part of the net Royalties received by the Doxford Company in each year in respect of any such [of the above] manufactured by persons firms or companies other than the Doxford Company, charged by the Doxford Company against the cost of [the above.]"

The text then clarifies that the calculation of profits includes fees from the cost of plans, supervision, technical advice and instructions given to such outside firms. What it does not include is an end date to this agreement, but it seems that it was intended to be a long term commitment, as the document makes clear that in the event of a death, the deceased's executors are entitled to payment of such profits and royalties. It also states that should the number of parties entitled to receive such payments reduce to below three, the money should still be shared by the two remaining alive.

The Indenture closes with a list of thirty nine shareholders. Thirty five were individual family members (though the trustees of Arthur Doxford were not included). Three joint holdings were AED & AOH, CDD and AOH, and AED and A. F. Maling. The list closes with Collective Industries Ltd., of 45 West Sunniside, Sunderland.

This may go some way to explain why the brothers and cousinhood agreed to hand away their patrimony. They continued to have a financial interest in the new Company, and they anticipated a healthy stream of income for years to come. Additionally, the debentures gave the Doxford family leverage over the NSBC through Kleinworts, who made efforts to force the NSBC to redeem them when they fell into difficulties in 1923, as described in Chapter Eleven. It also explains the strong incentive for Charles and Robert Doxford to keep the engine works in operation when the shipyard itself was closed from 1924-1927 and again from 1931-1934. Unfortunately, I have been unable to determine the value of the payments received by the family under these arrangements.

In the event, the business suffered badly from a drain on its working capital by the NSBC, and was brought almost to its knees. The new Directors began immediately to 'strip' its liquid assets, even to provide the cash for the original purchase. Additionally, although the agreement stated that fees and royalties should be paid within fourteen days of an Annual General Meeting at which accounts were published, no final accounts were produced for Doxford until 1922, so the original shareholders were forced to await payment.

Ten days passed, to allow the final negotiations with the NSBC to take place. The Doxford Board of Directors then met at 12.30 pm on Monday, 20 January 1919 at their Registered Offices at Pallion. Charles David was in the chair. The other two Directors present were William and Charles, Junior. The Secretary, Robert Haswell, reported "that he had received the resignations in writing from the following Directors, viz: Mr. R. P. Doxford, Mr. A. E. Doxford and Mr. Robert Doxford." These resignations were accepted, after which Mr. E. Mackay Edgar, (no address) Mr. Robert Alfred Workman (address given) and Mr. W. O. Workman (no address) were appointed Directors "to fill casual vacancies". The haste and secrecy of the decision is reflected in gaps in personal information about Edward Mackay Edgar and William Ord Workman (1880-1934).

116. The Workman family in a relaxed mood at Cowes. R.A. Workman stands on the right. From The Sketch, 15 August 1923.

C.D. Doxford, his son, Charles, and A.O. Hedley, their solicitor, then travelled down to London. On the morning of Thursday, 23 January, the Doxford Board was reconvened at Hotel Russell in Russell Square. C. D. Doxford took the chair, Charles Junior being the only other Director present. After the previous minutes had been confirmed and signed, A. O. Hedley, was appointed to act as temporary secretary. The Board then approved the transfer of 500 shares each to Edward Mackay Edgar, Robert Alfred Workman, Sir John Esplen and William Orr Workman. The secretary reported the acceptances by Mackay Edgar and the two Workman brothers of their Directorships. The Chairman then accepted the resignations of the remaining Board members, i.e. himself, William Doxford and Charles Doxford, Junior.

The first meeting of the new Board of William Doxford and Sons Ltd. then follows directly on the same page of the minute book. This took place at 12.30 pm on the same day at the 'London office of the Company', Basildon House, Moorgate Street, City of London. R.A. Workman was appointed Chairman of Doxford. E. Mackay Edgar, W.O. Workman and Sir John Esplen, K.B.E. were also present. Esplen (1863-1930) was Chairman of both Esplen, Sons & Swainston and of Furness Withy. He had been knighted in 1918 and was created the 1st Baronet of Hardres, in Kent, in 1921, for his services in WWI as Director of Overseas Ship Purchase.[17] Hedley had crossed London to report the proceedings of the earlier Board meeting at Hotel Russell, and the resignations of the remaining Doxford family were received and accepted. He then took no further part. Harvey Frapwell was appointed as London Secretary to Doxford at a salary of £100 per annum, and Sir John Esplen was appointed a Director. Messrs. Deacon & Co. of 9, Great St. Helens, London E.C. were appointed solicitors to the Company. They were represented by J.R. Marriott. Robert Haswell remained the Secretary to the Company at their headquarters at Pallion, so Frapwell was instructed to write to him, informing him of the change of directors. More importantly, Haswell was to be informed that the Board wished to receive the certificates of the Company's holding of War Loan and National War Bonds to the nominal value of £1,860,550. These were to be sent to Messrs. Kleinwort Sons & Co., to be held by them on behalf of the Company. Haswell was also instructed to send the seal of the Company to the London Secretary. Finally the Board, on behalf of the Company, agreed to lend to the NSBC £1,800,000 as a "temporary loan" from the first day of February 1919, with interest at 6%, to be repaid before 28 February 1919.

R.A. Workman was also the Chairman of the NSBC.

The new Board of Directors met again at Basildon House the following day. R.A. Workman was in the chair, the two other Directors being E. Mackay Edgar and W.O. Workman. Frapwell was in attendance as London Secretary, and A.O. Hedley and R.P. Doxford were present. As had been privately agreed with the Doxford family, their services were not dispensed with. The Board resolved that in future all cheques drawn on the Company's account at the National Provincial and Union Bank, Sunderland, should be signed by one of the following: R.P., C.D., A.E. or W. Doxford "as managers", and countersigned by a Secretary. (p 434 of the minutes) It was then resolved, "on the recommendation of the Managers", that Mr. James Yeames (1873-1961) be appointed Works Manager, Engineers' Department, for a period of three years, at a salary of £1,500 per annum.18 This was actually a family appointment, as Yeames was married to Jane Service Workman, a cousin of R.A. and W.O. Workman. The newly appointed Managers were instructed to report to the Directors each month "on the general position of the Company's business." A.O. Hedley was retained as a trustee of the debenture holders, and remained so until his death in 1926.

The weekend then intervened. On the following Monday, 27 January 1919, the Board of Directors reconvened, with only Workman and Mackay Edgar present. Their solicitor and the London Secretary were in attendance. It was resolved that Messrs. Sperling & Co. be instructed to take steps for the immediate sale of the entire holding of £1,860,550 in Government Bonds.

This took a little time. Although £1,604,856 of the loan to the NSBC was in hand by the end of January, the final amount was not received until 11 February. The Board met that day, again with just Workman and Mackay Edgar present as Directors. Frapwell reported that Kleinworts had confirmed receipt of £1,867,332. The London Secretary then reported that he had drawn cheques in favour of the NSBC for a total of £1,716,000 "on account of the loan to that Company authorised by the Board of Directors at the meeting on Jan. 23rd 1919." These measures were approved by the Board, after which, mundanely, the Company seal was affixed to contracts for the steam engines 531, 533, 535, 537, 539, 541 and 543, as requested by the Engine Builders Committee, based at Pallion. However, this demonstrates the changed relationship between the workforce at Pallion and their London masters. The Company seal was in London, and not one of the meetings of the Doxford Board of Directors took place at Sunderland over the next five years.

On Monday, 17 February, Workman and Mackay Edgar convened once more, to resolve the finance of the purchase as follows:

* By Doxford purchasing, through Sperling & Co., 18,200 First Mortgage Debentures of £100 each in the NSBC.
* By the Company purchasing 596 four percent debentures of the NSBC of £100 at the price of £65%, i.e. £38,740, and that such debentures, once purchased, should be cancelled.

Although there is no mention of the precise details, what seems to have happened is that the "temporary loan" by Doxford to the NSBC was replaced by Doxford taking the NSBC debentures. As a result it was starved of working capital. Today we would call this asset stripping, of the kind practised by private equity firms.

Press interest

So far, the takeover by the NSBC of Doxford had been conducted in private, though a short press release had been issued early in February. On the 18th of that month, full information reached the London and regional press, announcing the amount of money that had been paid by the NSBC.

As the Times put it, somewhat sceptically:

> "A £3,000,000 Debenture Issue
> It is announced that the purchase consideration for the acquisition, recently announced, of the undertaking of Messrs. William Doxford and Sons by the Northumberland Shipbuilding Company – an undertaking of which very little is known – amounts to over £3,000,000. We are informed that the purchase price will be provided by an issue of £3,000,000 of debentures, for the issue of which Treasury sanction has been obtained. There will, however, be no public issue, arrangements having been made, in deference to the wishes of the Treasury, to place the debentures privately. ...."

The amount is confirmed by the NSBC's entry in the 1920 Stock Exchange Official Intelligence. This notes that on 28 February 1919, the NSBC issued £3m of debenture stock secured by trust deed as a first specific charge on the land, buildings and fixed plant at Doxford, on 24,753 fully paid Preference Shares of £10 each in William Doxford, and as a floating charge on all remaining assets of the Company.[19] This sounds like using the assets of a Company to acquire its shares, which is an offence today. The 25,000 'B' Preference Shares and the 25,000 Ordinary Shares of £10 each are not mentioned.[20]

1919 - The decisions of the new Board of Directors

In February, the Board resolved to move the Registered Office of the Company from Pallion to Basildon House, Moorgate and, on Monday, 3 March, the London secretary reported that he had paid £20,000 to the NSBC on Sperling's instructions, and that the loan of £1.8m to the NSBC had been repaid in exchange for £1.8m of 6% NSBC debentures.

He also confirmed the purchase of 596 debentures in the NSBC by Doxford, and it was duly resolved to cancel these. This meant that over a few days Doxford had handed over £58,740 outright to the parent Company plus the £1.8m in debentures.

It is hard to believe that the Doxford brothers were unaware that the liquid assets of Doxford were to be grabbed by Sperling and the NSBC. Did they have no idea of their reputation? It is apparent from subsequent actions that when Sperling and the NSBC took over Doxford and other companies they were motivated purely by financial, not industrial reasons. It was not that the Doxford brothers were isolated in the North East. Robert was based in Hertfordshire, and Charles regularly spent time in London. If they did guess what might happen, but could not prevent it, then the pressure on them to sell from their relations must have been overwhelming. Everything that Charles and Robert did for the rest of their lives point to their continuing support for the family shipyard. What is not known is whether the brothers had approaches from other parties, as officialdom at that point was pushing for industrial consolidation.

On 8 April 1919, the Directors met briefly to appoint a new Shipyard Manager at Pallion, Hugh Gallacher. Meetings took place on a monthly basis, always in London. The early May meeting of the new Directors reported that agreements had been signed with Robert, Charles and Ernest Doxford, the family members who were remaining as managers. The 29th Annual General Meeting of the Company, the first under new ownership, took place on Tuesday, 27 May 1919 at Basildon House. This ratified that the auditors remained the same, and confirmed the purchase of 18,200 6% mortgage debentures of £100 each in the NSBC.

Ernest Doxford resigned from the Board of Managers at Pallion in October that year,[21] and moved to Yorkshire in 1922, but Robert retired only in his late seventies, and Charles remained with Doxford for the rest of his long life. It was Charles's direction that brought the Company through the coming lean years.

Work at the yard continued but it seems that as ships were completed the money received for them was automatically siphoned off to London. A further sum of £50,000 was authorised in June, so that by the middle of 1919 the NSBC had already taken well over £100,000 from its subsidiary in addition to the £1.8m debentures. From the estimated profit figures that the NSBC gave to Kleinworts prior to their acquisition in 1918, profit on nineteen ships on the order books from Norwegian and Italian shipowners ranged from about £24,000 to one at £102,000.[22] Presumably, profits were in this range for Doxford as well.

In 1919, Sperling took on another significant partner. This was Dr. Edward Philip Andreae (1879-1975). Andreae was a scientific engineer and a successful industrialist. He was the younger brother of Hermann Anton Andreae of Kleinwort Sons, & Co.[23] Dr. E. P., as Andreae was known, had served as Kleinwort's 'Company Doctor', in that he helped the bank ease back to health companies in which they had a significant holding, so that they could be disposed of.[24] Andreae later became Chairman of Doxford.

When the Board of Directors convened again on 16 October, the minutes of the meetings of 26 Feb, 3 March, 8 April, 8 May, 2 and 11 June and 24 July were read, and signed by R. A. Workman, as Chairman. It is somewhat surprising that such momentous decisions were taken during the summer months without such confirmation. However, all was going well. The Chairman was able to report that the trading profits, plus interest on investments for the first half of the year, and less allowances for Income Tax and Excess Profits Duty exceeded £65,000. Interim dividends had been paid on the Preference Shares, and a 20% dividend was authorised for the half year on the 25,000 Ordinary Shares, with a further 20% to be paid full year "free of income tax". The amount payable over the year was £50,000. At this meeting the report and accounts for 1915 were also presented and passed. Discussions with the Inland Revenue over Excess Profits Duty had prevented Doxford from preparing accurate accounts during the war.

Further acquisitions by the Northumberland Shipbuilding Company

As part of the Sperling Combine, as it became known, the NSBC headed the largest shipbuilding related conglomerate in Britain. After its first and immediate acquisition, in January 1919, of a majority holding in Doxford, and with major financial backing from Kleinworts they followed this with:

> * A controlling block of shares in the Fairfield Shipbuilding & Engineering Co. of Govan, near Glasgow, in June 1919, acquired from Cammell Laird. This was a warship builder, founded 1838, which transferred to passenger liners post WW1. R.A. Workman became Chairman.
> * A reverse takeover of Workman, Clark & Co. of Belfast, who built transatlantic liners and merchant ships and undertook repairs. It was

founded in 1880 and acquired in February1920, following a court case at the end of the previous year. This was the most contentious acquisition. Following the conglomerate's behaviour over Doxford, Workman's cousin, Sir George Clark, was well aware that his family company would be asset stripped by issuing debentures in favour of the purchaser, but failed to get the courts to disallow the takeover. Frank Workman remained Chairman, but R. A. Workman, Sir John Esplen and Sir E. Mackay Edgar became Directors and controlled the Company. This was the most expensive acquisition in the group.

* The Blythswood Shipbuilding Co. Scotstoun, Glasgow founded by Hugh MacMillan, formerly a Director of Fairfield, in 1919, produced oil tankers. This Company was sold in 1923, to alleviate the debts of the NSBC.

* A majority interest in the Monmouth Shipbuilding Co., Chepstow. Founded 1879, acquired 1920. R.A. Workman became Chairman.

* The Lanarkshire Iron and Steel Company and John Watson, coal miners, also in 1920, having been suppliers to Workman, Clark.

In each case, the original name was retained for these yards. The NSBC also took shares in Irvine's Shipbuilding and Dry Dock Co. Ltd. at West Hartlepool. R. A. Workman, Sir John Esplen and Hatry became directors of this. The demise of Irvine's in 1925 was to have far-reaching consequences for the Northumberland Group.

The inherent instability of the group, though, should have been evident. Rather than amalgamating a number of similar enterprises within a close geographical proximity, thereby saving on administrative costs and improved industrial efficiency, each of the constituent parts of the group lay in a different area of the United Kingdom. However, the sheer audacity of the purchases ensured that Edward Mackay Edgar, as Chairman of Sperling, was created a baronet in the New Year's Honours List of 1920, ostensibly for his war time work, in regard to British/Canadian trade. Also, despite being based in London, Edgar, Kennedy, the two Workman brothers, Sir John Esplen and four Strachan brothers appointed themselves Directors of one or more of the companies. These were not their only interests either. Sir John Esplen, for instance, was a Chairman of Wm. Esplen & Sons and controlled the British Maritime Trust, which acted as trustees for debenture issues. Not only was R.A. Workman Chairman of the NSBC, but also of Fairfield, Monmouth, Doxford and Irvine.

As a Director of the NSBC, Alexander MacAusland Kennedy attended the meeting of the Doxford Board held in January 1920. Kennedy was an experienced Clyde shipbuilder, who had worked at McMillan & Son of Dumbarton and Hamilton & Co, Port Glasgow, before joining R.A. Workman at the NSBC in 1919. He was appointed Managing Director of the NSBC and Managing Director of Fairfield, following its takeover shortly after that of Doxford. He was knighted in 1921. His background is described in Chapter Eleven, as he became Chairman of Doxford in 1924. The main business at this Board Meeting was to discuss the acquisition of Lanarkshire Steel and John Watson, the final companies listed above. Lloyd's Bank had undertaken to advance up to £1,500,000 to Workman, Clark for the purchases. The Directors resolved that Doxford should guarantee the repayment of this loan, together with interest, on or before 1 May 1920. The stated reason behind the purchase of Lanarkshire was to obtain steel plating for the group's ships as there was a general steel shortage in the UK at that time. However, Lanarkshire did not, and never had, produced such plating. Additionally, Lloyd's Bank held the upper hand in the transaction, as they already held prior lien debenture stock on the Company. The lack of a reliable source of coal was also viewed with concern and was the reason for acquiring John Watson.

An attempt had also been made to purchase the shares of Baldwins Ltd. of Port Talbot, another steel producer, and supplier to Workman, Clark, but this had not come to fruition. The failure had occurred between the signing of the contracts and completion, and resulted in a charge on all the subsidiaries of the NSBC. A settlement was agreed with the shareholders of Baldwins at the end of 1920. The NSBC agreed to pay five shillings per share held, and to purchase 35,000 tons of steel for up to three years from the Company. The matter was reported to the Doxford Board on 15 December 1920, who agreed that the Company should cover one third of these payments and orders, reflecting its importance within the group.[25]

During 1920, the shipbuilding business at Doxford proceeded as usual, and orders were still being fulfilled. The Board agreed an advance to the NSBC of £65,000, at 5%, from 2 February 1920. In June, the Managing Director, Charles Doxford's salary was doubled to £8,000, and those of Gallacher, Yeames, Keller and Haswell, were each raised by £500. However, Doxford were under constant pressure from their parent company. A further £85,000 was advanced to the NSBC "as a loan" on 15 July, and, by this meeting, the lack of steel plating from Lanarkshire had become apparent. During the spring, Sperling had been forced to enter into contracts for the purchase of steel plating with Dorman Long & Co., the South Durham Steel and Iron Co. and the Cargo Steel Iron Co. Ltd., for a 3% commission. Doxford, as one of the subsidiary companies, agreed to pay this commission. An EGM was held in May 1920 specifically to alter the articles of association to give remuneration to the Chairman and Directors, £1,200 in the case of Workman and £600 to each Director, backdated to 1919.

Only two weeks later, Doxford advanced the second loan in a month to the NSBC. This was of £60,900 at 6% interest. The meeting of 9 August 1920 was convened only to resolve a loan of £150,000, again at 6% interest. Between 15 July and 9 August, a staggering £295,000 was advanced in only 25 days. A further £100,000 followed on 8 September 1920, and £250,000 on 11 November, the Board having not met in October. But where did the money come from? 18 ships were completed at Pallion between March 1919 and December 1920, which may explain Doxford's profitability.

In this way, the NSBC used the advances of one company to purchase the next, with debentures issued to each company. These debentures paid a hefty 4% – 6% interest.

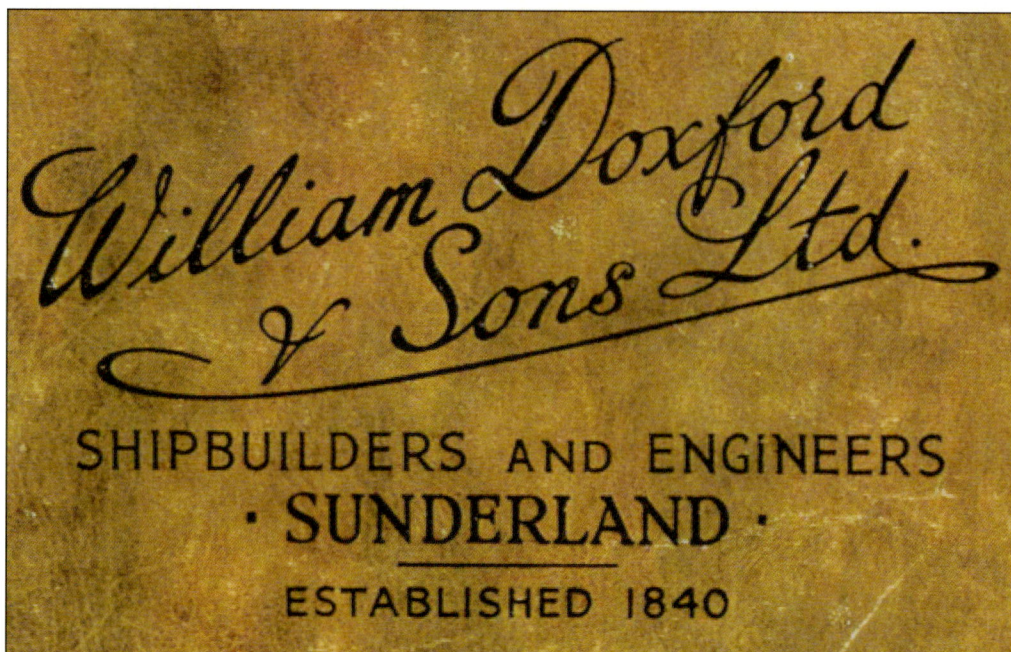

Trade began to slow in 1921 and, as early as 1922, the repayment schedule from the NSBC to its subsidiaries and debenture holders became unsustainable. However, for the moment life went on as before. By 25 February 1921, excluding dividend payments, Doxford had loaned or paid outright to the NSBC £771,165, and had guaranteed significant sums to both Baldwins Ltd. and Lloyd's Bank, probably reaching £2m. In addition there was of course the £1.8m debentures. The NSBC had been purchased by Sperling in 1919 for just £830,000.

In 1921, with the launch of the Yngaren, the Directors produced an expansive publicity booklet, 87 pages in length, about the history and current output of Doxford. The cover is shown here, and the first illustration was the composite photograph of all the family Directors of the Company, with William Doxford at their centre. These are the photographs shown earlier in this history.

The booklet has copious illustrations of the shipbuilding and engine works, and pays particular attention to the rebuilding of the yard in the early 1900s, when the new berths were built, the redesigned offices and the numerous workshops and mobile engines that performed the separate functions of building a ship and its propulsion. The section on government ships, showing the different standard ships of WWI, their boilers and engines, is also extensive. The final sections, on commercial work, show ships under construction, and other work undertaken, such as the development of a caisson for building bridges, and an electric coal elevator, an invention that helped to keep the yard open during the dreadful days to come. The booklet finishes with the opposed piston engine from its first prototype to the 58L4, the submarine and the auxiliary engines, and the sea trials of MV Yngaren and MV Dominion Miller.

The downturn

However, even before this celebratory booklet had been released, the downturn had begun. The London Secretary reported the cancellation of a number of contracts, but that agreement had been reached with Dorman Long & Co. to take only half the 300,000 tons of steel plates and sections ordered up to 1923. The companies in the Sperling Combine, excluding Workman, Clark, were asked pay £300,000 in compensation to Dorman Long. The Doxford share was £45,000. The NSBC was struggling, but was able to pay the interest on the debentures and dividends on the Preference Shares that summer.

On 17 October 1921, it was resolved that Doxford should apply for (previously their own) £1,650,000 non-Cumulative 6% 'B' Preference Shares in the NSBC. The Minutes give no indication how this was to be funded.[26] The text reads simply:

> "It was resolved that the London Secretary be and is hereby authorized to apply in the name and on behalf of this Company for One million six hundred and fifty thousand (1,650,000) Six percent non cumulative 'B' preference shares of One pound each of the Northumberland Shipbuilding Company Limited and to sign the application form necessary for that purpose." Signed R.A. Workman, Chairman.

Following the meeting of 4 January 1922, £500,000 of these were deposited with the National Provincial & Union Bank of England (now part of the National Westminster Bank), as part of Doxford's guarantee to the bank regarding the NSBC's overdraft.

1922 was the year that orders dried up throughout the shipbuilding industry. This was exacerbated by the UK government's decision to sell a substantial number of vessels confiscated from Germany after the war. Not surprisingly, the effect on the conglomerate under the direction of the NSBC was profound. The hefty interest payments on their existing loans and debentures were draining the parent company. In addition to debts to their subsidiary companies, they had built up a substantial overdraft at their bank. Therefore, in 1922, Doxford loaned a further £336,219 to the NSBC, and waived their right to £600,000 of their debentures, in favour of the N & P Bank. They then paid £36,000 for a further 450 NSBC Debentures, at 80% of their nominal value. They also made an agreement with and took a licence from the newly established Michell Bearings of Newcastle. This company had been formed in 1920 to make hydrodynamic oil bearings, principally for the aircraft trade. The partners at the launch were Vickers, Fairfield, John Brown Engineering and Cammell Laird. Fairfield were, of course, part of the group. Unlike so many other companies in this history, Michell Bearings continues in operation.

To strengthen the Board, Sir Alexander MacAusland Kennedy (1860-1939), the Managing Director of the NSBC, was appointed a Director on 28 July 1922. At that meeting, a General Purposes Committee was established, with just two members as a quorum. The powers of the GPC were wide ranging – Clause 3 was "To consider and decide all questions of policy and to issue the necessary instructions to the various officials of this Company or of the Associated Companies to give effect to the same" and Clause 5 was "To appoint at their discretion and remove all officials of this Company and any of the associated Companies and to determine their duties and fix their salaries and/or commissions." The General Purposes Committee seems to have been to facilitate matters without public scrutiny. A similar GPC had been set up for the NSBC. A management committee was appointed for Doxford, now to report to the GPC, rather than directly to the Board. Kennedy, as Chairman and Convenor of the GPC, appointed CDD as a member of the management committee, showing the confidence that he had in him. By November, a new agreement had been made with Messrs. Sperling & Co., and the Company's seal was affixed to this.

Could things get worse? Of course. At the end of January 1923 Doxford made a further loan to the parent Company of £30,892 10s, once more at 6%. The NSBC was struggling badly and running at a substantial deficit, but was committed to paying the interest and dividends to Doxford and the other participating companies, plus their bank overdraft. It is interesting that acquisitions were still being made. In early 1923, the NSBC purchased a parcel of shares in the shipbuilders and engineers, Richardsons, Westgarth of Hartlepool. The Doxford Board meeting held on 21 March 1923 states that:

> "The Chairman [R.A. Workman] reported that in accordance with his discussions with Mr. Charles Doxford the Managing Director – the Northumberland Shipbuilding Co. Ltd. entered into a contract for the purchase of 175,272 fully paid Ordinary shares of £1 each in Richardsons, Westgarth Company Limited at the price of twenty five shillings per share."

The minutes then continue: "these shares should be transferred to this Company."

Between 1919 and 1923, Doxford paid a staggering £4,000,000 to the NSBC. Additionally, at the Board meeting held on 26 April 1923, the Directors resolved that:

> "notwithstanding the Resolution previously passed by the Board fixing the rate of Interest to be paid by the Northumberland Shipbuilding Co. Ltd. on monies loaned to that Company, that as from July 1st 1921 no Interest be charged on any loan to the said Northumberland Shipbuilding Co. Ltd. and that all Interest (if any) debited since that date is hereby cancelled."

Annual statements of account under the new management

The 29th AGM (the first under new management) was held on 27 May 1919. The minutes first confirmed the election of the Directors and retained the same auditors. They then endorsed the action of the Directors to purchase the NSBC mortgage debentures above. No accounts were available, so the meeting was adjourned. In October the adjourned 26th Meeting (1916) was reconvened to receive the annual statement of accounts for that year, but this was not attached to the minutes. 1920 saw EGMs to authorise changes to the articles of association so as to remunerate £1,200 p.a. to the Chairman, and £600 to each Director.

As 1921 dawned, the Directors were finally able to finalise the reports and accounts for 1917, 1918 and 1919, meeting on 31 January at Basildon House and reconvening the respective adjourned meetings. R.A. Workman took the Chair, the Directors present were the newly elevated Sir E. Mackay Edgar and W. Orr Workman. C.P. Johnson represented the interests of the Canadian and General Trust Company. Harvey Frapwell, the London Secretary, was in attendance. This time the accounts for each year were attached, and the Directors reported that large claims against the Admiralty for work done were the subject of a Petition of Right to the Crown.

The nominal reserves of the Company had increased over the three years from c £2,570,000 to nearly £4,300,000 but, of this, £1.82m. was in the form of NSBC debentures. The order book was still buoyant at the end of 1919. The amounts received in respect of work in progress and on account of other vessels contracted for was £2,562,910, whilst expenditure on work in progress amounted to only £1,106,254. The figure for 1920 was £5,314,723, and the profit for the year was recorded as £1,162,873.

The first annual reports of the Northumberland Shipbuilding Company Limited

It was not until 1923 that the NSBC produced their first annual report and accounts since they started their acquisitions in 1919. The General Meeting planned in May 1923 had to be postponed on the day, because accounts had not been finalised. These were made up for three successive years to 30 June 1923, and were finally presented to the Annual General Meeting of the shareholders on Saturday, 6 October. The value of the subsidiary companies still stood on the books at over £8.8 million. However, when the papers were issued in September, the auditors refused to endorse this value, and marked them as of negligible worth. The press widely reported R.A. Workman's address, in which he stated that the accounts showed a deficit of £390,850, but that this had arisen only in the third year in operation. At the end of June 1920, the NSBC had accumulated reserves of £101,346, which grew the following year to £243,481. However, by June 1923 they were reduced by dividend payments of £108,481 on Preference and Ordinary shares, and the interest on debentures. Workman continued that it had not been possible to produce accounts before this, as the Excess Profits Duty remained outstanding. He conceded that the value of the subsidiary companies had fallen. To alleviate the situation, part of their holding in Fairfield had been sold, at a loss of £779,573, and further funds were sought in the near future. Workman then blamed the situation on the unprecedented slump in trade. This, he said, had led to postponement and cancellation of orders. However, their subsidiary Lanarkshire Steel were making a profit, and the NSBC had redeemed £1.5 million debentures, in addition to paying interest. At this juncture, the Government had received £1 million in taxes.

He continued that to his regret shipyards at present were a liability, as shipowners were not ordering new ships and that, "after the war the Government took over a large number of German ships and forced them on the market" at such prices that shipowners were induced to purchase. In Workman's opinion, these enemy ships should have been scrapped. His address to the shareholders was received in almost total silence, and few bothered to raise their hands to approve the accounts. In response to questions, he was forced to admit that the damages paid to Baldwins for the failed takeover had amounted to £1.3m. As has been seen above, these had been paid by the subsidiary companies. Finally, the Chairman stated that no director of the NSBC had received remuneration of his services since December 1921.

During the summer of 1923, Kleinworts had begun to take a more pro-active part in the direction of the Sperling Combine and its constituent parts. Although Doxford and Fairfield were hanging on, Workman, Clark had gone through a particularly difficult time, and they struggled to pay £72,000 debenture interest in August, though they eventually managed to obtain further funding from the National Bank of Scotland. Workman, Clark had suffered badly from orders either cancelled or held over (25 out of 32), but had managed to agree a three year moratorium with their debenture holders. The NSBC were in an even worse position, owing £145,000 in interest payments. Although Sir John Esplen's company had come partially to the rescue, both Sperling and Kleinwort were forced to step in over the shortfall of £85,000. This led to the resignation of both R. A. Workman and Sir Edward Mackay Edgar at the end of 1923 from all their commitments to the NSBC and its subsidiaries. Sadly, on 5 October, the two men had driven through the creation of £300,000 Second Debenture Stock of Doxford, "secured by way of a floating charge on the undertaking ranking next after the £150,000 First Mortgage Debenture created and issued and secured by a Trust Deed entered into by the Company dated the 11th day of June 1900." The Company Seal was fixed to the first tranche of these debentures. £25,000 were taken up by the Globe Shipping Corporation Ltd., a Canadian registered Company that was wholly owned by Doxford.[26]

Robert Alfred Workman endured further trauma in his life. He was made bankrupt in 1931, following fraudulent activity at one of his companies, British Oil. The home on Park Lane that he shared with his wealthy wife was sold in 1933, and Elizabeth's important collection of antiques and paintings was auctioned off. They moved to Hayling Island, near Portsmouth, where they lived quietly. Workman died there in 1949.

The new Board of Directors at William Doxford & Sons Ltd.

However, the change of leadership proved a boon for the Company. Sir Alexander Kennedy took control of both Doxford and the NSBC and direction returned to the North East. Kennedy had a hands-on attitude to the shipyard, and the Minute Books from 1924 clearly demonstrate this new direction.

Chapter Eleven

1923-1939
The Company survives two Depressions

Sir Alexander McAusland Kennedy assumed the chair of Doxford at their Board Meeting held at Moorgate on 28 November 1923 (though it was not until 26 August 1924 that he was officially appointed Chairman). W.O. Workman was the only other Director present at this meeting, at which the resignations of R.A. Workman and Sir Edward Mackay Edgar were accepted.[1] The meeting approved the transfer for sale of 7,380 shares in National Galvanizers and of £10,000 stock in the River Wear Commissioners. They then approved the sale of the freehold land on which National Galvanizers stood. The Directors agreed to release National Galvanizers from its debts to the parent company, and to put the subsidiary up for sale.

118. Sir Alexander Kennedy (1860-1939). From the Transactions of the Institution of Naval Architects, 1939.

For the next thirteen years, Kennedy was the driving force at Doxford. He was born at Dumbarton and, at seventeen, joined Archibald McMillan & Sons, shipbuilders in his home town. Having qualified as a naval architect, he became their chief draughtsman at only twenty five. For most of his long career in shipbuilding, Kennedy was with William Hamilton & Co. Ltd. at Port Glasgow. He was knighted in 1921 for services on a number of wartime committees whilst with Hamilton.

However, at the age of 59, Kennedy joined the Sperling Combine, taking the role of Managing Director of the NSBC. In 1920 he assumed the same post at Fairfield and was a Director of Workman, Clark. Having been a member of the Institution of Naval Architects since 1899, he was appointed to its council in 1929 and was made a vice president in 1937, this being after his retirement from Doxford and Fairfield. He held a number of other positions in the shipbuilding industry and was clearly an energetic man. Although committed to the shipbuilding industry in the North East, his home remained at Dumbarton, where he died on 14 January 1939.[2]

On 15 July 1924, under Kennedy's direction, the Doxford registered office reverted to Pallion, though it took until October to terminate the post of London Secretary.

For the next few years, Board Meetings alternated between Pallion, Govan and Newcastle, due to the cross Directorships of the participants. On 26 August George Strachan (1858-1929) was appointed a Director. Strachan was a Scotsman, one of four brothers involved in shipbuilding. He was a director of Fairfield, which he had joined as a boy. His elder brother, William Strachan, was the Chairman and Managing Director of Workman, Clark.

W. O. Workman attended his last Board Meeting on 1 October 1924, at which the minutes of all the meetings held since the beginning of the year were read and confirmed. Workman then tendered his resignation on 25 October. Charles Doxford, as General Manager, regularly attended Board Meetings, but was not a Director.[3]

119. Robert Haswell, O.B.E. (1865-1941) From The Shipbuilder and Marine Engine Builder, 1941. Courtesy of the World Ship Society.

Robert Haswell (1866-1941), on the other hand, was appointed a Director at the beginning of 1925, bringing the number to three. Haswell was the son of a joiner, who had joined the Company at the age of 15 as a junior clerk. He was the secretary to the Engineering Department until 1917, when he assumed the role of Company Secretary on the retirement of John Holey. He was awarded the newly created Order of the British Empire in 1918 for his wartime services. He endured the years under the control of the NSBC/Sperling, when his role was greatly diminished. After Charles Doxford's death at the beginning of 1935, Haswell assumed the role of Managing Director and remained in post until his own death on 9 September 1941. He was the Chairman of the Wear Shipbuilders Association between 1937 and 1939. The Association then went into abeyance during the war years. Instead, a joint committee was established for the duration of hostilities.

James Yeames, the General Manager of the Engineering Department, resigned, and K.O. Keller, was promoted to this position. Hugh Gallacher remained as Shipyard Manager. There was, therefore, a good measure of continuity in the management during the lean years of the 1920s.

1923-1928 – Financial Probity

The new Board set about putting the procedures for Doxford onto a clearer basis. The minutes written under the direction of Workman, MacKay and Esplen had always been brief and to the point (and for months at a time unsigned). From this point, they once again record items connected to the contracts negotiated by the shipyard. The minutes of January 1924, for instance, ratify decisions taken up to a year earlier.

The Directors faced problems on a number of fronts, the principal one being to set the Company once again on a sound financial basis. A serious cash shortfall required amending the terms of redemption of the £300,000 second debentures created by the previous Directors on 5 October 1923 from "on demand" to "payable six months after demand". The new Board now issued £115,000 of these debentures to Branch Nominees Ltd., the trustees of the Company's bank, the National Provincial Bank. However, these were still to be payable "on demand", and were to be held as security "for all moneys from time to time owing to them by this Company on their No. 2 account with the said Bank."[4]

It seems that only £25,000 of the second debentures had been issued, to The Globe Shipping Corporation Ltd. The corporation had gone into liquidation and the debentures were returned to Doxford "as the holders of the whole of the Share Capital of the Globe Shipping Corporation Ltd." It was quickly resolved to cancel the debentures.[5] Over the following months, Doxford were forced to lodge a number of guarantees that they received from their debtors with their bankers, but by November had negotiated with the National Provincial to halve the £100,000 guarantee of 1922 in respect of the NSBC overdraft.[6] They divested themselves of a second small subsidiary when Charles Doxford acquired the Company's shareholding in Superheat Liquid Fuel Limited for a nominal £50, plus ten shillings for the patent rights previously assigned to the Company. On a brighter note, though contracts had been cancelled, some of these were taken up by alternative shipowners.

On 6 January 1925 further significant measures were taken. It was reported to the meeting that 24,543 5% Preference Shares, 25,000 'B' Preference Shares, and 22,500 Ordinary Shares, together with 500 shares each in the names of Sir John Esplen and Sir Edward Mackay Edgar, all lodged with the British Canadian & General Investment Trust (on behalf of the Sperling Combine), had been transferred to new trustees, their London accountants, Sir Harry Peat and Sir Nicholas Waterhouse. The Company Seal had been affixed to these transactions,

> "and on 13th December 1924, to Agreement in Quadruple between Wm.
> Doxford & Sons Ltd., Northumberland Shipbuilding Co. Ltd., Robert Pile
> Doxford and others, re Oil Engine Royalties and Premiums; and on 23rd
> December 1924 to Agreement in duplicate between Wm. Doxford &
> Sons Ltd. and K.O. Keller re Oil Engine Royalties."

Sperling exercised no further direction from this point on, but Kleinwort retained an interest in the Company, in particular to protect its outstanding guarantee over the debentures in the NSBC and also their guarantee to the Doxford family. Kleinworts now played a significant role advising the companies previously held under the umbrella of the NSBC.

As 1925 progressed, the Board addressed the Company's financial position. At their April meeting, they made changes to the draft balance sheet to 31 December 1923 by transferring a substantial balance of nearly £990,000 from the Suspense Account to the Profit and Loss Account. £355,000 from this was then placed in a 'Reserve for Depreciation of Investments'. They resolved to write off the entire NSBC holding of 1,645,000 £1 'B' Preference Shares acquired in 1921. Depreciation provisions of nearly £84,000 were then written off under Capital Expenditure accounts for 1921-23. The Directors' fees of £600 p.a. agreed by the EGM of 1920 were rescinded and, from this point, Directors received only £100 p.a. They extricated the Company from an onerous undertaking to a third party made by the previous administration in 1922, and Sperling returned the document, duly cancelled. With these measures, it was possible to pay the interest on debentures at the half year. They were not, however, in a position to pay dividends on either Preference or Ordinary shares. This was partly due to the non-resolution of the Excess Profits Duty, and no dividends were paid for some years to come.

Following these difficult decisions and actions, the annual accounts for 1921 to 1924 were finally agreed at the 32nd and 33rd Annual Meetings, both held on 7 December 1925 at the Station Hotel, Newcastle. A credit balance of £202,253 12s 10$\frac{1}{2}$ d stood on the profit and loss account at 31 December 1923.[9] However, it was still a tough situation, and the income from the continued ownership of MV Yngaren and MV Eknaren had to be assigned to the Company's bank. This situation continued for some years more.

Octavius Hedley died on 26 April 1926, having given exceptional service to William Doxford & Sons for over thirty years. He had been Charles Doxford's friend and right hand man, and was a trustee for the debenture holders. His partner, Ernest Cuthbert Thompson, was appointed as a trustee in his place, Lord Daryngton[9] being the other trustee. In due course Thompson became one of CDD's executors.

Unfortunately, all the companies under the former Sperling Combine were in difficulties, as orders were so difficult to win. The NSBC was still run from London, and its Howdon yard lay idle during 1921 and 1922, with only one ship launched in 1923. During 1923, their yard numbers 283-382 were unassigned, as were 390-400, and only seven ships left their yard between 1924 and 1925.

1923 was also a bad year for Workman, Clark, with only one ship under construction. However, their yard then partially recovered. Seventeen ships were completed from 1924 to the end of 1926, mainly steam ships and mainly for British shipowners. Workman, Clark reneged on the payment of £10,000 for their licence to build Doxford engines, and this amount was eventually written off. Like Doxford, they had loaned huge amounts to the NSBC and they were simply not building marine oil engines at this time. Instead, Doxford supplied any engines required.[10]

Resolution of Excess Profits Duty

The dispute over the Excess Profits Duty outstanding to the Inland Revenue dragged on but, by mid-1926, there was movement on the matter. In March 1927, the Board were able to confirm that negotiations with the Inland Revenue over EPD had gone to judgement and had finally been concluded. Doxford did not challenge the decision, and consented to pay £662,563 4s 0d, the original demand having been over £1.5m. Another year passed before the matter was finally concluded.[10]

The Company did not hold cash reserves to pay this amount, so agreed to allocate to the Inland Revenue 24,783 of the original 5% Preference Shares of £10 each, previously held by the NSBC. This seems very generous of the Government, but probably reflects its interest in helping the yards recover. On 18 September 1928 an EGM was held to alter the articles of association and to rename the share classes as (a) 5% Cumulative Preference shares (25,000), (b) 6% Cumulative 'B' Preference shares (25,000), and (c) Ordinary shares (50,000), and to allow the Inland Revenue, as long as its trustees held these shares, to nominate a Director to the Company. This right was not taken up until 1931.

It was at this March meeting that it was reported that Charles Doxford was willing to pledge £20,000 personally to support an order for four steamships. The Board agreed to pay him £1,250 on each of these four ships, "thus enabling the Shipyard to be re-opened and saving of Establishment Charges." In April 1927 they came to a second agreement with CDD over ships for the Moor Line, for which the details are given in the following chapter. SS Stonegate (C585), 5,044 grt, was launched on 10 November 1927 and handed over to Turnbull Scott Shipping Co. Ltd, London in January 1928. By the end of the year, Doxford were again in a position to pay interest on their debentures, and had successfully concluded the saga over EPD.

The Shipbuilders' Investment Company

By mid-1926 the situation at the NSBC had reached the point of no return and in 1926 the yard was closed, along with five others on the Tyne. The NSBC was put into receivership in July. One bonus for Doxford was that their outstanding guarantee to the National Provincial Bank for £50,000 was finally cancelled. Kennedy and the other Directors then sold Blythswood and Monmouth shipyards, but Lanarkshire Steel and John Watson remained under the umbrella of Workman, Clark.

With Kleinwort's backing, in May 1927 the Shipbuilders' Investment Company (the SIC) was established, as a holding company. Its registered office was at 9 Victoria Street, London S.W., and a number of Board Meetings were held there. The SIC purchased the NSBC Howdon shipbuilding yard from the receiver, on behalf of the prior lien bondholders. The price was just £320,000, though the yard had been purchased by R.A. Workman and his associates for £8m. only eight years earlier. The SIC also acquired 24,580 (of 25,000) £10 Ordinary Shares in the Fairfield

Shipbuilding and Engineering Co. Ltd., 43,200 £25 Ordinary Shares in Workman, Clark & Co. Ltd, and virtually all of the issued £250,000 in 6% 'B' Preference, and £500,000 Ordinary Shares in Doxford for £125,000, though the Inland Revenue retained their £250,000 in 5% Preference Shares. At the time, the press predicted that Fairfield would provide most of the profit for the new Company. Both the Belfast News-Letter and the Scotsman reported on 18 May 1927 that "the shares of Workman, Clark & Company and Wm Doxford & Sons are considered of no present value." Considering the work undertaken by the new management, this was a harsh judgement, and was subsequently proved false. In the event, only two of the companies held by the SIC survived into the 1930s: Doxford and Fairfield.

Charles personally provided half the money to the SIC to acquire Doxford. It is understood that he and the other family members saw a chance to recover the family business. Once under its umbrella, the Directors resolved to change the Company's annual year end from 31 December to 30 June. Annual meetings from henceforth took place in the autumn. The accounts presented to the 36th AGM held on 17 December 1928 were for eighteen months. Doxford were finally in a position to pay dividends on their shares after six years of struggle. A helpful consequence of the closure of the NSBC was that the guarantee given in 1924 by Doxford to the National Provincial Bank in respect of the £50,000 overdraft to the NSBC was returned, duly cancelled, on 23 July 1927.[11] By mid-1928, agreement had also been reached with the South Durham Steel & Iron Co. Ltd. and with the Cargo Fleet Iron Co. Ltd. to release Doxford from their liabilities to these companies. However, on 5 November 1928, the Directors were obliged to write off the loan to the NSBC of £102,892 16s 1d and the 6% Debentures of £1,156,400.

With these measures, and the resolution of the Excess Profits Duty, financial stability was now achieved. The difficult decisions taken over the previous three years had come to a successful conclusion. However, Doxford were forced to grant further indemnities and transfers of mortgages to their bankers for a few years more.

Sir Alexander Kennedy bought the defunct NSBC and revived this as Northumberland Shipbuilding Company (1927) Ltd., with himself as Chairman. He reopened its yard. In 1928 and 1929 its seven berths launched 78,059 grt, all medium sized steam cargo ships, ranging from 3,859 to 6,903 grt, but during 1930 this output dropped to only 13,855 grt. The Howdon yard was then transferred to the newly established National Shipbuilders Security Ltd. (the NSS). This had been set up by Sir James Lithgow as a shipyard rationalisation agency, underwritten by the Bank of England. The NSS closed the yard.

Frank Workman, the long term Chairman of Workman, Clark, died in November 1927, and the following year his shipbuilding yard went into liquidation. An acrimonious court case was brought against the former Directors by one of the shareholders, and took years to resolve. Like the NSBC, Workman, Clark was revived as a new Company in 1928, but it did not thrive, and was also sold to the NSS in 1935. Both its yards lay idle until WWII, when the North Yard was dismantled. However, the South Yard was reopened by Harland & Wolff.[12]

By 1932, the NSS had closed nine shipyards in the North East. Those that vanished from the Wear were Robert Thompson, Osbourne Graham and a site at Pallion formerly occupied by William Gray & Co., who remained in operation at Hartlepool. So many shipyards were closed by the NSS that thousands of workers were thrown out of work, leading to abject poverty and the Jarrow march of 1936. Fairfield went through a particularly bad patch at the end of the 1920s, when orders collapsed, but survived by building small paddle and steam turbine ferries for railway companies. They also managed to achieve some naval orders.

At the start of the 1930s, Doxford were still forced to deposit mortgage bonds with their local bankers. In addition, on 9 September they gave a form of assignment to Kleinwort, Sons & Co. in respect of a mortgage bond on the Minister Wedel (C605), a 6,833 grt tanker, built for Rederi A/S Norske Transatlantic, Oslo. They also signed two deeds with the Silver Line, which was having cash flow problems with Harland and Wolff. The situation did not improve in the coming years.

120. Visit of the Prince of Wales. Charles Doxford, in light coat at rear, and Keller by door to the General Office.

A Second Royal visit

On 3 July 1930, Edward, Prince of Wales paid a brief visit to Sunderland. He chose to visit Doxford, as the representative shipyard and marine engineering business in the town. This was a very special honour, and shows the reputation that the Company had retained over the previous decade, despite all the problems that the 1920s had brought. The yard spruced itself up for the celebrations, and these were a huge success. The photograph shows the bunting and union flags over the door of the general office. The slight figure of the Prince is greeted by Kennedy.

153

The Directors and Management during the 1930s

George Strachan died at the end of 1929, leaving a vacancy on the Board. Charles was made a Director at the 38th AGM held on 27 October 1930, one of his first actions being to recruit Dr. John Ramsay Gebbie, aged 41 and a naval architect, who came to Doxford as the Shipyard Manager. Frederic Statham Towle (1881-1953), a tax specialist, joined the Board a year later, as the nominee of the Inland Revenue. During the early 1930s, the Board of Directors comprised Sir Alexander Kennedy, Chairman, Robert Haswell, Company Secretary, F. S. Towle, as Inland Revenue appointee and Charles Doxford, Managing Director. In 1930 the SIC held only two companies: Doxford and Fairfield. They sold a controlling interest in Fairfield to Lithgow Ltd. in 1935, after which Doxford stood alone.

Dr. Edward Philip Andreae joined the Board after Charles Doxford's death, attending his first meeting on 10 July 1935. Sir Alexander Kennedy retired at the 44th Annual Meeting in November 1936, and Andreae then took the chair. Two new Directors were appointed, one from each division. These were K. O. Keller and J. R. Gebbie. Doxford was now the only Company under the umbrella of the SIC. Sperling and Kleinwort disbanded the holding Company in March 1936, distributing the 328,482 of the 360,000 shares issued amongst existing shareholders. Kleinwort received 456,224 of the 500,000 Doxford issued Ordinary Shares, and c £220,000 of the 'B' 6% Preference Shares.[13] Sperling, had operated as a registration company since the demise of the combine, but was finally dissolved in November 1945.[14]

Dr. E.P. Andreae (1879-1975)

Andreae came to the Chairmanship of Doxford through his connection with Kleinwort, Sons & Co. Ltd. His mother was Sofie Kleinwort, daughter of the founder. His elder brother, Herman Anton Andreae, was a Director of the family bank, so Dr. E. P. joined the Sperling Combine as a way of becoming involved with a financial institution, despite having training as a chemist. Andreae proved to be a successful Chairman for Doxford, because of his understanding of the world outside shipbuilding and his lack of bias over the two enterprises within the Company: shipbuilding and marine engineering. He was the first southerner to lead the Company and remained based in Surrey. He travelled north for meetings, but ensured that some took place in London. Andreae oversaw two

121. Dr. Edward Philip Andreae. Chairman of William Doxford & Sons, 1936-1957. From 47th Annual Report, 1939.

major changes to the structure of Doxford. He took the Company public in 1937 and, just prior to his retirement in 1957, restructured the enterprise as a holding company with two operational subsidiaries. His retirement lasted for many years, as he lived to the great age of 95.

The Board of William Doxford & Sons Ltd. during the final years of the decade and into the Second World War was, therefore,

* Dr. E. P. Andreae, Chairman,
* R. Haswell, Managing Director until his death in 1941,
* F. S. Towle, Inland Revenue appointee,
* Dr. J. R. Gebbie, Shipyard Manager, Managing Director from 1941,
* K. O. Keller, who died in 1942,
* W. H. Purdie, who succeeded Keller.

The Management

Robert Haswell became the Managing Director in 1935, after the death of Charles Doxford. He was succeeded as Company Secretary by William Rawlings (1877-1954), another very long serving employee at Doxford. Bill Rawlings had joined the Company in 1891, the year that the Doxford brothers set up the Limited Company. He began as a clerk in the Engineering Department and in 1928 was appointed departmental secretary. At the outset of WWII, Rawlings had reached retirement age, but he stayed in post until the end of 1945. During his last twelve months he also served as Chief Accountant. He was an energetic man, who played many sports. His daughter was the successful actress Peggy Rawlings, who was married to the radio comedian, Richard Murdoch.

K. O. Keller died in service in 1942, and his role as Director of Engineering was assumed by W. H. Purdie. E. G. Fletcher took the role of Shipyard Manager.

1937: William Doxford & Sons Ltd. becomes a public company

By the end of 1936 the Shipbuilders Investment Company had been dissolved. The Board decided to restructure Doxford as a public company. Following the Board Meeting of 8 January 1937, changes were made to the £1m share capital. Agreement had been reached with the holders of the 5% Cumulative Preference shares and of the 6% Cumulative 'B' Preference shares that accrued dividends and the right to receive Cumulative dividends in the future should be cancelled. EGMs were held and all £10 shares in the Company were subdivided into non-Cumulative £1 Preference shares and £1 Ordinary shares. The 6% 'B' Preference shares then became Ordinary shares, so that the capitalisation of the Company became 250,000 £1 non-Cumulative 5% Preference shares and 750,000 £1 Ordinary shares. Application was made to the London Stock Exchange, to convert to a public company and this was announced in The Times of 23 February.

The first accounts of the Public Company were presented to the 45th AGM, held at Winchester House, Old Broad Street, on 28 October 1937. These showed that the profit had more than doubled over the year from £108,077 to £249,642. A debit balance of £402,466 on the profit and loss account was standing on the books at 30 June 1936. This debit had been mainly due to writing off loans to Workman, Clark, which had gone into liquidation. This was now cleared by using £116,015 of the current year's profits and by taking the remainder from reserves. In spite of this write down, c £133,500 was available to pay dividends on the Preference Shares of 5%, plus an extra 1%, and 10% on the Ordinary Shares.[15] After placing a further £45,000 in taxation and general reserves, more than £23,000 was available to carry forward. Doxford's earning power, expressed as a percentage of Ordinary Capital, was in the region of 47%. Additionally, £300,000 in 4% First Mortgage Debentures had been redeemed on 1 July 1937. A modest £30,000 was set aside for future reserves. It was a remarkable turnaround. Only eight months after going public, the £1 shares were quoted on the stock market at £2 9s 4$^{1}/_{2}$d.

Chapter Twelve

1919-1939
The Pallion Yard in the Interwar period

122. The Pallion shipyard in 1921, with the ten year old Queen Alexandra Bridge down river.
The main offices, with skylights can be seen on the lower left, beside the Wear.

Work barely faltered as the sale of the business was carried out during 1919. Apart from the ongoing development of the marine oil engine, ship construction in the yard was buoyant. A number of commissions were under construction as peacetime conditions returned. The first ship completed under the chairmanship of R.A. Workman was launched on 4 February 1919. This was the SS War Balsam (C530), 5,292 grt, initially ordered under the aegis of the Shipping Controller. She was transferred to the British India Steam Navigation Co. Ltd., Glasgow and renamed the Homefield in May that year. She was one of seventeen steamships built between April 1918 and June 1920 with the prefix 'War'. All were later renamed. They were standard ships, ranging from 5,171 grt to 6,698 grt, and were owned by both British and foreign shipping companies. However, the situation then changed rapidly in the early 1920s. Freight rates dropped dramatically. A contributing factor was that the British Government took over German vessels as war reparations and offered them for sale at reduced prices, rather than scrapping them. By mid-1920 it was apparent that there was a surplus of ships, and orders dried up. The last that Doxford received was SS War – (C543) 6,695 grt. This became the Koranton, owned by R. Chapman & Son, Newcastle. C544-576 had been ordered by Norwegian shipowners in 1917, for post war construction. C544-556 were built, but only five of these went to Norway. Four were purchased by the Transatlantic Rederi of Gothenburg, Sweden, and two of these, MV Yngaren (C549) and MV Eknaren (C556), contained the new

157

Doxford opposed piston engines. One more went to Sweden, and the Moor Line, (W. Runciman), stepped in to take the final two. Of C557-576, only the general cargo ship SS Castlemoor (C562), 6,574 grt, was built. She was registered in August to the Moor Line.

As shipbuilding orders dried up, together with other Wear shipbuilders Doxford cut back their workforce. As early as May 1921, they reported to the Wear Shipbuilders Association that "a number of under foremen have reverted to the tools." Other shipbuilders were in a worse position; some were working only two to three days a week, others doing "practically nothing". The J. L. Thompson yard was closed.[1]

123. 1920 Plan of alterations to the Engine Works for building oil engines and to install a 20 ton crane.
Courtesy of the Sunderland Antiquarian Society.

Despite the downturn, in 1920 the new management carried out a major redesign of the engine works for the production of the new oil engines. The plan, pointing downwards towards the River Wear, shows the location of each shop. An overhead crane was placed to the north of the building, beside a small tool room. The engine works were further extended, possibly in the late 1920s. When even more space was required in 1939, the floor plan of the works already stretched further to the east.

124. The Sun Shipbuilding & Dry Dock Company, Chester, Pennsylvania, was the first to take out a licence to build Doxford marine oil engines in 1923. Public Domain.

The first overseas licensee for the Doxford Opposed Piston Engine

There was interest in the Doxford opposed piston engine from other engine builders, both in Britain and abroad. The Sun Shipbuilding & Dry Dock Company of Chester, Pennsylvania, was the first overseas company to take out a licence to build the engines. Agreements between the "Licence Holder (William Doxford & Sons Ltd., Sunderland)" and the licensee established certain strict rules, such as adhering to the Doxford patent. This was to maintain the standard of the engine, but licensees then had the freedom to change the performance of engine parts to suit their particular market.

The contract was for a stipulated number of years, though Doxford could terminate the contract before this with notice. By the end of the 1920s, Doxford had four British licensees and two from abroad. By 1939, more engines were manufactured annually by licensees than in the Doxford engine works. This demonstrates how important the opposed piston oil engine was for the survival of the business.

125. MV Silvercedar, C581, the third ship financed by Charles Doxford for the Silver Line. The launch on 2 June 1924. Courtesy of the Sunderland Antiquarian Society.

Despite difficult trading conditions, between 1924 and 1928, the engineering team under K. O. Keller had the confidence to pioneer engine development in advance of an upturn. Only ten ships left the Pallion yard between 1922 and 1928. Without the engineering work and payments from licensees, the business could easily have foundered.

The great majority of ships constructed by Doxford over the following years, seventy two from 1923 to the outbreak of WWII, were powered by internal combustion engines. Only eleven vessels built between 1924 and 1930 had steam engines installed, and these were supplied by other engineering companies.

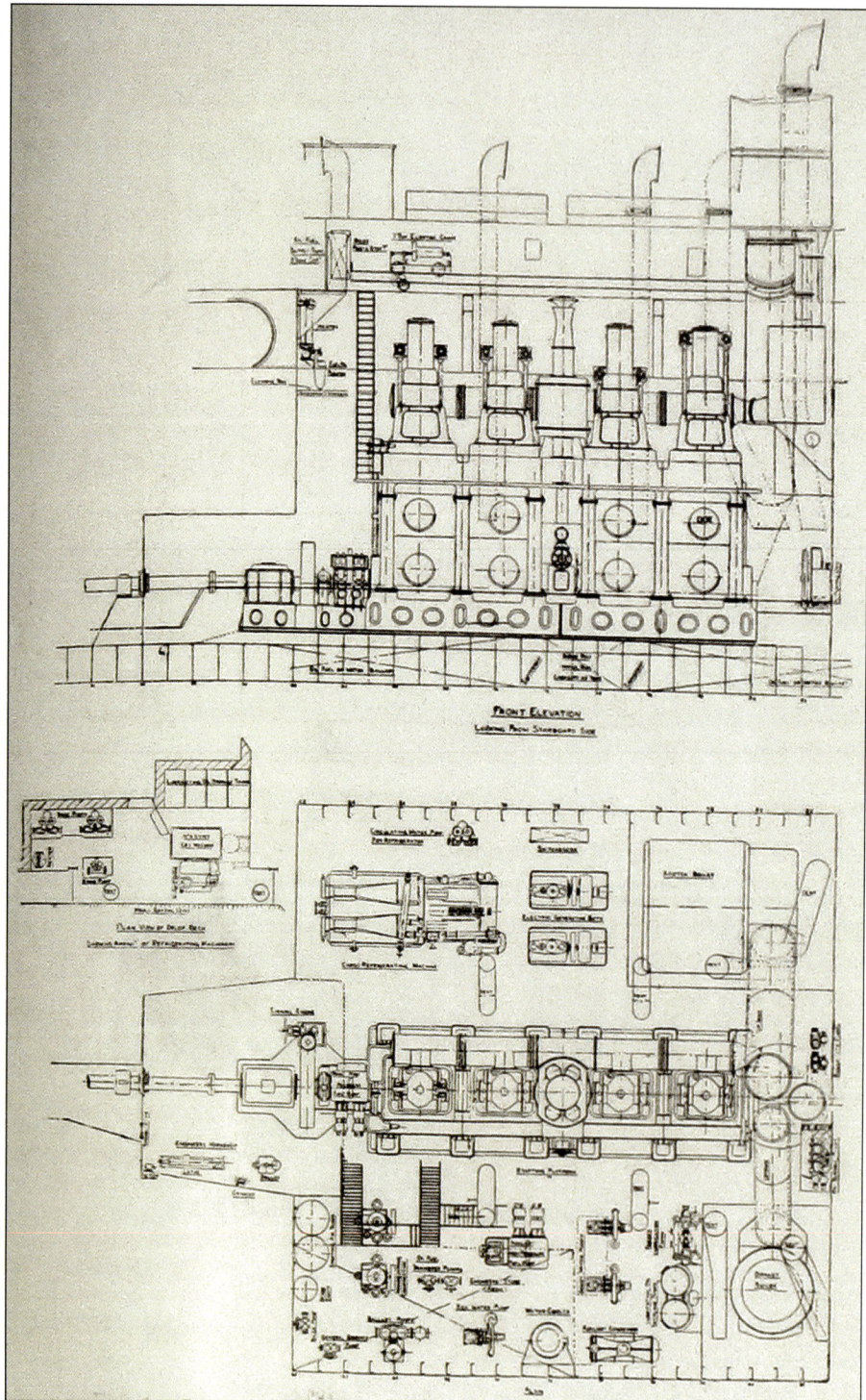

126. Plan of the engine room of Pacific Trader, 1924. From The Shipbuilder, Feb 1926, p 103.

Shipbuilding

The situation deteriorated further. The only ship that Doxford launched in 1923 was MV Pacific Shipper (C577), 6,304 grt. She held the fourth opposed piston engine, and was registered to Furness Withy & Co. Her sister ship, Pacific Trader (C578), also 6,304 grt, left the yard in February 1924 and both were completed by mid-year. Reflecting the interest the Doxford engine attracted during the lean years of the mid 1920s, The Shipbuilder of February 1926 gave a full report on the Marine Oil-Engine Trials Committee investigation of this ship, which by then had been in operation for eighteen months. A plan of its 56 ft 10 in engine room was included, and a diagram of the 4-cylinder Doxford engine.

127. Pacific Trader (C578), launched 20 February 1924, for Furness Withy & Co., sister company to Doxford. Courtesy of the Sunderland Antiquarian Society.

As recorded in Chapter Eight, Charles Doxford then personally ensured that three 'sister' ships were built for the new Silver Line, run by Stanley and John Thompson. Stanley Miller Thompson was married to CDD's niece.[2] The first, MV Silverelm (C579), 4,351 grt, suffered an abortive launch on 24 March 1924, and entered the water at 4.45 am the following morning. Despite this set back, Robert Haswell, the Company Secretary, reported to 'Mr. Charles', who was in London at the time, that twenty people boarded her on 7 May for her sea trials. The second ship was launched as Oristano (C580), 4,357 grt, but quickly renamed Silverfir. The third was MV Silvercedar (C581), 4,354 grt. These ships held a 3-cylinder 54L3 Doxford marine oil engine of 1,760 bhp. Two were sunk by the Germans during WWII, but MV Silverelm was not broken up until 1960. The Moor Line (Sir Walter Runciman) also accepted two ships in 1924. The Vinemoor (C580) and the Westmoor (C584) had the same engines as the ships built for the Silver

161

Line. These contracts enabled the Pallion yard, now under the direction of Sir Alexander Kennedy and George Strachan, to remain open for most of that year.

Charles Doxford continued to spend part of each week in London, attending the Baltic Exchange, but cash flow management was critical. Robert Haswell wrote to him at the Savoy Hotel on 19 September 1924, as the financial situation deteriorated further.

> "We have managed to pay the Engine Works night shift from Office cash and as the wages bill for tomorrow is within the current account amount, it will not be necessary to draw on No. 2 account." [3]

128. 4-cylinder engine 680L4 for MV Silverash. 1926. The Shipbuilder, November 1926. Courtesy of the World Ship Society.

However, closure of the shipyard took place only a month later, following the handover of the Westmoor. No ships left the yard during the next three years, but the £105,285 received from Walter Runciman allowed the No. 2 account which, it seems, was used as an emergency source of funds, to be discharged. Engine production and development continued. Capital expenditure of £12,000 was agreed for the Engine Works in 1925-26, and the Board Minutes also record fees paid to Charles for contracts on engines during the period of closure, as had been agreed with Sperling at the takeover. The Company's finances were also assisted by the installation of six more 4-cylinder, 2-stroke opposed piston oil engines in Silver Line ships between 1925 and 1930. Three were built by J. L. Thompson & Co. at North Sands and three by Sir James Laing & Sons at Deptford. The service speed of the 'Silver' ships was officially 13 knots, though they could achieve $14^1/_2$ on a favourable sea trial. They were built on the open shelter-deck principle, and had eleven winches and seventeen derricks to facilitate rapid loading and discharging of cargo. The sea trials of one of these, MV Silverash, 5,299 grt, were reported in detail in The Shipbuilder of November 1926.[4] She was one of the J. L. Thompson built ships, their yard no. 555, launched on 10 June 1926.

129. Doxford Foremen on a day out from the works during the 1920s. Skilled men were retained and some worked beyond retirement age during the Second World War. Courtesy of the Sunderland Antiquarian Society.

So during the closure Doxford retained its Engineering Department, but only the managers, key foremen, some skilled men and apprentices remained in work in the shipyard.

130. Drawing of an elevator barge, typical of work undertaken at Pallion during the 1920s recession. Courtesy of the Doxford Engine Friends Association.

Some work was undertaken. The yard had already diversified into designing and building coal conveyor systems, such as pontoon elevators and elevator barges. These sat alongside colliers and raised the coal with the aid of steam engines. Jack Jordan advised me that some engines used on such conveyor systems were termed 'semi-diesel' and may have been similar to the small Doxford generator engines in MV Yngaren, but there is no written proof of this. The conveyor systems kept some workers in employment, but most of the men were on short time, and many were laid off for prolonged periods. Once again, the community of Sunderland suffered widespread hardship. The labourers in particular were forced to turn up at a dockyard gate, known as a 'market', twice a day, most times to be turned away. The frustration was in trying to find which market was hiring that day.

131. MV Port Hobart, 1925. Built and engined by Swan Hunter, with twin 54L4 Doxford Engines. Photograph by Allan Green.

MV Port Hobart, 7,448 gr, was a refrigerated cargo ship launched on 10 March 1925 by Swan, Hunter & Wigham Richardson at Wallsend (yard number 1257) whilst the Doxford shipyard was closed. Swan Hunter also built and installed her twin 4-cylinder Doxford engines, 54L4, under licence from Doxford. She was fitted out in four months for the Commonwealth and Dominion Line, London. The total construction time was only eleven months. She was employed for the run to New Zealand, and her lines are similar to the Silverash. However, she was about a third larger in capacity. Sadly, she was shelled and sunk by bomb action off Bermuda on 24 November 1940 on her way from Liverpool to Auckland.

The worsening trade situation meant that ship and marine engine builders were actively seeking to reduce fuel consumption. The engineering department experimented with different cylinder sizes, and modifications were introduced such as a dished piston to give a spherical combustion chamber. Vibration was a problem that discouraged shipowners from placing Doxford engines into passenger ships. In

164

1926, work began on a balanced engine to counteract this. Instead of the piston strokes being equal a differential stroke was introduced.

Adjustments were also made to the weight of reciprocating parts and the boring of the centre crankpins. The designation of SB (i.e. Short Stroke, Balanced) was given to the

133. One of four 60SB4 engines installed in MV Bermuda, 1928. Note the flattened shape for a shallower draught. From The Motor Ship, Jan 1928,

new engine. Two of the first four engines with this designation were actually built by the Doxford sister company and licensee, Workman, Clark of Belfast. All four were installed in the passenger liner MV Bermuda, 19,000 tons, 14,600 bhp, built by Workman, Clark for the Furness Bermuda Line as their yard number 490. The Motor Ship of January 1928 recorded that because the ship had a shallow draught, a lower height of engine was needed, so four were installed to power such a large vessel. They were 4-cylinder, 60SB4 engines.

The Bermuda was luxuriously furnished and her cost was reported to be a staggering £1.5 million. She sailed between New York and Bermuda, and was well received by passengers, but had a very short career. She suffered a fire whilst in Bermuda in mid-1931, which destroyed the super-structure and some of the accommodation, but was able to return to Belfast for repairs under her own steam. These were nearly completed at the Workman, Clark yard when she caught fire again in November that year. The damage this time was catastrophic, and she

132. The lavish interior of MV Bermuda. The 'Smoke-room' illustrated in Motor Ship, January 1 1928. Courtesy of The Motor Ship.

sank. She was refloated, and a court case was brought to judge whether the second fire had been started deliberately. Workman, Clark were exonerated, but her damage was deemed beyond repair by the insurers. The engines were removed, and in 1934 two were fitted by Workman, Clark into MV Incomati, as their yard no. 532, for the Bank Line. On her way under tow for scrapping at Rosyth in July 1933, the Bermuda ran aground. It was a sad end to a luxurious ship.[5]

Shipyard output on the Wear during the 1920s

The Shipbuilding Employers' Federation conducted a survey of employment on new ships during the 1920s. During this period there were eleven yards on the Wear. Under normal trading conditions, Laing, Doxford, and J.L. Thompson were the three largest employers, and the table below shows that although no yard escaped closure for new work, there was some work on the river each year.[6] The figures do not give a true picture for Doxford, as their marine engineering department was still in operation, but they show how quickly the company recovered once the depression eased. In 1930 Doxford were employing the largest number of men, women and boys on the Wear, plus, of course those involved in engine production that are not included in these figures. The smaller firms had barely recovered their original position, and during the 1930's three were closed.

Firm	No. of work-people, including apprentices, boys, youths and women, engaged in new work, as shown in periodical return for 31 March in each year									
	1921	1922	1923	1924	1925	1926	1927	1928	1929	1930
Laing	1934	1427	1008	500	552	634	1202	843	929	1293
Doxford	894	897	405	1096	-	-	31	1256	956	1582
J. L. Thompson	960	930	626	751	487	562	673	1031	353	808
W. Gray, Wear Yard	967	624	771	745	789	-	310	742	693	479
Pickersgill	595	-	68	565	537	621	217	715	494	480
Bartram	426	-	195	504	119	-	165	627	591	545
Robt. Thompson	338	172	495	480	-	-	189	516	507	500
Austin	297	247	401	276	151	-	173	47	271	430
Crown	224	234	246	244	220	-	-	204	84	176

Four generations work in the shipbuilding industry in Sunderland from 1924 to 1988

The Jordan family story is typical of the skilled people who gave their time and energy to Doxford during the twentieth century. Despite the problems experienced at the yard, and its changes in constitution, the Jordan family were one of a number of families where son followed father into the Pallion Yard.

John William Jordan (1878-1925) was born in Sunderland. He was the eldest son of a policeman, Alexander Jordan, who came to Sunderland from Cumberland. After retiring from the force, Alexander took up a second career as a private investigator. He and his wife, Elizabeth, had nine children, and John William was the first to join the shipbuilding industry. John became an accountant/timekeeper with S.P. Austin & Son Ltd., at Southwick. He married and had a son, Robert Alexander Jordan, who was only sixteen at his father's death.

134. Robert Jordan, (right) at Malta, with the Captain of Cingalese Prince after pay off at Malta. Courtesy of Jack Jordan.

Rather than joining his father at Austin, Robert (1909-1986) had come to the Doxford yard at Pallion in 1924, aged fifteen. This was just as the shipyard closed for three years, so he was fortunate that Doxford were still taking on apprentices. Robert worked under Mr. McCoy, the foreman in the workshop and the oil engine shop. Most of the Doxford workforce had been paid off due to the recession, and work that might have been done by skilled men was carried out by apprentices. His most memorable jobs during his five year apprenticeship were turning piston heads on a Gisholt vertical lathe for MV Freshmoor (see below) and for a 3-cylinder exhibition engine that was then shown at Newcastle. In 1926, Robert moved to the Drawing Office, making drawings related to upgrading the Doxford engine from a cast iron frame work to fabricated steel. However, in 1930, all the workforce were reduced to part time work, two days one week, three days the next. As there seemed little chance of improvement, Robert decided to go to sea. He obtained a post as Junior Engineering Officer on the Cingalese Prince, 8,474 grt, built in 1929 by the Blythswood Shipbuilding Co. Ltd. at Glasgow for the Furness Withy Group. She had twin Doxford 60LB4 engines built by Richardsons, Westgarth & Co., Hartlepool. He sailed with her to China, but on the return voyage the crew was laid off without pay at Naples.[7] The British Embassy loaned him £10 to make it home only after his mother sent a telegram to confirm that she would repay this. In 1933, Robert married and, for reasons of job security, joined the police force. He served with the Durham County force for twenty six years but, in 1956, took a half pension and returned to the Doxford Drawing Office. There he had to start on 'improver's pay'. Three years later he became a Section Leader, and retained this position until his retirement at the end of 1969.

Two of his sons came to Doxford, John William (Jack), the second, (b. 1935), and Robert Alexander (Bob) (b. 1945). Jack worked under Percy Jackson from 1953-55, in the Research and Development Drawing Office and at the Palmers Hill test site on the north bank of the Wear, which had been acquired by Doxford in 1946

167

(Chapter Fourteen). He was part of the team developing the experimental single-cylinder 'P' engine, but had to leave for National Service. On his return in 1962 he worked on the 'J' engine. Bob, ten years younger, joined his father and brother in the drawing office, but emigrated to Canada in 1966 to work with Rolls Royce. Jack remained at Pallion until shortly before the site closed for all work in 1988. He was the assistant Drawing Office Manager at the engine works.

Jack's son, Leslie John Jordan (b. 1960) served his apprenticeship with Doxford Engines and, after completing some time in the works, was promoted to the Production Drawing Office,

135. Jack Jordan, Sep 2018.
Photograph by Patricia Richardson.

under the Works Engineer and Manager. His work involved installing new multi-tool machines for specialist processes. However, by 1984, Doxford engine works were no longer building new engines, and were reducing the workforce prior to full closure. Leslie decided to join the police force, taking the family back to the work of both his grandfather and his father. Now retired from the force, Leslie uses his engineering skills as a volunteer at Ryhope Colliery Museum.

The Yard reopens

During 1926 there was widespread frustration amongst the working men in the country, culminating in the miners' strike and the General Strike. However, in a way, this was not the disaster for shipbuilding as might seem the case. Coal had to be imported from the United States, leading to an increased demand for ships and bringing better freight rates. Shipowners put in tentative new orders, and shipbuilders were finally able to refuse such contracts at a loss, as they had done to keep their yards open. However, Doxford faced tough conditions as they received their first enquiries.

136. MV Freshmoor (C588) on sea trials in 1928. From Doxford Publicity book of 1929, p 12.

As recorded in Chapter Eleven, the yard was reopened in the autumn of 1927 through the personal pledges of Charles Doxford. The first contracts were steam ships: SS Stonegate (C585), for Turnbull Scott Shipping Co. Ltd., London, SS Carica Milaca (C586), for Atlanska Plovidba, Dubrovnic and SS Forthbridge (C587), for Crosby, Magee & Co., Liverpool. MV Freshmoor (C588) was built via a contract between Charles Doxford and the Company, but sold to Freshmoor Navigation Ltd., managed by Harris and Dixon, London. She was a small coastal tanker of 1,074 grt, with an operating speed of 10 knots.

During these difficult years, Keller and his team at Doxford produced the balanced engine, both SB (Short Balanced) and LB (Long Balanced). The first 3-cylinder 40SB3 engine was installed in the Freshmoor in September 1928. Charles had also been approached by the Moor Line (Sir Walter Runciman) to build a further two ships. However, the shipowner demanded that payment should be 'cash on delivery', something that the financial position of the Company precluded. Charles

137. 3-cylinder 40SB3, i.e. Short and Balanced, engine fitted to MV Freshmoor, 1928. Courtesy of the Doxford Engine Friends Association.

made an offer to the board to undertake the contracts on his personal account, and to provide cash instalments to the company during the period when the ships were under construction, on an agreed 'time and line' basis (the actual cost of labour and materials, plus a percentage for profit, which would now be called cost plus.). His incentive was that he would be:

> "entitled to retain for his own use and not accountable for the excess (if any) in the price payable by the Shipowner to Mr. Doxford over the price payable by Mr. Doxford to the Company on such time and line basis."[8]

The contracts were nos. 591 and 592, MV Glenmoor and MV Innesmoor, and they each had a 3-cylinder opposed piston oil engine of 2,200 bhp. The Shield Daily News reported that the ships achieved a speed of 10 knots at 80 rpm. The Moor Line also requested an option for another four similar ships. The Board agreed that, should these options be taken up, Charles would provide finance on the same basis. According to the yard list only two came to fruition. There was also a delay in starting the work, as Runciman insisted that this should not begin until September. Charles Doxford continued to help the Company by accessing engine contracts. In September that year, for the sum of £60,000, Short Brothers ordered a set of 4-cylinder opposed piston oil engines, 2,250 bhp (engine contract 164) and two more licences were granted to companies to build these engines. However, some of the arrangements that existed from the time when the Company was in family ownership were terminated. In 1928 Robert Doxford and Otto Keller relinquished the patents granted to them personally in favour of the Company.

1928 saw seven ship launches and rising income from engine licensees. By the end of 1929, seventeen ships had been launched from the re-opened yard: nine steamships and eight motor vessels. One of the engine licensees, Richardsons, Westgarth, of Hartlepool, reported to their annual meeting in August that they had five orders for Doxford opposed piston engines on their books, in addition to their general engine work.

Shipowners were still in difficulties. Contracts were agreed that allowed payments to be staged by bills of exchange, secured by a mortgage on the vessel. If a shipowner defaulted on the mortgage payments, the decision had to be taken whether to take the vessel in hand. This was unattractive when so much shipping was laid up. In most cases, the ship was left in its original ownership, awaiting resumption of payments, but sometimes there was no hope of this. Two ships fell into this category and the saga was described by J.F. Clarke.[9] SS June (C594) and SS Juliet (599) had been delivered to Hans Hannevig of Horten, Norway, in 1929. Hannevig defaulted, but Doxford allowed him to retain ownership. By 1932 the two ships faced impoundment abroad. Doxford took possession, and did a deal with a new shipping company, Essex Oak Ltd., run by Messrs. Meldrum & Swinson, with Doxford having an interest in the company. Charles Doxford personally invested £1,500 to bring them into serviceable condition. The ships were then renamed Essex Oak and Essex Noble. This seems to have been successful as both vessels, under later ownership, lived out their natural lives. They were scrapped during the 1960s.[10]

The Doxford Economy Cargo Ship

Once the yard reopened in 1927, Charles Doxford began to consider the development of a marine oil fuelled 'economy' general cargo ship. Tramp steamers typically consumed thirty to forty tons of coal per day, and were capable of a speed of just under 10 knots. The aim was to construct a motor ship which could reach this speed, but with a consumption of only about six and a half tons of fuel per day. Although oil was more expensive than coal, more space was created for cargo. In 1930, as a new Director of the Company, he recruited Dr. John Ramsay Gebbie (1889-1968) into the firm as General Manager of the shipyard from the now defunct Northumberland Shipbuilding Company. It was Gebbie's design, which he developed with Charles, which became known as the Doxford Economy Cargo Ship. Gebbie was born at Greenock. He attended the Royal Technical College, Glasgow and then obtained a degree in Naval Architecture from Glasgow University. He was later granted a doctorate. He served his apprenticeship at Scotts' Shipbuilding and Engineering Co. Ltd. on the Clyde, becoming their assistant chief draughtsman before moving to the NSBC after it was acquired by the Sperling Group. Gebbie married Edith Slater at Gateshead in 1936. They had no children, and lived at 11 Valebrook, Sunderland until his death in 1968.[11]

The 1930s – The Second Closure of the Doxford Shipyard

However, to begin with, things did not go to plan. MV Lise (C611), 6,286 grt, a steel tanker built for A/S Lise (Ivar N. Christensen), Oslo, was launched on 18 December 1930, and handed over in March 1931, after which the shipbuilding yard at Doxford was closed once again. This depression was far deeper than that of the 1920s. Eighty eight ships were built on Wearside between 1924 and 1926, but there were virtually no orders for five years between 1931 and 1935. Only thirty small ships were launched from the yards that remained open, and these had an average tonnage of just 2,243.[12] Sales of Doxford engines were also at a

138. Empty Berths in the West Yard, Pallion, 1932.
Courtesy of the Sunderland Antiquarian Society.

virtual standstill. Only two engines were sold in 1931, none in 1932, one each in 1933 and 1934, though things began to improve in 1935, when five were built.[13] The two photographs show the situation at Pallion during 1932.

As during the mid-1920s, the engine department remained open, and experiments began in waste heat recovery. Doxford engines needed a lower input air supply than other types of engine, due to the scavenge air design. Scavenge air was needed to expel the spent fuel/combustion products from the cylinder. This was necessary because some fuel components such as vanadium pentoxide were very corrosive to the pistons and cylinders. The scavenge pump design allowed the exhaust temperature to be cooled by very little excess air. Experiments indicated that this could be reduced from 30% to as low as 10%, unlike other types of engine that needed 60%. An excess air supply of 20% or lower allowed a reduction in scavenge

139. Ships laid up on the Wear by the Doxford yard 1930s. The West yard is empty in this photograph. Public Domain.

pump size. In addition, the exhaust temperature of 375 degrees Celsius made it possible to generate 0.6 kg of steam per kW engine power at a pressure of about

10 bar. A system using rubber hoses introduced for the upper pistons during the 1930s remained standard until the development of the 'P' engine, designed by Percy Jackson in the 1950s. (See Chapter Thirteen)

Development work also continued on the opposed piston marine oil engine. In 1931, Keller found that placing the side crank-webs in circular form, as main journals (61 inches in diameter), shortened the engine and reduced both its weight and

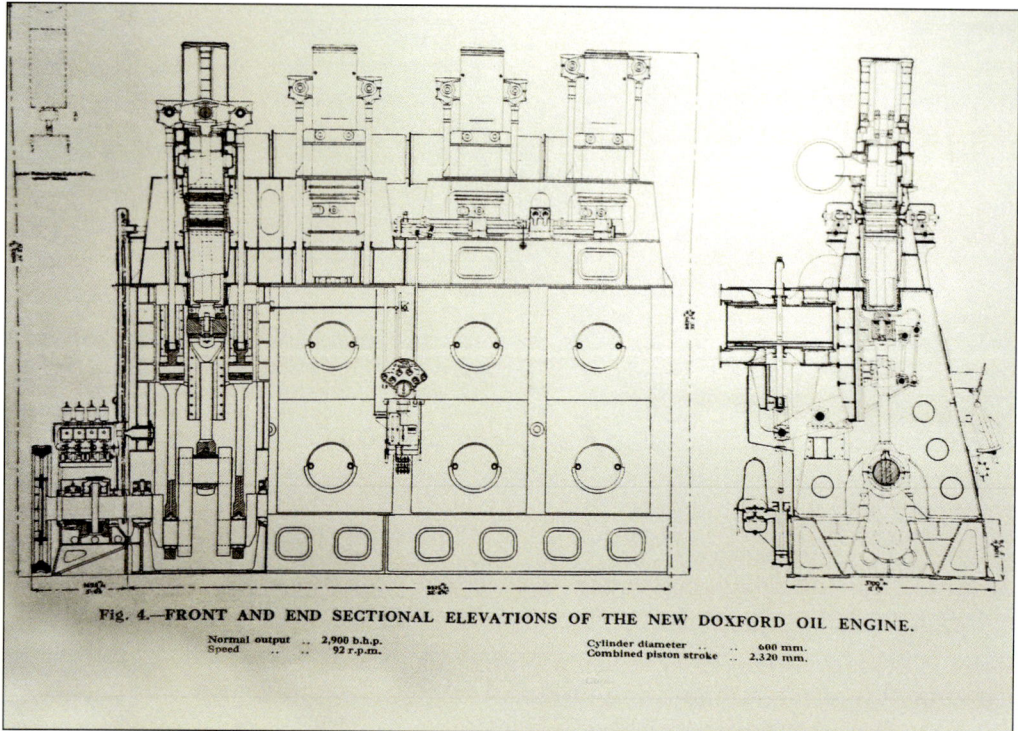

Fig. 4.—FRONT AND END SECTIONAL ELEVATIONS OF THE NEW DOXFORD OIL ENGINE.

Normal output .. 2,900 b.h.p.   Cylinder diameter .. .. 600 mm.
Speed .. .. 92 r.p.m.   Combined piston stroke .. 2,320 mm.

140. Development of the Doxford Engine in the 1930s, despite the closure of the shipyard.
From The Motorship, February 1933, p 305. Courtesy of The Motor Ship.

cost.[14] Then, in 1933, Keller, Purdie and Ker Wilson designed all welded, fabricated steel superstructures for the engines, and supporting frames were used for the first time. The eventual engines that powered the Doxford Economy ships were 3-cylinder, 52LB3 and 60LB3, (mainly the latter) both of welded construction.

141. MV Sutherland (C612) 1934. The first Doxford Economy Cargo Ship.

Meanwhile, Doxford and Gebbie worked on the ship design that proved to be profitable even in the worst trading conditions. Economy did not necessarily mean that a ship was cheaper to build, though it required few tools and had a partly welded hull. Economy meant that such a ship was designed to be economical to run, and needed little maintenance. Additionally, the Doxford Economy Cargo Ship had a wider beam than a conventional cargo vessel, so could carry more cargo for its length.

A glimmer of light appeared 1934, when an order for the new design was received from Sir Arthur Sutherland of B.J. Sutherland, Newcastle. In 1929, B.J. Sutherland had commissioned SS Roxburgh, from the Burntisland Shipbuilding Co. Ltd, Fife. She was an economical steam ship with a triple expansion engine, but the order had been put on hold, and was only completed in early 1935. The Roxburgh could achieve nine knots on a coal consumption of about sixteen tons a day, considerably less than other coal burning ships of her time, but Sir Arthur was seeking an even more economical vessel. The ship built by Doxford as C612 was given the name MV Sutherland, and was launched on 16 December 1934, almost exactly four years after the Lise had left the Pallion yard. The Sutherland, 4,956 grt, was 412 feet long (125.7 metres) with a speed of $10^3/_4$ knots. She was powered by an updated 3-cylinder engine, the 52LB3, i.e. Long and Balanced, 1,800 bhp, running at 115 rpm. Doxford took a cover advertisement for the engine in the February edition of The Motor Ship. In this edition, the magazine reported on the sea trials that took place on 29 January, stating that "scarcely a trace of vibration was noticed, quietness of operation being a performance feature of the main engine".[15] The Sutherland then sailed to India, and made five more voyages before being sold to the Rio Cape Line, part of the Prince Line. She was renamed the British Prince, but was

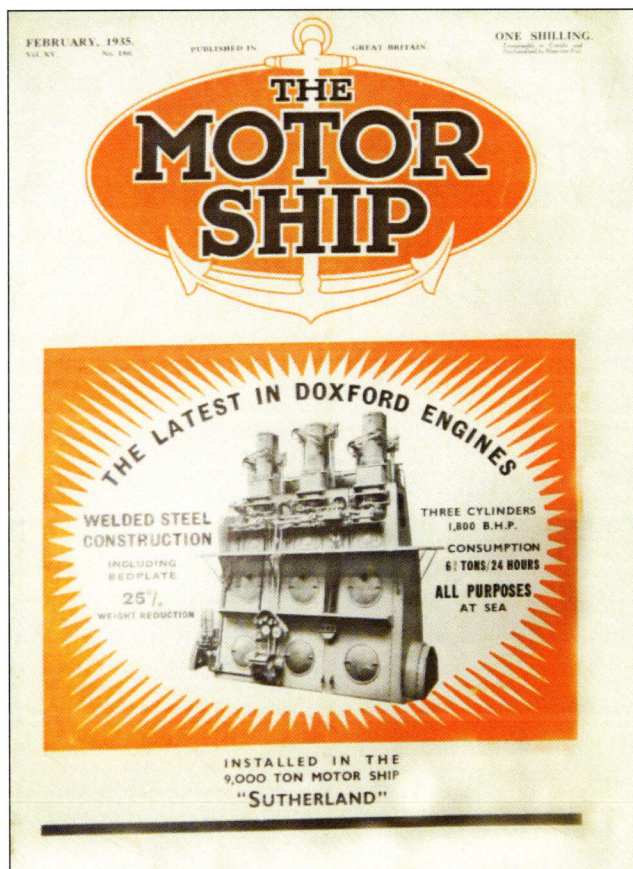

142. The Motor Ship, February 1935 cover advertisement for William Doxford & Sons. Courtesy of The Motor Ship.

bombed and sank off Hornsea on 26 September 1941. In 1940 a second MV Sutherland (C658), 5,172 grt, was built by Doxford for the same owner. This second vessel was of a similar size as the first but with a slightly greater capacity.

173

Between April 1935 and May 1936, the Sutherland was followed by the Kinross (C613), Stirling (C615), Caithness (C616), Peebles (C625) and Ross (C626), for B.J. Sutherland, all very similar. Between these orders a further twelve economy vessels were built for other shipowners up to the end of that year. The number indicates the speed that could be achieved in construction of economy ships. Economy ships were also built under licence to Doxford in Britain and on the Continent.

Scrap and Build 1935

Finally, the government introduced the 'Scrap and Build' scheme (The British Shipping (Assistance) Act, 1935). Its first provision was to set aside £2m as an operating subsidy for shipowners, with the intention of ending the intense competition for freight rates. In fact, freight rates were already improving, and the full amount was never taken up. Secondly, all new ships and all scrappage had to take place in British yards, as a measure to alleviate unemployment in the shipbuilding and repair industry. Part II of the Act brought into being the term 'Scrap and Build'. Loans were made available on the basis of scrapping one ton for each new ton built. The proviso was that the new tonnage should use modern methods of construction, such as prefabrication, something that was in any case

143. SS Virgo, built by Doxford as Elgin (C367).
The single turret ship scrapped in 1936. Photo R.A. Snook.

happening. The Act provided an incentive to shipowners to commission medium sized ships to replace a variety of out of date vessels. In fact, one of those scrapped was an elderly Doxford turret ship. This was the Virgo, built in 1906 as Elgin (C367), 3,835 grt, for B.J. Sutherland & Co. She had been sold on to become Gwynmead and finally met her end as Virgo. She was part of a package of five ships scrapped for Cadogan S.S. Co. Ltd. after which they obtained a loan of £91,000 to enable Barclay Curle & Co. of Glasgow to build the Queen Anne, 4,937 grt, and others in the Queen Line. The Queen Anne had a Doxford 52LB3 engine, installed by the builders.[16] The new ships were overwhelmingly of open shelter deck design, in the 5,000-5,500 grt range. During the 1940s their capacity grew to over 7,000 grt, but this did not mean that the ship's length or breadth increased. Instead, the draft was deepened for heavy wartime cargos and the ships changed from having open shelter decks to closed shelter decks. Both these modifications gave higher figures for deadweight and gross tonnage.[17] The scrappage scheme worked reasonably

144. MV Ripley (C623) a ship financed by Scrap and Build. 1936. Public Domain.

well through to 1937. In 1936, 338 ships were built with a gross tonnage of 1,091,446. However, output fell to 243 ships and 854,095 the following year and to a mere 300,000 grt in 1938, as freight rates slumped once again. The Government had been slow to take on board the challenge from subsidies given by foreign administrations, but eventually responded with the British Shipping (Assistance) Act, 1939. Loans were from now on provided without the need for scrappage. These were extended to cargo liners and short sea tramps, and shipbuilding grants were made available, linked to the freight index.

Doxford were the company that benefited most by the provisions of these Acts. They built six ships through the Scrap and Build legislation, and a further ten under the Shipping Loan arrangements of 1939. The 1936 ships, of whom three were sunk during WWII, were:

Yard number	Ship	Owner	Manager	Subsequent history
618	Rugely	Red 'R' S.S. Co. Ltd.	Stephens, Sutton Ltd.	Convoy duties, scrapped 1972
620	Riley	Whalton Shipping Co. Ltd.	Stephens, Sutton Ltd.	Subsequently Anoula A., Kien Ping, wartime service. Scrapped 1968
621	Rothley	Whalton Shipping Co. Ltd.	Stephens, Sutton Ltd.	WW2 service, hit by torpedo by U-332 and sunk with loss of 2 lives.
622	Ridley	Stephens, Sutton Ltd.	Stephens, Sutton Ltd.	Hit submerged object in Dec. 1938, but limped home, and survived the war.
623	Ripley	Thomasson Shipping Co. Ltd.	Stephens, Sutton Ltd.	Sunk by U-161 on 12 Dec 1942 off Brazil. Crew survived.
629	Queen Maud	Queen Line (T. Dunlop & Sons,)		Sunk by U-38 on 5 May 1941, off West Africa, carrying coal. 1 life lost.

In 1936, whether in response to the new Government legislation, or already planned, fabricated steel bedplates were used for the first time. These replaced cast-iron, and reduced the deadweight. However, the engines were of equal importance. In 1937, Andreae authorised significant expenditure of £69,352 on the extension of, and new equipment for the Engineering Department.[18] This was to facilitate the development of the 3-cylinder economy engine that became an integral part of the Doxford economy ships.

145. QSMV Dominion Monarch at Sydney. Fitted with four 5-cylinder Doxford engines. Postcard.

Outside the scheme, Doxford were, however, also producing larger engines. In 1938 they completed two 5-cylinder engines (725SB5) for the 20 knot QSMV (quadruple screw motor vessel) Dominion Monarch, 27,000 grt. These engines generated 8,000 bhp each. The Dominion Monarch was constructed at the Swan Hunter and Wigham Richardson yard at Wallsend on the Tyne as their yard number 1547. Swan Hunter was one of Doxford's licensees, and built two further identical engines for the same ship, giving her a total output of 32,000 bhp. She went into commission in early 1939 under the ownership of the Shaw Savill line. As the depression lifted, three more licensees came on board: John Brown, David Rowan and Alexander Stephens, all based on the Clyde.

Apart from carrying passengers, the Dominion Monarch was a refrigerated cargo ship. She sailed between Britain and New Zealand, via Australia. She was

146. One of the 5-cylinder engines, developing 8,000 bhp, fitted to Dominion Monarch.

176

requisitioned as a troop ship during WWII and in its immediate aftermath. Instead of carrying just 535 first class passengers, she accommodated 3,556 servicemen and women. She resumed operation as a passenger liner in 1948, after reconditioning by Swan Hunter. In 1951, Robert Pile Doxford's grandson, Denis, returned to Britain in her from Australia with his family. The Dominion Monarch was sold to a Japanese company in 1961, who displayed her as a floating hotel for a short time at Seattle. She was broken up in late 1962.

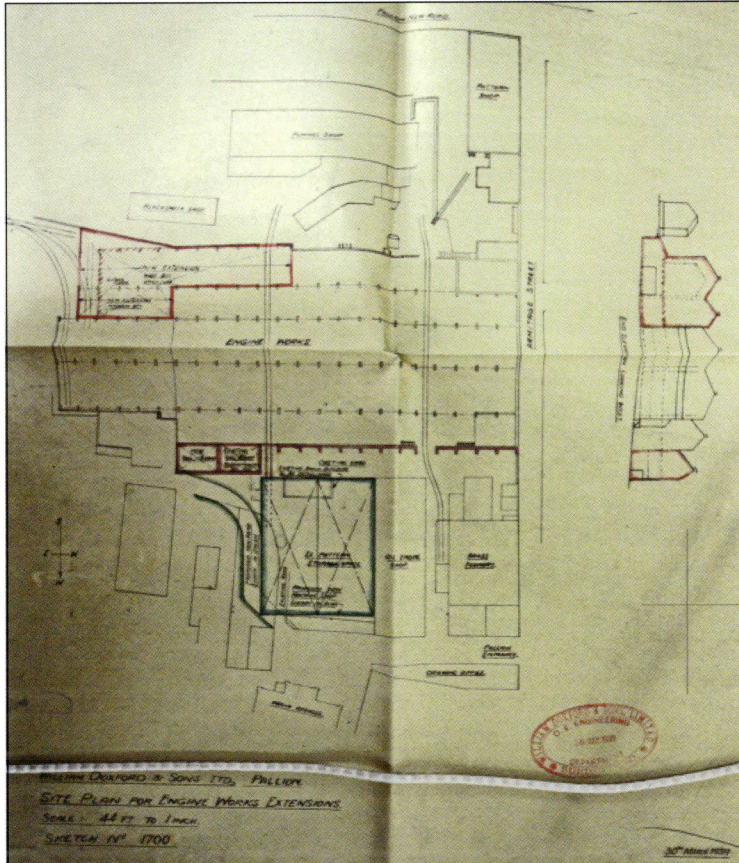

147. Further extensions to the Oil Engine Works, 30 March 1939. The main offices are at the bottom of the plan. Tyne & Wear Archives Service, Newcastle. DS.DOX/2/82/1.

In fact, immediately prior to WWII Doxford were confident enough to extend the Engine Works. Part of the design was to enlarge the main building to the South, towards the blacksmith shop. The extension had two floors, with a wide and a narrow bay on the upper floor. Amendments and additions were made to the fitting out areas beside the river, and alterations and extensions to the tool rooms beside the erecting pits. To the south of the main engine works, the existing tool room was doubled in size, a small building was demolished and a substantial machine shop placed beside the oil engine shop, with a new access off the main entrance road.

Shipbuilding output in the North East immediately prior to WWII

A remarkable fact is that despite two periods of closure, Doxford produced the highest gross tonnage of all the Wear shipyards between 1920 and 1938, at 461,000 grt.[19] The output of their nearest rival, Sir James Laing & Sons, was 283,000 grt. Shorts and Thompsons produced c 250,000 grt each. Doxford were also the largest employer on Wearside, with a workforce just under 1,600 in 1936, only two years after the yard had reopened. Theirs was nearly 50% higher than that of J. L. Thompson. At the end of 1938, the Sunderland Echo and Shipping Gazette reviewed the situation on the river. They recorded that the merchant tonnage launched from the Wear yards had surpassed that of 1937 by 33,000 grt; 169,898 grt from 35 ships. (Though, of course, some of the launches may not have gone into service until later.) The Wear was then pre-eminent on the North East Coast for merchant tonnage, as shipyards on Tyneside had launched only 24 merchant vessels (154,095 grt).[20] This does not reflect the true output from the Tyne, though, because the river's shipyards built warships for the Admiralty. Although Hartlepool and Teesside produced 29 ships between them, the gross tonnage was only 99,776.

148. Ship under construction at Pallion in the interwar years. The continuing use of wood is graphically illustrated. From 'Where Ships are Born'.

In 1938 Doxford built nine ships totalling 51,153 grt, with engines generating 26,850 ihp. The same year J. L. Thompson launched only six, of 40,752 grt and 21,500 ihp respectively. Three of the Doxford ships (C645-647) were the last powered by steam to leave the yard. SS Starstone and SS Themoni were powered by engines from Richardsons, Westgarth. SS Ittersum held one built by NEM. From 1939, all production was diesel powered. The Doxford economy ships were now achieving nearly 11 knots in service, but fuel consumption had increased to nine tons per day.

149. A 5-cylinder Doxford engine developing 8,000 bhp, built just prior to WWII. The Motor Ship September 1938. Courtesy of The Motor Ship.

Chapter Thirteen

1939-1945
The Second World War

The output from Wear Shipyards during WWII

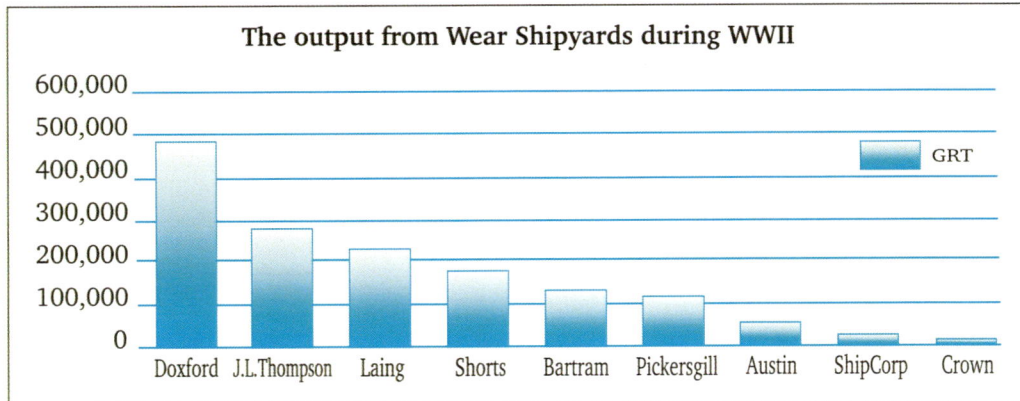

Strangely, despite the increasing threat of war, business was subdued in 1939, and only four ships were launched from Pallion before the declaration on 3 September. MV Kassos (C650), 5,215 grt, which was delivered to the Kassos Steam Navigation Company, the Greek shipping line, in July 1939, was the first to go into service during the war. She was followed by Merchant Prince (C651), 5,229 grt, which was delivered in September to the Drake Shipping Co. Ltd., London.

150. MV Kassos (C650), completed in July 1939, the first Doxford Standard ship to go into service during WWII. Courtesy of The Sunderland Site.

MV La Estancia (C652), 5,185 grt, was then launched on 14 September for Buries Markes Ltd., London. She was the first of ten to be built by Doxford through the Shipping Loan scheme described in Chapter Twelve. All three ships were similar, and two suffered attack from German U-boats. The Merchant Prince was badly damaged in 1943, but survived with one loss of life. She remained in service until 1963. La Estancia was less fortunate. She was sunk in the Atlantic by U-47 on 20

October 1940, almost midway between Iceland and Britain. She had a complement of thirty three, including one passenger. A crew member died, but the rest managed to launch the lifeboats and all were eventually picked up by British ships.

151. La Cordillera (C655) One of the ships built under the second scheme. Author's collection.

In fact, the first Doxford built ship to become a casualty of war was MV Vancouver City (C598), built in 1930 for the Reardon Smith Line. She was sunk by U-28 on 14 September 1939, seventy five miles south west of Milford Haven. Convoys had not yet been set up, and she was zigzagging, supported by an aircraft, so the U boat did not give a warning. Three of her complement of thirty three were killed, but the rest were picked up by a Dutch oil tanker called Mamura, directed to the scene by the aircraft. Doxford went on to build a second ship named Vancouver City for the Reardon Smith Line in 1942, as yard number 689. She survived the war. One of the most interesting stories is that of the Troma (formerly Rodsley). The ship was purchased by a Norwegian company. When loading coal at Moss, Norway, on 9 April 1940 she was taken over by the Germans when they invaded. Under the German flag, she suffered damage on a number of occasions during the war, including from an air attack on Hamburg in 1943. On 24 November 1944 she sank at Oslo following sabotage, but was raised in 1946, and acquired by the Norwegian war insurance organisation. After repairs at Antwerp the Troma was renamed Max Manus. As such, she was sold in 1963 to Loucas Nomikos of Greece and renamed Flora N. Just a year later she was destroyed by a fire when at Ibiza, and was finally broken up.[1]

A website gives details of allied merchant shipping damaged or sunk by German U-boats. This lists over three thousand ships, including thirty seven built by Doxford between 1924 and 1944. Four pre-Great War turret ships were also sunk, one being SS Nyland (C403), built in 1909. At the outbreak of war, she was in neutral Swedish ownership. She was sunk very early into the conflict. Just after midnight on 28 September 1939 she was boarded by U-16, off Norway. The Nyland's captain tried to pretend he had no papers, but orders to divert from Amsterdam to Ramsgate were found. The crew were ordered to abandon ship and she was then sunk by a torpedo. Cargoes varied considerably, and included explosive materials, coal, steel, ore,

180

The table here shows the ten ships built through the second scheme. Five were lost through enemy action, though one was anti-German.

Yard No.	Ship	Owner	Manager	Subsequent history
652	La Estancia (1939)	Nolisment S.S.Co. Ltd London	Morel Ltd	Sunk by U-47 on 20 Oct 1940 in Atlantic south of Iceland. One man lost.
638	Rodsley, launched 5/37, renamed Troma 8/37, later Max Manus and Flora N.	A/S J. Ludwig Mowinckels Rederi, Bergen	Originally Stephens Sutton.	Vessel taken over by Germans at Moss, Norway. See below for her story, scrapped in 1964.
655	La Cordillera (1940)	Buries Markes Ltd., Londonsunk		Torpedoed and by U-163 85 miles east of Barbadoes. 3 men lost. Doxford built a second ship with this name in 1946, C740.
659	Putney Hill (1940)	Putney Hill S.S.Co.	Counties Ship Management Ltd.	Hit by torpedo from U-203 on 26 Jun 1942 off Puerto Rico, and sunk by 53 rounds. 3 men lost.
660	Tower Grange (1940)	Tower S.S. Co. Ltd.	Counties Ship Management Ltd.	Sunk by torpedoes from U-154 on 18 Nov 1942. 6 men lost.
661	Rawnsley (1940)	Red 'R' S.S. Co. Ltd.	Stephens, Sutton Ltd.	Bombed and hit by an aerial torpedo on 8 May 1941 and taken to Crete. She sank in Hierapetra Bay.
663	Rookley (1940) later Despoina, Jumbo and Ibis II	Thomasson Shipping Co. Ltd.	Stephens, Sutton Ltd.	Took part in convoys, but survived. Sold to Greek companies in 1956 and 1960. In 1966 renamed Jumbo, on Panamanian flag and final name given in 1970. Broken up at Split in 1971

Yard No.	Ship	Owner	Manager	Subsequent history
665	Duke of Athens (1940) later Breeze, San John P, and Theokletos	Trent Maritime Co Ltd., London		WWII convoy duty, including of tanks, other heavy equipment and as a troopship. From 1954 chartered to Palm Line. Sold 1961, 1965, 1967 and broken up Pakistan 1969.
666	Reaveley (1940) later Grenehurst, La Barranca, Westwind and Universal Mariner.	Stephens, Sutton Ltd. Newcastle	managed by owners	WWII convoy duties, steel, timber, grain etc. Sold 1948, 1956, 1959 and 1966. Broken up 1969.
668	Antar (1940) later Garbeta	New Egypt & Levant Shipping Co. Ltd.	T. Bowen Rees & Co. Ltd.	WWII Convoy duty, grain and flour, steel, general cargo. Sold 1948 and renamed. Broken up 1963

essential minerals, timber and grain. All were vital to the war effort. There was clearly an advantage to travel in a convoy, as twenty two of the casualties were unescorted. Some journeys in life rafts lasted for many days, but there were surprisingly few deaths amongst the crew, gunners and passengers on board all these vessels. 1,404 survived, and only 222 died. The greatest loss of life was from MV Lady Glanely (C640), built in 1938 and sunk by U-101 in the early morning of 2 December 1940 four hundred miles off Ireland. She was carrying a cargo of wheat from Vancouver, via the Panama Canal and was torpedoed, despite being in a convoy. All thirty three lives were lost, her master, 31 crew and one RM gunner.

As 1939 drew to a close, the order list built up. Sixteen launches took place in 1940, though some were not completed until 1941. At the start of the conflict, contracts were agreed with shipowners from all regions, but from 1940 the Ministry of War Transport (MoWT) and the Admiralty controlled all new building orders. For the North East, they appointed managers exclusively from the region for their commissions, unlike elsewhere. The yards on the Wear were told to concentrate on merchant shipping, and together produced over 1.5m grt. Not only did the Doxford output outstrip that of the other yards on the river, Pallion launched the greatest general cargo ship output of all shipyards on the mainland during the course of the War. Doxford built seventy five ships, of nearly 500,000 grt. Of course, to put this into context, Harland & Wolff at Belfast greatly surpassed this figure. From 1939 to 1945 they built 140 warships and 123 merchant ships. Doxford also carried out repairs to 3,000 vessels. Swan Hunter, Wigham Richardson on the Tyne produced only fifty five merchant ships, but a great output of warships, including battleships, cruisers and destroyers.

152. The Doxford Economy Cargo Ship Kafiristan (C675), 1941. She survived the war and was later renamed Avisglen by Purvis Shipping Co. Ltd. Author's collection.

Up to the end of 1940, Doxford built ships in the range from 4,998 to 5,217 grt, with a standard ship's complement of thirty three, but they then quickly passed 7,000 grt, due to the modifications needed for wartime use, in that the ships were deeper and carried more cargo. The ships were the same length, and the crew complement did not increase significantly. The activity of German U-boars precluded sea trials, which were suspended between September 1939 and July 1945. Additionally, as merchant ships of the standard design were produced rapidly and efficiently, trials were not necessary. Only two contracts were for the Admiralty. They came late in the War. C726 and C727 were built in preparation for D-Day as HMS LCT (3) 7067 and 7068, two petrol engined Mark 3 landing craft for carrying tanks, hence L C T(ank), and each of just 625 tons displacement.

The Kafiristan, seen above, carried out convoy duties throughout the War. She was built for the Hindustan Steam Ship Co. Ltd., managed by Common Bros. Ltd. She made at least twelve voyages across the Atlantic as a grain carrier and also journeyed to the Mediterranean and the Indian Ocean. She was converted to act as a Catapult Aircraft Merchantman (CAM), and as such was equipped with a Hurricane aircraft, that could be launched from a rocket propelled trolley in the bow. The post card shows her as the Avisglen, during the mid-1950s. Her final name, Noelle, was given to her in 1961 by the Compania de Navegacion Skiathos S.A., Beirut, Lebanon, but she was sold yet one more time, to the Carmelia Shipping Co. Ltd. of Famagusta, Cyprus. Noelle was finally broken up in 1972.

Doxford were fortunate not to receive devastating bomb damage to their yard, though J.L. Thompson was successfully targeted twice, both in May 1943. A ship was sunk at the Doxford fitting out quay and the joiners' shop severely damaged, but the yard recovered swiftly. On the whole, German bombing was inaccurate; and the yards had barrage balloons to protect them but, though the docks and yards survived virtually unscathed, the centre of Sunderland was less fortunate. 273 people were killed in the town and it is estimated that damage of some sort was suffered by most local homes.

153. King George VI and Queen Elizabeth at Pallion. 19 June 1941.
Their majesties are greeted here by K.O. Keller.

The Pallion yard received a great morale boost on 19 June 1941, when King George VI and Queen Elizabeth came to Sunderland. They chose to visit the engineering depart-ment, where they watched a quay trial of the engine in MV Daltonhall (C672), 7,250 grt, built for the West Hartlepool Steam Navigation Co. Ltd. They are seen here being greeted by K.O. Keller, whose diary records the names of the men introduced to their Majesties. They were Messrs, J. Botwright, the Engineering Works Manager,[2] W.H. Purdie, the Chief Draughtsman, E.G. Fletcher, Shipyard Manager, H.W. Jeans, Assistant Yard Manager,[3] Walker, the oldest Engine Works Foreman, H. Gibson, Foreman Plater, Morrison and Ferry, both Engine Works men, Gibson, Watson and Clarke, Shop Stewards, and Captain Temple, of the Home Guard. Keller also noted: "Mr. Haswell here first time since 18th Feb." It seems likely that the Managing Director had been unwell, as he died in September that year.

The Engine Works in Wartime

During the war years engine production was prolific. 107 were built at Pallion during the 5^1/$_2$ years of conflict, about a quarter for ships built at other yards. At one period, a new engine was being tested every fortnight. Doxford Engine Works benefited from the Government Loan Scheme, in that many of the ships delivered under this had Doxford engines from other manufacturers, built under licence. Additionally, the Sun Shipbuilding and Dry Dock Company, their American licensee, produced a medium speed geared 6-cylinder engine. The Motor Ship recorded: "These comprise two 6-cylinder Sun-Doxford engines with cylinders of 21 inches in diameter by 60-inches combined stroke. The normal rate was 4,500 bhp per engine at 180 rev/min, though each engine was capable of 25% overload, thus producing 5,625 bhp at 195 rev/min." This compares to the prototype Doxford engine of 1921 running at 77 rev/min. Fuel consumption could be as low as six tons per day, but the engines of ships in a convoy had to be run at full capacity to keep up, so was usually much higher. Despite this, the engines were considered extremely reliable.

William Hamilton Purdie (1888-1971)

154. William Hamilton Purdie, Engineering Director, William Doxford & Sons Ltd.

In 1942, following the sudden death of his mentor and long term colleague, Karl Otto Keller, W.H. Purdie succeeded him as General Manager of the Engine Department. Purdie had by then been with Doxford for over thirty years.[5]

William Purdie, known as Bill, was a Scotsman, born at Innerwick, East Lothian, in 1888. He served his apprenticeship in the drawing office of David and William Henderson Ltd., shipbuilders and marine engineers at Glasgow. He completed his training at Rugby. In 1911 he visited Doxford and accepted a year's employment with them at Pallion. He never left, and his career at Doxford ended over forty five years later. Bill Purdie and Keller together led a formidable design team for the Doxford marine oil engines.

After the sale of Doxford in 1919, W. H. Purdie was appointed Chief Draughtsman and Designer in the oil engine drawing office, so was one of the team that developed the first engine to go into service in the Yngaren. Like Keller, he was meticulous in finding the best improvements to Doxford engines, endeavouring to make them lighter and more economical in use. At the time of his election to the Institution of Mechanical Engineers, his departmental responsibilities included the supervision of eighteen draughtsman, six apprentices and six lady tracers. These last were some of the very few women who worked for Doxford, but they were a vital component of the workforce.

After Keller's death, Purdie continued the series of improvements and weight reductions, and in 1943 the Doxford 3-cylinder engine received its nickname 'Economical'. Doxford led in marine engineering as well as ship building mainly because its engines had been fully fabricated since the mid 1930s. Steam still held sway with other marine engineering firms. Two thirds of engines built for merchant ships on the North East coast during the War were steam reciprocating, just under a third were heavy oil engines and only 4% were powered by turbines, though this last figure was probably much higher for warships. Boilers were heated equally by coal and oil.

In 1944 Purdie was made a Director of the Doxford Board and, in 1947, he recruited the third principal engine designer at Doxford, Percy Jackson. He retired in 1953, just as Doxford celebrated the sale of their one thousandth marine oil engine. At the presentation, he displayed his modesty and commitment to the firm, stating how sad he was that Charles and Robert Doxford and Otto Keller were no longer present to witness the remarkable success of their engine. After his retirement, he was persuaded to stay on the Board as a consultant for a further five years. After this, he returned to Lanarkshire, where he died in 1971.

Labour shortages and relations

Unlike WWI, between 1939 and 1945 the government recognised the need to keep essential industry manned and introduced the designation of reserved occupations into conscription. These obviously included the shipbuilding industry, but the exemption was not extended to management. Therefore, current managers and foremen were asked to remain in post, even if over retirement age. George Henry Chappell (1868-1945), joined Doxford in 1895 from a local shipbroking firm. He served as a clerk with Doxford for fifty years, lastly as Head of Accounts and Advertising. Chappell was still in post when he died in August 1945, despite being over seventy when the war began. At least three more men celebrated fifty years with the firm during the war: Matthew Brown, Chief Cashier, William Rawlings, Company Secretary, and F. W. Hall, Secretary of the blast foundry.

During the War there was persistent unemployment on the Wear, but a shortage of skilled labour for the shipyards. Many men had been forced into other occupations during the mid-1930s and were now settled. Others had left the North East and moved to the more prosperous south. An examination of 229 cases of unemployed men on the Wear showed that more than half those

155. Women 'humpers' helping platers during WWII, c. 1943.
Courtesy of the Sunderland Antiquarian Society.

registered as unemployed were considered unsuitable for returning to work.[6] The workforce allowed very few women to be recruited to fill essential jobs, arguing that as long as there was a single local unemployed man, this should be barred. But this photograph shows a group of women 'humpers' assisting their plater colleagues at Pallion. It is clear that the three men training the women are of a mature age. Women were paid considerably less than men. Their wages for semi-skilled work were only a half to two thirds that of a male labourer. Women working on naval ships were categorised as 'dilutees', agreement having been reached between the Amalgamated Engineering Union (AEU) and the Admiralty for them to work until cessation of hostilities. However, the agreements reached on Tyneside and elsewhere had little effect on Wearside, as the river was asked to produce very few naval ships. Virtually all these women returned to home duties in the immediate post war period.

There was no protracted industrial action on Wearside during WWII, unlike in other shipbuilding areas and in other industries elsewhere in the U.K. The Labour Supply Committee was established under the aegis of the Wear Shipbuilders Association. The employers were represented by R.N. Thompson, (J.L. Thompson), J.R. Gebbie (Doxford) and A.J. Marr (Laing). The union representatives were J.J. O'Donnell (Boilermakers' Society), W.L. Barker (Amalgamated Society of Woodworkers) and L. Mitchell (Ship Contractors' and Shipwrights' Association) (who was followed by G. Steele, National Society of Painters). Agreements over labour were then made

156. The Pallion yard in 1943, showing ships under construction in both yards, the newly opened Shipbuilding Corporation yard and two Pickersgill yards. From Where Ships Are Born.

locally with a larger number of unions, rather than the AEU. Individual shipyards set up wartime Works Committees, again with three representatives on each side. Although not perfect, through these mechanisms there were no stoppages through demarcation difficulties and labour was interchangeable between trades when needed. Wages, as in WWI, grew steadily, and families regained a standard of living unknown for many years. The average working week was forty eight hours, but overtime was often required, and the yards and engine works operated seven days a week. The blackout, though, brought particular problems during the winter, as no outside work could be done after dark.

Despite the wartime need for extra capacity, just one shipyard was reopened on the Wear, and this was only due to pressure from Norman (later Sir Norman) and Cyril Thompson (though they were supported by Doxford's new Managing Director, J.R. Gebbie). Southwick Shipyard was opened on the former Swan Hunter site, under the aegis of the Shipbuilding Corporation, set up by the Shipbuilders' Conference. It came into operation in late 1942, but is considered to have failed to increase output significantly on the Wear, owing to the shortage of labour and materials. Recruitment had to be mainly from existing yards on the river, thereby reducing their capacity in turn.

A fourth Royal visit to Pallion

On 1 July 1943, King George V's daughter, Mary, the Princess Royal and Countess of Harewood, came to Pallion. She toured the shipyard and the engine works and was the first member of the royal family to launch a general cargo ship. This was MV Greenwich (C707), 7,297 grt, built for the Britain Steamship Co. Ltd, (Watts, Watts & Co.), London. HRH is seen wearing the uniform of Controller Commandant of the A.T.S., saluting members of the

157. Visit of HRH the Princess Royal to Doxford, 1 July 1943. HRH is accompanied by J. Botwright, Engineering Works Manager, and J.R. Gebbie, Managing Director.

Doxford home guard, who were on parade for her visit. The Greenwich survived WWII, and was still in service into the 1950s, but Watts, Watts & Co. launched the fourth of that name in 1959.

Administration during WWII

From press records, it seems that during WWII the £1 Ordinary Shares in Doxford traded at around £2, ranging between 35 and 47 shillings. Income was satisfactory, and reserves increased, but the outstanding profits of WWI were not repeated. During the War years the dividend paid on Ordinary Shares was 12.5%.

There was no change of Chairman, but the Managing Director, Robert Haswell, died in 1941. The post passed to Dr. J.R. Gebbie, who was extremely active locally during WWII. Gebbie served as President of the NECIES in 1942, and was one of the employers' representatives on the Labour Supply Committee set up under the aegis of the Wear Shipbuilders' Association. He was intelligent and innovative, but also a strongly opinionated man. Despite his energy and commitment, he is still considered a controversial figure, not only at Doxford but in the wider shipbuilding industry on the North East Coast. His further career follows in Chapter Fourteen. Ernest G.

Fletcher (1889-1970) replaced Gebbie as Shipyard Manager, having been Chief Draughtsman in the Shipyard. He held this post until his retirement in 1953.[8] During the war, Doxford also lost K.O. Keller. He was followed as Director of Engineering by his protégé, W. H. Purdie. F. S. Towle remained a non-executive director throughout the War years.

Unlike the situation in WWI, and despite constructing the largest number of U.K. built ships during the conflict, the profits of the Company do not appear to have increased exponentially, though they rose as the years passed. The balance sheet for the year ending 30 June 1939 shows a valuation of the Company as £1,314, 316, this rose to £1,749,278, a figure below that of 1918.

Within the 1939 figure, the fixed assets were given as £460,207. Doxford held £244,480 in Government securities, and the current and deposit accounts at the bank contained £306,627. The net profit for the year as reported to the 48th AGM was £258,572. £25,673 was brought forward from the previous year, £100,000 was set aside for taxation, £50,000 was transferred to the general reserve and £77,500 was distributed as dividends to Preference and Ordinary shareholders. £31,072 was carried forward.[9]

Comparative figures for the year ended 30 June 1943 show that further extensions and additions had been made to the freehold premises and plant over the previous four years. With allowance for depreciation the fixed assets had, therefore, risen to £530,376. Doxford's investment in Government securities had nearly doubled, to £458,626, but their bank deposits had fallen to £111,678. The profit in 1943 was to £211,127. No provision for taxation was made in the 1943 accounts, but £27,436 was appropriated to the staff pension scheme, £25,000 was transferred to the general reserve and £20,000 to the contingency reserve. £90,000 was paid in dividends, and £48,691 was carried forward.

On 25 October 1945 the 53rd AGM was held in London. This was for the first time since the outbreak of War. Dr. E.P. Andreae, as Chairman, reported that since hostilities began in September 1939 until VJ Day in August that year, seventy eight ships had been built by Doxford totalling 535,000 grt. Seventy three engines had been installed in Doxford built ships and a further thirty five delivered to other shipbuilders. The net profit was £184,817, within the average for the previous five years. Andreae foresaw reliable work in the near future, as orders in hand were sufficient to keep the yard and engine works occupied "well into 1947". However, he stressed that:

> "I have limited my forecast to two years. You may this unduly cautious, but shipowners and shipbuilders have not forgotten the disasters which followed the last post-war boom, with its spate of orders accepted on ridiculously long term contracts, which could never be fulfilled. We are wiser today. Before we can take a longer view with any confidence, many problems will have to be solved, and the greatest of these will have to be the subject of international agreement."[10]

He mentioned the arbitrary position that similar companies faced over the Government's Excess Profits Duty. Some were treated detrimentally, but Doxford were gainers. The following year he was able to report that Doxford had received a refund on the Excess Profits Duty, and would be allowed to use this for improvements to equipment and premises.

The robustness of a Doxford 'Economical' engine

A coda to a wartime loss is that of engine of the Dallas City. She was built by Furness Withy in 1936, and during the war was owned by Reardon Smith. On 4 July 1940, she was sunk whilst in a convoy off Dover by three bombs from a German aircraft and effectively blown apart. Luckily all the crew survived. The Doxford engine continued to run as the ship sank. In 2018 Hamish Morrison led a team to the wreck and found that although the ship's wreckage was flattened, the Doxford engine (60LB4) was still standing upright on the sea bed.

158. Pundua (C725). First ship to be delivered under peacetime conditions.
Collection of Clive Ketley, from The Sunderland Site.

End of hostilities

The first ship to be delivered to her new owners under peacetime conditions was the Pundua (C725), 7295 grt, a general cargo ship launched on 27 February 1945, but not handed over to the British India Steam Navigation Co. Ltd. until 14 June.[11] She had a long service record. She was renamed Shun On in 1967, her new owners being the Jebshun Shipping Co. Ltd. of London and Hong Kong. She was laid up at Singapore in 1971, and broken up two years later.

Chapter Fourteen

1945-1961
Post war Boom and Bust

Doxford emerged from WWII in a strong position. The Chairman of the Company was the financier, Dr. E. P. Andreae, supported by directors Dr. J. R. Gebbie, Managing Director and Deputy Chairman, F. S. Towle, the tax officer, and W. H. Purdie, Director of Engineering. The new Secretary was John George Hugall F.C.A. (1911-1993), a Sunderland man and the Chief Accountant, who had joined Doxford a year earlier. Hugall was appointed Financial Director in 1953 and was a later Chairman. The Pallion yard still had three open berths with cranes in the West Yard and three longer berths with overhead gantries in the East Yard.

In March 1946 the Company took over a local marine engineering company, John Dickinson and Sons Ltd, and thereby acquired a 650 foot fitting out quay at Palmers Hill, north of the river, close to where the Glass Museum now stands. Dickinson had been a family run firm, established in 1853. In June 1940 it was acquired by the North Eastern Marine Engineering Company (NEM) of Wallsend to support wartime work. NEM were the lead Company in a conglomerate known as the Richardsons, Westgarth & Co Ltd. NEM was the largest Company in the group, but only Richardsons, Westgarth was listed publicly, so that name was used as the parent.[1] The Palmers Hill engine works were now used for testing and developmental work, and the fitting out quay was equally important, as the larger post-war ships took much longer to fit out than previously, and space was tight at Pallion quay. However, W. H. Purdie, Director of Engineering, admitted to the Sunderland Daily Echo that few staff employed by Dickinson had moved to Doxford. Most of the 450 men transferred to other members of the Richardsons, Westgarth group.[2]

159. At work on a 60LB3 engine at Doxford works for the MV Clarkeden, built by Short Bros. in the post war period. Courtesy of the Sunderland Antiquarian Society

1946 was a time of optimism, and the year when 'Where Ships Are Born' was published. This was written by J.W. Smith, 'Blue Peter' of the Sunderland Daily Echo, and T.S. Holden, as celebratory propaganda. Gebbie was one of its promotors, as the new Chairman of the Wear Shipbuilders' Association. The book proved very popular, and a second edition was printed the following year. As Gebbie wrote in the Foreword:

> "The craftsmen of Sunderland are without superiors anywhere, and I look forward to a prosperous future for the Industry and its workpeople."

Sadly, Doxford would never surpass the gross tonnage of 116,090 delivered in 1942, (from seventeen similarly sized ships), but the order books were buoyant. In 1946, they built five tankers for the British Tanker Co. Ltd. of London, a subsidiary of the Anglo-Iranian Oil Co., (renamed British Petroleum in 1954). These were contracts 734 to 738, and the tanker names each had the prefix 'British'.[3] Two were under 7,000 grt and had 3-cylinder 60LB3 engines of 2,500 bhp, but the other three, of 8,600 grt, had the 4-cylinder 60LB4 of 3,100 bhp installed. Doxford built a further eight tankers for this Company. None of the first seven exceeded 8,600 grt, because of the limitations of draft and breadth in the shallow Suez Canal. Following the nationalisation of the Iranian oil industry in 1951, and loss of their refinery at Abadan, the British Tanker Co. made new alliances in the Middle East. They demanded larger tankers, and were using ships of up to 70,000 dwt by the 1960s, then the largest through the canal. The last tanker that Doxford built for them was the British Envoy (C798), 11,243 grt, delivered in December 1953. The one shown here was completed in July 1950. She was the British Defender (C779), 6,138 grt (8,420 dwt). After the seizure of the Suez Canal in 1967, the route round the Cape

160. British Defender (C779), 1950. Owned by the British Tanker Co. Ltd. Courtesy of Ian Buxton.

had to be used, and tankers of over 200,000 dwt were deployed. A number of their earlier tankers were sold to new owners. None of the Wear yards could offer such sized ships. The British Defender had a varied life, lasting thirty two years. She was sold in 1965 to Trustee Secretaries Ltd., managed by F.C. Strick of Newcastle, and renamed El Flamingo. Under their ownership, in 1969 she was converted to a self-unloading suction/hopper dredger, with bottom doors. She retained this name as she passed through three more hands before being broken up at Bruges in 1982.[4]

As the decade proceeded, the size of ships afloat continued to grow. At the end of 1954 the Doxford Board committed itself to modernising and lengthening its two fitting out quays at Palmers Hill, so that ships of up to 20,000 tons deadweight could be accommodated.

161. The 3-cylinder engine installed in the Trawler Lammermuir.
Courtesy of the Doxford Engine Friends Association.

At the 62nd annual meeting, held at Winchester House, London E.C. on 29 October 1954, Dr. Andreae announced another milestone for the Company. The 1,000th Doxford marine oil engine had just been installed, a yearly average of 18.5 between 1921 and 1945, but 69.3 from 1946 onwards. The number included those built by licensees.

Two special engine designs

British shipyards were flexible in the type of ships they provided, how they were engined, and how they were fitted out. They responded to the needs of shipowners, and their directors often had strong personal links with their customers. At the time this co-operation was seen as a strength, as it resulted in repeat orders, but in the second half of the century it proved a disincentive to actively seek new markets, or to design a modern 'branded' ship. Austin & Pickersgill were the exception on Wearside, as they developed the very successful standard cargo ship known as the SD14.

162. The trawler Lammermuir, 1,400 tons displacement, fitted in 1949 with a bespoke Doxford 3-cylinder engine.

193

The Doxford engineering department was also responsive to specialist demands. In 1947, 5-cylinder 60SB5 engines, developing 5,150 bhp, were installed in two small mail ships for MacAndrews & Co., part of the Royal Mail group, in response for the need for speed. The Pinto (C743), and the Pelayo (C744), both 2,579 grt, provided express services to Gibraltar and Barcelona.

In 1949, the department was asked to build a specific 3-cylinder engine for a fishing trawler to be based on the Tees. The specification was to develop an engine (no. 284) that would run at low speed for trawling purposes, but then be able to quickly achieve full speed ahead for her return to port with the catch. The Lammermuir, 729 grt, was built by John Lewis & Sons Ltd. at Aberdeen, their yard no. 220, for a consortium of St. Andrews Steam Fishing Co. Ltd., Hull, James Marr & Son Ltd. and the West Hartlepool Steam Navigation Co Ltd. The ship's hull was towed to Sunderland, where the engine was installed. This was a fully balanced 3-cylinder engine with a 440 mm bore, upper piston stroke of 620 mm, lower piston stroke of 820 mm, i.e. a total stroke of 1,440 mm (44SB3). The engine developed 1,100 bhp at 145 rpm, but could be operated as low as 15/17 rpm. At 145 rpm she achieved a service speed of 13 knots. John Lewis then applied for a licence and built a further five ships for other owners with similar Doxford type engines 40SB3 to 48SB4.

163. Tanker Caltex Kenya (C784) beneath the gantries in the East Yard.

The Caltex Kenya (C784), 8,523 grt, was the first of a number of similar tankers built for the Overseas Tankship (U.K.) Ltd., London to the specifications they demanded. She was powered by a 5-cylinder 67LB5 engine. Her bridge and most of her accommodation was midships and one innovation was that all the officers and cadets had a private bathroom attached to their cabin. Her ship's complement was sixty five, almost double that of the Doxford Economy Cargo Ships of WWII. Caltex Kenya was launched from the yard on 19 September 1951, shortly before its reconstruction, and delivered in March 1952. She had an honourable career, and was renamed Texaco Kenya following a change in ownership in 1968. She was broken up in Taiwan during the autumn of

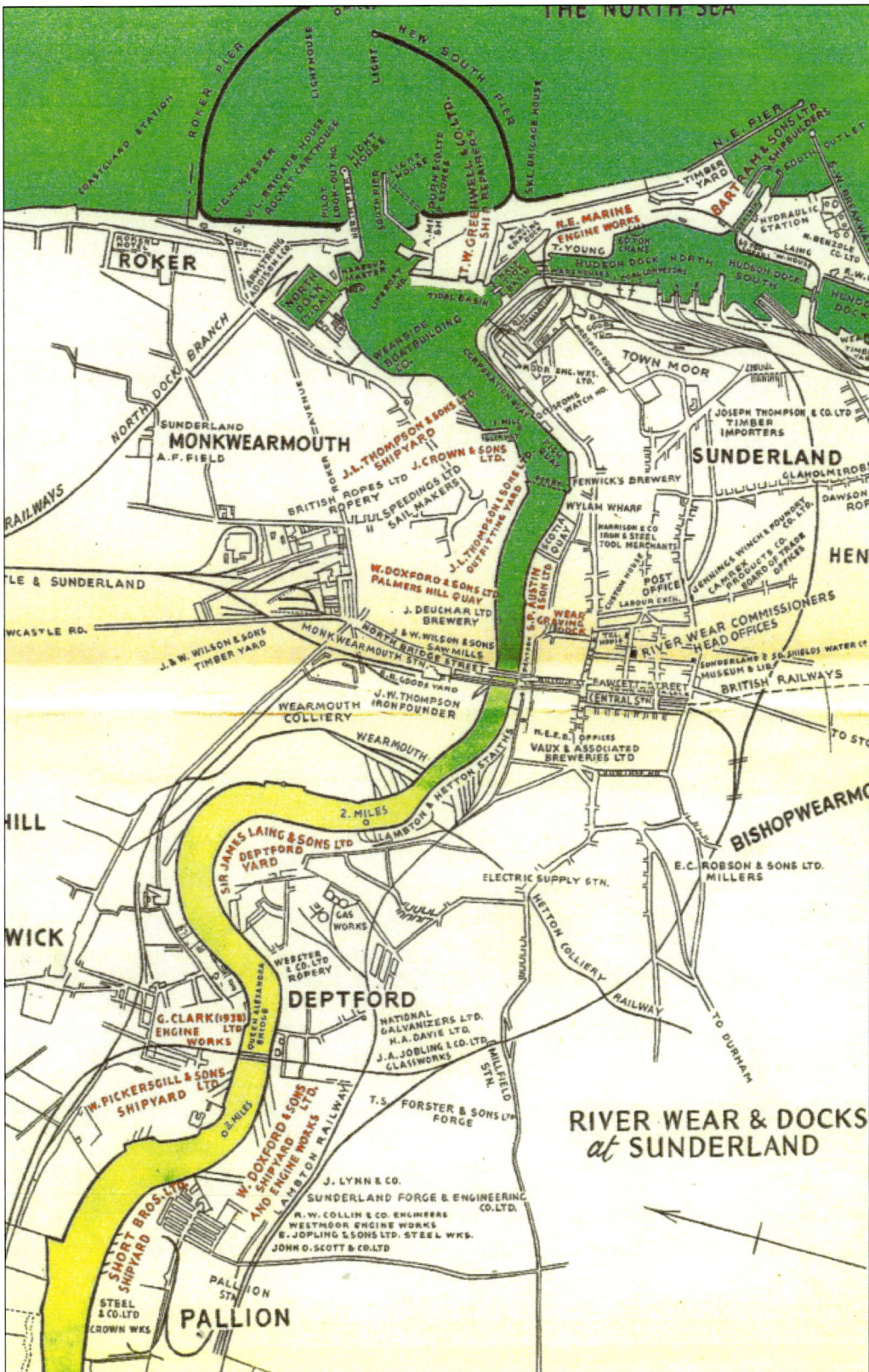

164. A map of the River Wear showing the shipbuilding and other industries in operation in the early 1950s.

1971.[5] Sadly, one of her sister ships, the Caltex Tanganyika (C787), suffered a disastrous launch on 31 October 1951. An experienced shipwright, Norman Levitt, aged forty nine, was killed and three others badly injured when the signal to launch was given incorrectly and one of the supports to be knocked away remained in place, causing the huge ship to veer.[6] Launching a ship was always a risky operation, and such accidents left indelible memories on those who witnessed them.

At the start of the 1950s the number of shipyards operating on the River Wear had dropped to just seven: J.L. Thompson & Sons Ltd., William Doxford & Sons Ltd., Bartram Sons Ltd., S.P. Austin & Sons Ltd., Sir James Laing & Sons Ltd. (under the control of the Marr family), W. Pickersgill & Sons Ltd., and Short Bros Ltd. The three large marine engineers were William Doxford, G. Clark (1938) and Richardsons, Westgarth/N.E.M. TW. Greenwell continued as ship repairers and a number of smaller companies associated with shipbuilding were still in operation. In the mid-decade Short Brothers closed and S.P. Austin merged with W. Pickersgill.

The re-ordering of the Shipyard to facilitate prefabrication

In the immediate post-war period, the Doxford Board decided to introduce prefabricated welded ship construction. Some plate welding had already replaced riveting at Pallion, especially for oil tight structure in tankers. Welding used less steel and manhours than

165. The new welding sheds, showing access by rail. From Paper to the Institute of Welding by Clement Stephenson. Courtesy of Ian Buxton.

riveting, and many of the skilled riveters who left the yards in the 1930s had not returned. However, hull construction was still carried out using plate-by-plate erection. The East and West yards each had their own platers' shop, frame furnaces, scrieve boards

196

(portable floor boards for drawing full size ships' lines), plus punching and shearing machines, though both yards were served by a common stockyard. This duplication was wasteful in both space and cost. Prefabrication also led to reduced construction time, leading to same amount of work undertaken on half the number of berths.

In 1951, Clement (Clem) Stephenson (1913-2001), a naval architect who had recently joined Doxford, was asked to take charge of re-ordering the shipyard, keeping production ongoing whilst this was underway. On 17 April 1952, he read a paper to the Institute of Welding on the reorganisation that had recently taken place at Pallion in relation to pre-fabricated welded construction.[7] Following E.G. Fletcher's retirement in 1953, Clem Stephenson became the Shipyard Manager, and was appointed a Director the same year. Once on the Board, his position was confirmed as Managing Director of the shipyard.

The reconstruction took place by firstly demolishing the three berths in the West Yard, along with their associated buildings. Three large covered welding sheds for the prefabrication process were then built on the site of the old West Yard, in alignment with the engine shops. These are shown on the plans as similar in size. However, the photograph on page 196 shows two main sheds, with a third, somewhat smaller, set back, to the right. The following plans show the layout of the shipbuilding yard before and after reconstruction. The third plan is of the welding sheds. The Engineering Works area is not included.

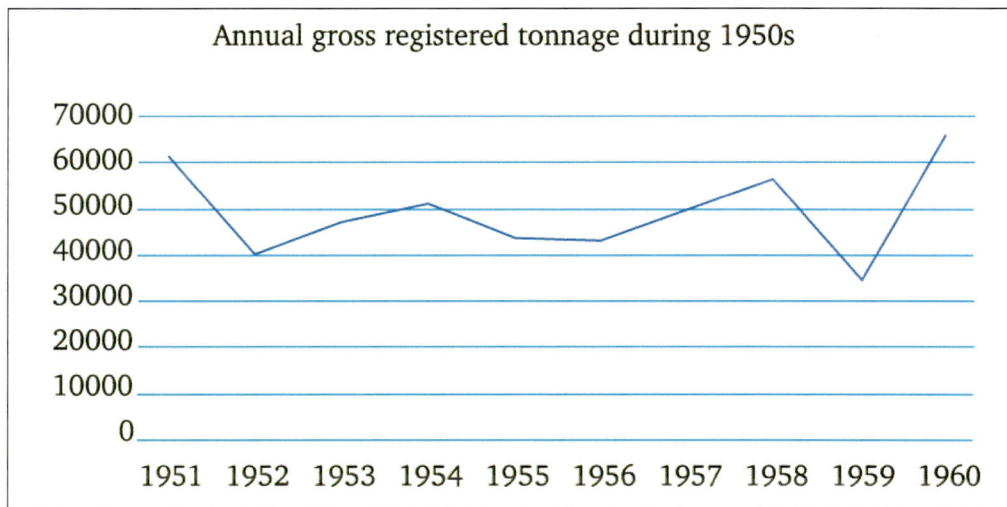

By 1953, the modernisation of the yard had cost £1m and work continued until about 1957. From figures presented to the Board in 1956, the work was achieved within budget.[8] In 1959, the Journal of Commerce reported output did not falter during the reorganisation of the yard, though the Doxford yard list belies this. A dip can be seen from the chart, but it seems that this was due to a shortage of steel in 1952, according to the report given by Dr. Andreae to the 60th Annual General Meeting held on 5 November that year.

166. Plan of the shipyard prior to installation of welding sheds.

167. Plan of shipyard showing position of the new welding sheds.

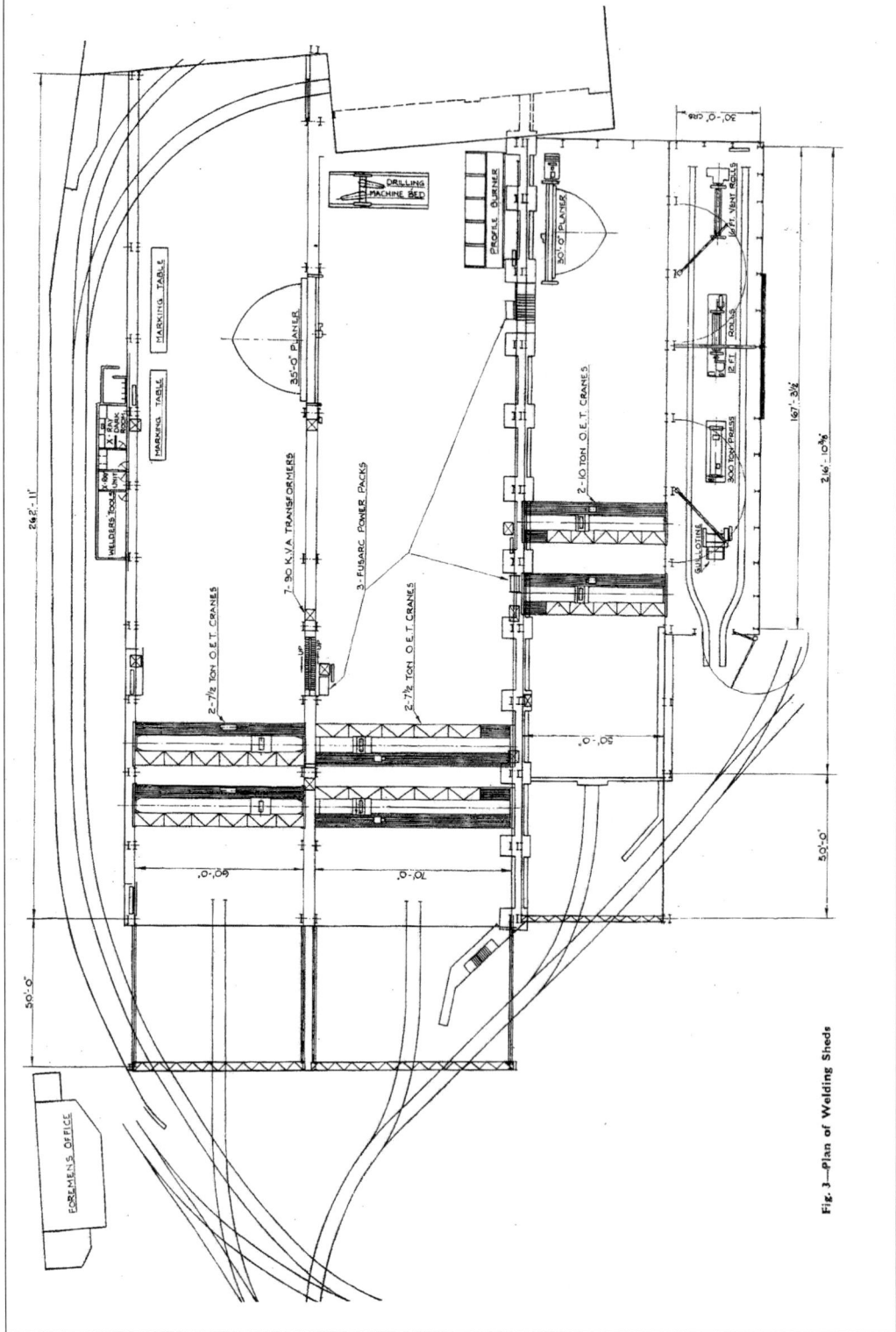

Fig. 3—Plan of Welding Sheds

168. Plan of the welding sheds. Clem Stephenson paper.

As foreseen, there was a severe shortage of steel available for commercial ship production, due to the Government's export and re-armament needs. This prevented the full use of the new facilities. Seven ships were delivered in 1951, with a total of 61,378 grt (average 8,768 grt). This number of ships was not matched until 1958, and that year the gross registered tonnage was only 56,552, as two were small ships under 7,000 grt. In the year ending 30 June 1952, the shipyard completed and delivered only three oil tankers and two general cargo vessels, all Doxford engined. Engine production was buoyant as a further four were supplied to other shipbuilders. It was not until the 1960s that ships regularly topped 10,000 grt.

However, the profitability of the yard increased because the labour force in the shipyard fell over the decade by 15%.[9] The Journal of Commerce article stressed that this was achieved by an agreement with the steel workers to replace the 'squad' method of working (who completed a whole section using a discreet number of workers) with a flow system, whereby each operation was performed by one or two men in turn. Electric travelling cranes shifted the heavy material into position, and welding was done by a 'down hand' system, with plenty of welding points available. The associated workshops were also modernised, and the fitting out quay was rebuilt. This now provided marshal-

169. Lifting a double bottom unit in No. 2 Welding Shed.
From Clement Stephenson's paper.

ling areas for materials to be brought on board by a fifteen ton level-luffing crane. This is a crane mechanism where the hook remains at the same level whilst luffing; moving the jib up and down, so as to move the hook inwards and outwards relative to the base. New joiners' and other workshops replaced the duplication that had previously existed, with the emphasis on an efficient layout. The output from the re-ordered yard would have been higher still, but was constrained by the downturn in orders at the end of the 1950s. The engine works were also substantially extended during the decade, at a further cost of half a million pounds.

201

Following the Board Meeting held on 1 February 1956, chaired by Andreae, Arthur Storey, who had become General Manager of the Engine Works on Jackson's retirement, submitted a six year development plan for the Engine Works, which was approved. J.R. Gebbie took over as Chairman the following year, and asked for changes to be made to this. The Board minutes of 18 September 1957 discussed the revised programme of capital expenditure,[10] but because of resistance by Gebbie to allow engine building to encroach on 'his' shipbuilding land, Storey was told to purchase and demolish some terraced housing to the west of the yard. This, of course, caused great distress to families who had lived there throughout their lives. However, the extension allowed the Engineering Works to increase production substantially. Employment in this division rose by 500, due to Storey's energy and drive. On the other hand, the shipyard began to falter in obtaining orders, a trend that accelerated at the start of the 1960s.

170. *The machine tool room of the engine department, known as Oily Bay, late 1950s, showing how men worked alongside each other as they produced the variety of special parts needed to build an engine. The foreman in the white coat is George Scott. Courtesy of of the Doxford Engine Friends Association.*

Daily life in the yard

The working day during the 1950s was from 7.30 am to 5.30 pm, five days a week, with an hour for lunch, plus three hours on a Saturday morning, though even apprentices had to work a thirteen hour night shift on occasion. Bringing their 'bait boxes' with them for a mid-morning snack, men, women and boys streamed through the gates at Pallion, clocking on at the time office. Dinner was served in a subsidised canteen, but this was in the shipyard, and at some distance from the engineering works.

There was huge camaraderie amongst the workforce. Most lived close to the yard and had grown up knowing all their neighbours. Many had followed a relative into the yard. A Doxford pension was a perk awarded to staff; workers only received one for exceptionally long service, rather than as a right. As a result, many worked into their sixties or seventies, to delay the poverty of retirement on the low state provision. This meant that three generations were often working side by side. Relationships with the management were not close, but were pragmatic, and there were surprisingly few strikes. Those that did occur were of short duration. Unions were respected by the management, and becoming a shop steward was a source of pride. The early to mid-fifties were a time of full order books, so that the tensions that arose in the sixties throughout the industry were less obvious.

In 1947 the school leaving age was raised to fifteen, so boys now joined as apprentices shortly after their fifteenth birthday. Recruitment was local, and most were brought into the Company by a family member. Training still lasted for five years, whether learning a trade on one of the machines or by using a pen/pencil in the drawing, financial or managerial offices. To a new apprentice the machines seemed huge, the noise overwhelming, the foremen formidable, and the managers remote and awe inspiring. There was no systematic training schedule. A new drawing office apprentice started by making tea, delivering post and material around the site and bringing lunch to managers who refused to eat in the canteen. An engineering apprentice was introduced to Mr. Jack Taylor, the foreman storekeeper, who had held the post for decades. In many cases he was taking on apprentices whose fathers had also been in his care. Taylor wasted very little time in allocating the new boy a job whereby he must climb about the store like a steeplejack to obtain small items from unlabelled metal pockets.

171. Firbank (C817) launched on 22 October 1956. Journal of Commerce, 25 September 1959. Courtesy of Ian Buxton.

They also watched and learned, began to handle tools and implements and gradually gained knowledge of the different processes. Whilst this was the time-honoured way of doing things, it caused British industry to fall behind its overseas rivals, whose technical training of young people was far superior. At any downturn, apprentices were not taken on, leaving gaps in skills at a later date.

However, men also had to learn to work under a new corporate structure, as Doxford met the challenges of the post war period. The Firbank, pictured here, was one of the last to be launched under the 'old' regime, but she benefited from the reorganisation of the yard with prefabricated, welded construction. Throughout the life of the Company, a launch was a cause for celebration and satisfaction, and the Firbank, one of many built for the Bank Line, Glasgow (A. Weir & Co.), had a thirty two year career as a general cargo ship. She was renamed Aegis Beauty in 1973 and Maldive Seafarer in 1978. She was finally broken up at Howrah, Calcutta.[11]

The restructure of William Doxford & Sons Ltd

In response to commercial demands, in 1956 Dr. Andreae and his Board restructured Doxford into three units, a holding Company under its original name, and two supposedly equal subsidiary companies: William Doxford & Sons (Shipbuilders) Ltd., and William Doxford & Sons (Engineers) Ltd. The allotment from the parent Company to each subsidiary was 499,998 ordinary shares of £1. The Board of the parent Company was Dr. Andreae, (Chairman) Dr. Gebbie (Deputy Chairman), W.H. Purdie, Managing Director, Engineering, J.G. Hugall, Financial Director and C. Stephenson, Managing Director, Shipyard. The Secretary (since 1953) was J.W. Holey. John Walton Holey (1918-1998), was the grandson of John Holey, Secretary to the Company at the turn of the century. He was a chartered accountant, who joined Doxford from their local auditors, Messrs. Rawlings & Wilkinson. When Andreae stepped down as Chairman in 1957, Roy Patterson Key came on to the Board. R.P. Key was an advisor on production efficiency to the Board of Trade from 1949, and was formerly with ICI. He was a director of a number of engineering companies, and an associate of Cuthbert Wrangham, a later Chairman of Doxford.[12] Each subsidiary had its own Board, but there were cross directorships. The Chairman and deputy chairmen of the holding Company held the same role on the subsidiary Boards, giving them the ultimate decision making power. The directors of the subsidiaries were executives, and some were also on the main Board. All appointments as a director of the subsidiaries were from the executive. Holey also assumed the role of Secretary to both these.

Stephenson and William Jobling, the Technical Manager, were appointed to the Board of the shipbuilding subsidiary, which met for the first time on 30 May and was incorporated on 8 June 1956. On 15 June, the New Westminster City, C814, became the first ship to be delivered under the new arrangement, to Sir William Reardon Smith & Sons Ltd.

The holding Company set out terms on the relations between the two subsidiaries, in the form of a directive. The first paragraph reads:

> "That as a matter of settled policy, the Engineering Subsidiary Company shall at all times and in all respects give preference in its construction programme to the machinery requirements of the Shipbuilding Subsidiary Company."[13]

The Three Boards 1956-1961

Holding Company	Shipbuilding	Engineers
E.P. Andreae, Chairman, retired 1957	E.P. Andreae, Chairman, retired 1957	E.P. Andreae, Chairman, retired 1957
J.R. Gebbie, M.D. & Dep Chairman 1956, Chairman 1957-1961, resigned as M.D. Dec. 1958.	.J.R. Gebbie, Chairman 1957-1961	J.R. Gebbie, Chairman 1957-1961
J.G. Hugall, Financial Director: 1956, M.D: 1958 Dep Chair 1957-1961	J.G. Hugall, Dep. Chairman 1957-1961	J.G.Hugall, Dep. Chairman 1957-1961
R.P. Key (Nov 1957-1961) (replacing E.P. Andreae)	C. Stephenson, Shipbuilding, 1956-1961. Chairman from 1958.	W.H. Purdie, (1956-1958), Consultant
W.H. Purdie, retired 1958	W. Jobling, Technical Manager, 1956-1962	A. Storey, M.D. Engineering, 1956-1958
C. Stephenson, 1958-1961	R.P. Key, Nov 1957-1961	R. Atkinson, M.D. Engineering 1958-1961
G.C.L. Thompson, 1956-1961		
R. Atkinson 1958-1961R.	Atkinson, 1959-1961 (as M.D. Engineers)	C. Stephenson, 1959-1961 (as M.D. Shipbuilders)

At the time, this seemed sensible, but its unintended consequence was to deny the engineering subsidiary the funds, facilities and manpower to develop its research capabilities for the much larger engines demanded by the market at the end of the decade. The shipbuilding subsidiary was allowed to remain within its 'comfort zone', working with British shipowners who still demanded ships within certain defined ranges, served by engines up to six cylinders. The Chairman and Deputy Chairman saw no reason why larger engines should be designed and built. There was also pressure from the strictly confined space within the Pallion site; any potential encroachment by the engineering works into the shipbuilding area was strongly resisted.

To be fair, Gebbie came in at the peak of Doxford's profitability. At the end of 1957, a bonus of 25% of salary was awarded to the officials of the Company. However, even at the beginning of 1958, shipbuilding orders began to falter and shipowners became anxious to delay or cancel existing contracts. The time from the receipt of an order to delivery of a vessel could be three years or longer, depending on the contract and the number of ships already in the order book. An empty berth resulting from a completion or cancellation might not materialise for some time. For instance, Sir William Reardon Smith had provisionally ordered eleven ships for delivery between 1963 and 1968, but in 1958 asked for two to be treated simply as options for berth allocation. As 1958 progressed the situation deteriorated further. Meeting after meeting of the Board recorded that "enquiries were almost negligible and mainly from Brokers." There was a reluctance to deal through brokers, because of the terms they demanded. The comfortable world of time and line was gone, purchasers demanded fixed prices and flexible payment terms. Whilst understandable, Doxford Shipbuilders failed to forge new relationships with these broking firms that could benefit them when conditions improved. Gebbie also declined to deal with booming Japanese shipbuilding and engineering companies, refusing them a licence to build Doxford engines or to develop a working partnership with them. He is reported to have said: "If they want Doxford engines, we will build them." There was such widespread prejudice against the Japanese in the post war period that a group of businessmen had to be protected from angry workers when they visited the Pallion Yard.[14] Japanese companies turned to Sulzer and to Burmeister & Wain, whose diesel engines were better suited for the size of tankers and cargo ships now being built in their yards. To understand Gebbie's attitude, one has to appreciate this background, and also his age. He had given great leadership on the Wear during WWII, but in the end let down the Company he had served with such diligence.

John Ramsay Gebbie D.Sc., C.B.E. (1889-1968)

By the time J.R. Gebbie took the chair at Doxford, he had been with the Company for twenty seven years, and was aged 68. Gebbie was born at Greenock and, at seventeen, was apprenticed at Scotts. He later worked for the Northumberland Shipbuilding Company until its demise. Charles Doxford then recruited him as the Pallion Shipyard Manager. Gebbie's energy and drive, plus his design of the Doxford Economy Cargo ship had been a major factor in the Company's wartime and post war success. Gebbie was appointed to the Board in 1936, became Managing Director in 1941, and Deputy Chairman in 1942. He was awarded the O.B.E. in 1943 for his wartime work on the River Wear. With a 'hands off' Chairman such as Andreae, Gebbie had become the driving force at Doxford. He was also involved in all aspects of shipbuilding on the Wear throughout the war, and was one of the main protagonists of the Labour Supply Committee, and in re-opening one of the shipyards on the Wear that had closed in the 1930s. Gebbie was President of the NECIES in 1942, President of the Shipbuilding Employers' Federation in 1944, and Chairman of Wear Shipbuilders' Association in 1946.[15] In 1951 he received the C.B.E. in the New Year's Honours List whilst President of the Shipbuilding Conference. Gebbie had an excellent grasp of shipbuilding needs, and he oversaw the re-building of the Doxford Yard in the immediate post war period. He was innovative on the technical side of shipbuilding, and served on the General and Technical Committees of Lloyd's Register of Shipping. From 1952-54 he chaired the Council of the British Shipbuilding Research Association. He was a ship designer through and through, but it is still strange that he had quite so little interest in the profitable engines that took them around the world.

However, he was by now an old man, and very much set in his ways. An example of his viewpoint is the statement he made on engineering to the 66th Annual Meeting held on 30 October 1958, at the end of his first year as Chairman. After mentioning the introduction of the diaphragm and of exhaust turbo charging for the larger engines, and presaging the 'P' engine (though this was still three years from coming into service), he stated:

> "The opinion has been expressed recently in the Press that British oil engines have fallen behind those of their foreign competitors, especially in regard to the design and construction of engines of very high powers up to, in fact, over 20, 000 bhp on a single screw, and as your Company is the only British licensor of large marine oil engines, I feel I should say something here on this matter. Until now our largest Doxford engine in service has developed up to 9,000 bhp, e.g. our latest six cylinder supercharged engine of which several are in service and of which over fifty are building or on order. This type of engine can be built in powers up to about 12,000 bhp, whilst our new engine is intended to provide powers up to around 14,000 bhp. Beyond these powers we do not at present intend to go because your Board and their technical advisers are not yet convinced that the oil engine is necessarily the most suitable prime mover for the propulsion of ships requiring these very large powers on a single screw. It is not, therefore, complacency or lack of enterprise which has prevented your Company from developing these very large oil engines, but, quite simply, that we are not yet satisfied of its acceptance, nor that the introduction of such engines would be a profitable venture for your Company, at least at the present time." [16]

Sadly, this attitude denied the development by Doxford of the larger engines now required by the industry and lost him a valuable employee, namely Arthur Storey. During the first year of his Chairmanship, Dr. Gebbie retained his position as Managing Director of the holding Company, but he then ceded this role to the Financial Director, J.G. Hugall. Although his obituary in the Transactions of the Institution of Naval Architects states that "his guidance during the initial stages of the formation of the group was invaluable because of his intimate knowledge of all aspects of the industry," this does not take into account his seeming indifference to the engines that drove Doxford-built ships.

The Engineering Department

The chief motivation of the Doxford engineering department was to keep its pre-eminent position in the market. The Company had fourteen British licensees building its engines and eleven based abroad. In 1947 W. H. Purdie was nearing retirement, and recognised the need to bring a new pool of talent into his team. He recruited Percy Jackson (1897-1984) as Chief Development Engineer, to run a new Research and Development Department, based at the newly acquired Palmers Hill site. This became known as the Palmers Hill Research and Development Test Station. Jackson was born in Halifax, Yorkshire, and had worked principally on stationary engines. He was apprenticed in 1915 with the Campbell Gas & Oil Engine Company, in his home town, and studied at the local technical college. His studies were interrupted by WWI, in which he served in the Royal Naval Air Service, but he eventually obtained a B.Sc. (Eng.) from London University, followed by a master's degree.[17] During the 1930s, he was with Blackstone at Stamford but, after their takeover by R.A. Lister in 1937, moved to Mirrlees, Bickerton & Day at Stockport, Cheshire, as their chief engineer. There he worked through WWII on stationary diesel engines for defence purposes, such as in ordnance factories. In 1945, the Company became part of Associated British Oil Engine Group, and Jackson was appointed their Technical Director.

172. Percy Jackson, Chief Development Engineer, later Technical Director, Doxford. Designer of the 'P' and 'J' engines. Courtesy of Alan Jackson.

Mirrlees, Bickerton & Day gave their engines alphabetic names. Jackson followed this practice with the two engines that he designed for Doxford, the 'P' engine (Percy) and the 'J' engine (Jackson).

173. The great length of the Engine Works is seen here. Photograph taken 1957/8 by W.E. Wiseman, who worked at both Pallion and Palmers Hill. Courtesy of the Doxford Engine Friends Association.

On joining Doxford, initially on a five year contract, he was the first 'outsider' to be recruited to the engineering division for many years and had to prove his worth. Another outsider in his team was Ernest R. Groschel, an instrument mechanic. He was appointed at the same time as Jackson, seconded from the British Shipbuilding Research Association on a three year contract. When this ended in 1961, Groschel left Doxford, but returned to the Palmers Hill site for a further secondment in the mid-1950s to continue the technical work on the 'P' engine. John George (Jack) Gunn (1907-1966), a long term Doxford employee and Chief Draughtsman was promoted to Chief Engineer of Research & Development at Palmers Hill, where he was Jackson's second in command. Gunn was born in St. Luke's Terrace, Pallion, and lived all his life close to the Doxford yard. When the North East Coast section of the Institute of Marine Engineers was formed in early 1953, Gunn served on its first committee.[18]

The development team at Palmers Hill was only about five men, dwarfed by their continental rivals Sulzer, Burmeister & Wain and M.A.N. Even after Gunn's death at 59, much regretted due to his strengths as a practical engineer, the team never expanded. It was eventually subsumed into the Design Department at Pallion. George G. Jackson (no relation to Percy) was later the Chief Designer.

Development of the Doxford engine during the 1950s

With Purdie's encouragement, Percy Jackson first set about addressing deficiencies in the common rail system of fuel injection, aiming to make Doxford engines lighter and more efficient. From very early days, Doxford had used this system of airless injection, common rail being a method of opening the priming line to make it common to all cylinders. This had been mostly satisfactory and was notably efficient. However, it was costly, due to the number of components, and their physical size. Jackson first tried a jerk pump method, but this involved a separate pump for each cylinder, so was quickly rejected. His team then experimented with a number of other methods, including compression, pneumatic and hydraulic operation and an accumulator pump. The work took a number of years, with incremental improvements to existing engines. W. H. Purdie retired in 1953, but remained as a consultant until he finally left the Board in 1958. Arthur Storey was now the head of the engineering department.

From 1950, all Doxford engine production changed from running on light petroleum distillates to thicker high viscosity fuels (HVF), known as boiler fuel. The use of distillates, hydrocarbon solvents such as mineral spirits, kerosene, white spirits and naphtha, had avoided residue entering the crankcase from the lower pistons, though Doxford engines had been capable of running on HVF from the outset, and some already used this fuel. This was to ships' advantage in early days, as ports away from home had ample supplies of boiler fuel, but little of the distillates. However, with HVF, contaminants were a problem, and the lubricating oil had to be purified on a regular basis to prevent corrosion of the running gear components of the engine.[1]

In 1950 Doxford Engines built a 6-cylinder 750 mm bore x 2,500 mm combined stroke engine, developing 8,850 bhp at 110 rpm. This was Doxford's largest non-turbocharged normally aspirated engine and one of the first to use high viscosity fuel. It was installed in the converted tanker, MT Paludina, built by Swan Hunter for Shell in 1949 (Yard No. 1771). She was originally powered by a 3-cylinder Doxford type engine, built under licence at Wallsend.

174. MT Paludina, 1949, first built with a 3-cylinder Doxford engine, but replaced by a 6-cylinder engine designed by Jackson. Collection: Richard Cox

A particular challenge was that Doxford ships began to suffer from broken crankshafts, due to torsional vibration problems. As can be seen from this photograph, crankshafts were extremely large and heavy, and returning them to Pallion for investigation was a major undertaking. The Sunderland Daily Echo reported on 29 August 1951 that a 44-ton crankshaft from the Moor Line's Dartmoor (C 771), a general cargo ship only 18 months old, had to be transported to Pallion from the John Readhead yard at South Shields up river to Newcastle and then via twenty one miles of mainroad, as the

175. Working on a crankshaft in the Doxford Engine works.
Photograph: W. E. Wiseman. Courtesy of the Doxford Engine Friends Association.

direct route via minor roads could not accommodate its bulk. The breakages were not necessarily to do with engine size, though the majority were 75LB6 engines, and most were installed in tankers. These engines had recently been uprated to run faster, and a few crankshafts failed, though most gave no trouble throughout the working life of a ship. It was difficult to find a solution, especially as some breakages were identified as poor maintenance and incorrect operation. They were catastrophic when a ship was at sea, especially when on the other side of the world. Bringing a crankshaft back to the test bed from abroad was a major and expensive operation. The problem persisted throughout the 1950s. Eventually, Jackson's team identified that introducing flexible coupling to replace the connecting rod for the centre scavenge pump and the fillet radii in the shaft, (i.e. the rounded corner that the bearing has to fit over, and which had been recessed into the web to shorten the engine) solved the problem. Doxford engines lost some of their reputation through broken crankshafts, though the problem was affecting marine engineering companies on the Continent as well. The Company's openness appears to have done them no favours.

Introduction of the Diaphragm

A further change was that between 1950 and 1955 all Doxford engines were designated LB (long balanced), ranging from three to six cylinders. The majority were 4-cylinder, developing 3,300 bhp. Universal use of HVF forced a redesign of the engine. Testing began in 1954 on a barrier, in the form of a diaphragm, to prevent corrosion of the crankshaft. The circular diaphragm plate and gland completely isolated each cylinder from the crankcase, whilst allowing access to the piston rod gland. It also improved the overall cleanliness of the crank chamber, and ships' engineers reported that it even smelt better![20] One of its advantages is that it could be fitted retrospectively to existing Doxford engines.[21] They also began work on an experimental 6-cylinder diaphragm engine, but this took three years. The

67LBD6 was installed in the Northbank (C819), for the Bank Line in mid-1957. This developed 6,180 bhp and with a service speed of 15 knots, matching similar ships of the time.

The Leeds City (C807) was the last Doxford ship with a 4-cylinder 70LB4 engine. She was 6,162 grt, 436 feet in length, built for the Reardon Smith Line, Bideford, and delivered in June 1955. Her engine ran at 112 rpm, developing 4,800 bhp, and she had a service speed of $13^1/_2$ knots. The Tyria (C808) was a similar sized general cargo ship, delivered to the Anchor Line, Glasgow only a month later. However, she had a 4-cylinder 60LBD4 (long balanced diaphragm), 108 rpm, generating 3,300

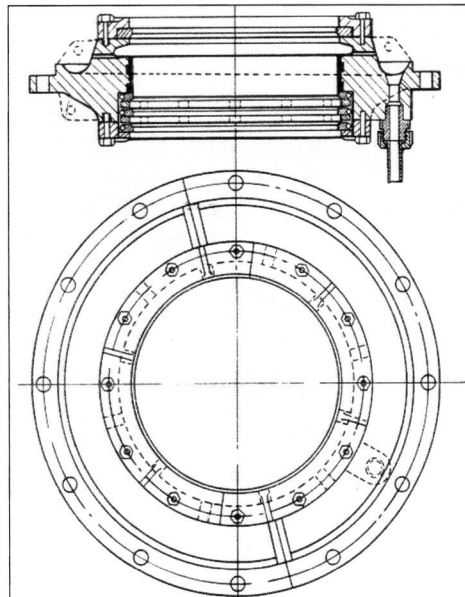

176. The Diaphragm Gland. Courtesy of Jack Jordan.

bhp, with a service speed of $12^1/_4$ knots. The diaphragm, therefore, was not originally designed for a faster service speed, but to prevent contamination. However, as the decade moved forward, the 70LBD4 engine, running at 112 rpm, developed 4,800 bhp, and the service speed increased to between $13^1/_2$ and $14^1/_4$ knots.

Turbo-charging the engine

In the early 1950s, Jackson was also working on exhaust gas turbo-chargers, as they operated at a higher pressure than could be achieved with mechanical scavenge pumps. John Jordan, who worked under him, told me that when turbo-charging was first used, both engineers and shipowners were concerned about their reliability, so installed scavenge pumps beside them, operating in series. Doxford built a turbo-charged test engine to this design at the Palmers Hill site in 1953/4. This was a 600 mm bore, 3-cylinder 2,000 mm stroke engine, called 60SB3. Tests were lengthy, but proved that the new engine generated the same power as an unsuper-charged 4-cylinder engine. At the Doxford AGM held in November 1954, Dr. Andreae heavily promoted this new engine, and stressed its importance in keeping the Doxford licensees on board.

In 1955 the first turbo charged engine went into service. This was engine no. 302 (60SBDS3 - 600 mm short balanced diaphragm supercharged 3-cylinder) and was fitted into an existing ship, the British Escort, built at Swan Hunter in 1943 as Empire McCabe, yard no. 1726, but renamed in 1946 by her new owners, the British Tanker Co. Ltd. She was originally fitted with a standard Doxford 'Economical' engine 60LB4. On test, the new engine achieved 4,000 bhp at 130 rpm, but in service this reduced to 3,600 bhp at 115 rpm. The engine was, however, considerably more fuel efficient, and increased the ship's average speed by half a knot.

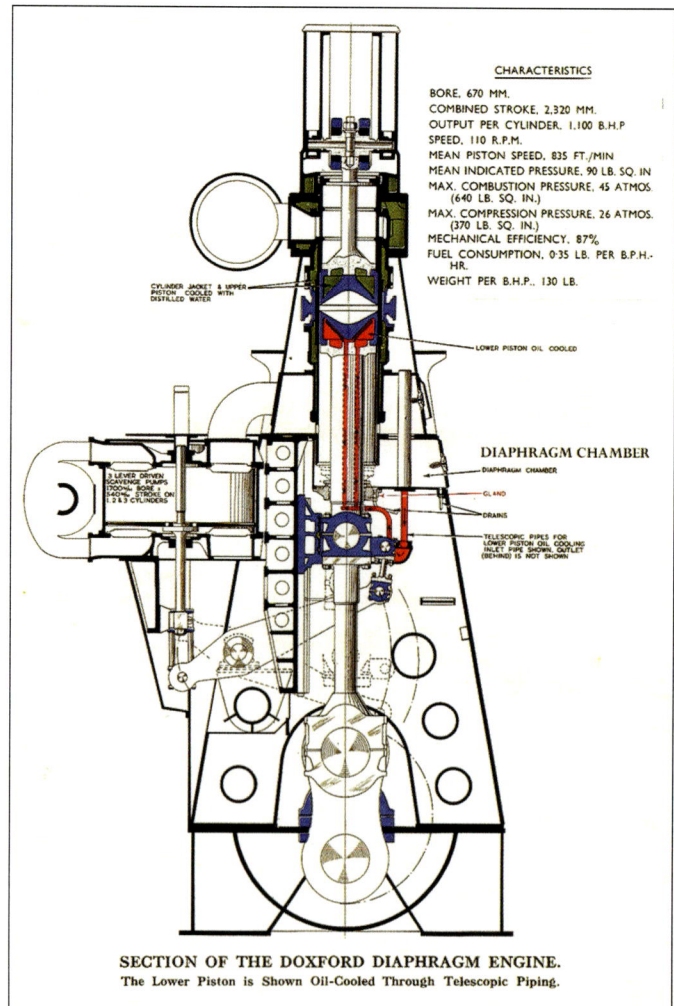

CHARACTERISTICS

BORE, 670 MM.
COMBINED STROKE, 2,320 MM.
OUTPUT PER CYLINDER, 1,100 B.H.P
SPEED, 110 R.P.M.
MEAN PISTON SPEED, 835 FT./MIN
MEAN INDICATED PRESSURE, 90 LB. SQ. IN
MAX. COMBUSTION PRESSURE, 45 ATMOS. (640 LB. SQ. IN.)
MAX. COMPRESSION PRESSURE, 26 ATMOS. (370 LB. SQ. IN.)
MECHANICAL EFFICIENCY, 87%
FUEL CONSUMPTION, 0·35 LB. PER B.P.H.- HR.
WEIGHT PER B.H.P., 130 LB.

SECTION OF THE DOXFORD DIAPHRAGM ENGINE.
The Lower Piston is Shown Oil-Cooled Through Telescopic Piping.

177. Drawing demonstrating the diaphragm. Courtesy of Jack Jordan.

It was later appreciated that scavenge pumps were no longer needed, and engines were then fitted with turbo-chargers only. The air flow increased, developing power up to 50% greater than obtainable from the same bore and stroke, with a lower fuel consumption. The first fully turbo-charged engine, 65LBD6S was completed in

178. 6-Cylinder 67LBDS6 engine under test in the Engine Works for MV Stuart Prince (C840) 1960.
Photograph by W.E Wiseman. Courtesy of the Doxford Engine Friends Association.

February 1957 by the Doxford licensee Scotts of Greenock (their engine no. 762) and installed in the Egori (their yard no. 673), which they built for the Elder Dempster Line. This developed 9,000 bhp at 16 knots. The ship had a twenty two year service under various owners, until broken up in 1979.[22]

Later in the decade, Jackson's team at Doxford introduced further modifications to stiffen the crankshaft. They shortened the upper piston stroke, reducing the side rod crank throw and allowing an overlap between the side crankpins and main journal. The overlap increased the stiffness. The stiffer crankshaft meant that spherical bearings, used in all Doxford opposed-piston engines from the outset, could be replaced by plain ones. Spherical bearings were complicated to insert, as they had to be added one by one, so this was a saving in time. His team also dispensed with upper piston guides and introduced a three piece cylinder liner. This facilitated maintenance and ensured supplies from a wider range of foundries. There were still problems, though, in maintaining a temperature that did not produce the damaging thermal stresses that limited the size of an engine. For the later, more powerful 'J' engine, cylinder liners were redesigned as a single piece liner.

Arthur Storey left Doxford in 1958, his post being taken by Robert Atkinson. In February 1960, Percy Jackson and Robert Atkinson presented a paper to the Institute of Marine Engineers, detailing the problems over the crankshafts and the remedial measures undertaken, but the long delay to achieve a satisfactory outcome had dampened the enthusiasm of ship purchasers and engine licensees. Their honesty and openness are also reputed to have disadvantaged Doxford. Continental rivals, Sulzer, M.A.N., Burmeister & Wain and Götaverken of Sweden were the beneficiaries. Therefore, by the end of the 1950s, Doxford had lost many of its licensees, as British engineering firms took licences from these continental firms. Doxford themselves were asked to install Sulzer engines in some of their ships.

By 1965, the twenty five licensees on board in 1950 had reduced to only seven, six British and one abroad:

* Alexander Stephens Engineering, Linthouse, Glasgow (renamed)
* Barclay Curle & Co. Ltd., Whitechurch, Glasgow
* George Clark & NEM Ltd. (NEM had been an earlier licensee), Wallsend
* Hawthorn Leslie (Engineers) Ltd., St. Peters Works, Newcastle-upon Tyne
* Scotts Engineering of Greenock (part of the original Company)
* The Commonwealth of Australia
* Vickers Ltd. Barrow (also renamed).

They had gained only one new licensee. This was the Department of Supply, Victoria, Australia. Amongst those lost was their first licensee, the Sun Shipbuilding & Dry Dock Co. Chester, Pennsylvania. All the Scandinavian licensees had discontinued their agreements, as had two in the Netherlands, one each in France and Italy and the Taikoo Dockyard & Engineering Co. of Hong Kong, which had built Doxford engines for five years.

Two of the last ships to be fitted with a 6-cylinder 67LBD6 were built for the Charente Steamship Co. Ltd., managed by T. & J. Harrison Ltd., Liverpool in 1961. These were Custodian (C844 - pictured opposite) and Tactician (C845). They were specially designed with a Stulcken heavy lift derrick amidships, four holds forward

179. & 180. The Custodian, C844, 1961. Courtesy of The Motorship, March 1961.

of the engine room and one aft, which held four refrigerated compartments. The acceptance trials were reported in great detail in the Motorship of March 1961.[23]

The 'P' Engine

During the second half of the 1950s, Jackson worked on a redesigned turbo-charged engine with the designation 'P'. The project did not come to fruition until 1960, but during this experimental period he was awarded prizes for his development work from the Institution of Mechanical Engineers, of whom he was a life member, and from the Institute of Marine Engineers.

The first prototype single cylinder engine was built at the Doxford Palmers Hill Research site in 1956. It was known as the 67PT1, the P standing for Percy and the T for turbo.[24] Development of this engine continued in parallel to improvements in the standard Doxford range. Engine contracts 815-841 were built up to August 1960. In May that year, the Board took the

181. Percy Jackson's fore-runner to the 'P' engine, on test at Palmers Hill. This was the 67PT1. Courtesy of Jack Jordan.

215

decision that an engine type 85PT6 should be designed and built, at an approximate cost of £400,000, and that the engineering subsidiary should also proceed with designs within the range 56PT3, 4, 5 & 6, but without building a prototype.[25] It took another four years, and 5,000 hours testing, first in the Pallion yard and then at Palmers Hill, before the first 'P' engine, engine no. 330, went into service on 1 February 1961. During the testing, one of the last innovations was to dispense with the bottle guides for the upper pistons, another feature of the opposed piston Doxford engine that had survived for over forty years. Bottle guides had been used to mitigate the slight motion of the upper pistons and protect them from wear, particularly in stormy weather. However, during testing it was found that the guides played no part in alleviating this movement, so they were removed. Their removal also meant that the upper piston stroke could be reduced.

The engine that first went into service was designated 67PT6. This was a six-cylinder 670mm bore engine, designed to develop 10,000 bhp. The engine speed was 112 rpm, giving a service speed of 16 knots when fully loaded. It was both shorter and lighter than its predecessors for the same generation of power, and was installed into the tanker, MT Montana, 13,628 grt, built by Sir James Laing & Sons Ltd., as their yard number 822. The Montana was owned by A/S Tanktransport (Thorvald Berg), Tonsberg, Norway. Percy Jackson spent the first eighteen weeks of the maiden

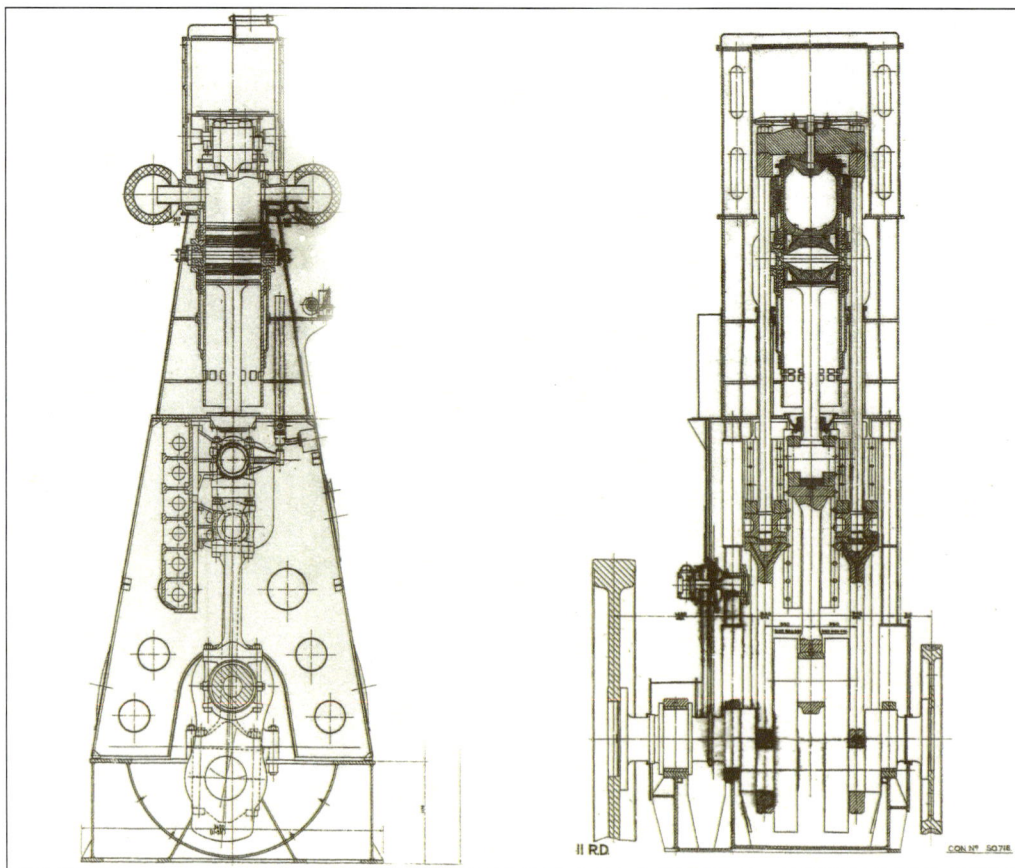

182. Sectional Drawing R 511 of the 1956 test engine. Courtesy of Jack Jordan.

216

voyage on Board, and gave an extensive report to The Motor Ship for their June 1961 edition. Almost immediately after leaving port, the ship ran into five days of stormy weather in the Channel, giving Jackson the opportunity to observe that there was no obvious difference in the movement of the upper pistons, whether the ship was rolling or not, thereby justifying the decision to dispense with bottle guides. Examination of the crankcase and entablature (the housing which holds the cylinder liner, the scavenge air space and cooling water spaces) at Rio de Janeiro showed that the combustion was clean, as there was no sludge or carbon deposits.[26]

183. The Crankshaft of the 'P' engine, illustrated in the Publicity Brochure of the new Doxford & Sunderland Shipbuilding and Engineering Group, 1961.

At the end of her eleven month maiden voyage around South America, the prototype engine was reported to be 'completely reliable', and the new Managing Director of Doxford Engineering, T.W.D. Abell, announced to the press that thirty three further orders had been received, totalling £5,000,000 and that larger engines up to nine

184. Doxford engine no. 330, 67PT6, the prototype 'P' engine of the Montana, on test at Pallion. It was a much shorter engine than a 67LBD6. Courtesy of the Doxford Engine Friends Association.

cylinders were envisaged.[27] However, over the life of the engine there was some criticism over its reliability.

Forty five 'P' type engines were built, twenty for Doxford built ships, sixteen for other British shipbuilders, and nine by licensees. Two thirds were four-cylinder and one third were six. None exceeded six-cylinders, as these were judged by Jackson and his team to be the optimum for this engine. In fact, even before the first 'P' engine went into service, Percy Jackson and his team were turning to the development of the larger 'J' engine, and this went into service only three years later, as described in Chapter Fifteen.

The second 'P' engine was described very fully in The Motor Ship, only a month later.[28] The Prince Line ordered two tankers from Doxford, which were both under construction in 1960, and both of 12,958 grt. The first of these, Stuart Prince (C840), was delivered to the Prince Line Ltd. (Furness Withy), London, in November 1960. She was fitted with the last of the LB or SB ranges. The second tanker, Tudor Prince (C842), was delivered in April 1961, with an identical engine to that in the Montana. The Motor Ship report included the following table showing the comparison between the balanced diaphragm engine installed in the first ship and the second 'P' engine installed in the second, both engines having six-cylinders.

Comparison of the Doxford engine characteristics

	Stuart Prince	Tudor Prince
Main Engine	Doxford 65LBDS6	Doxford 67PT6
Number of Cylinders	6	6
Diameter of cylinders	650 mm	670 mm
Combined Stroke	2,320 mm	2,100 mm
Service Output	8000 bhp	8000 bhp
rpm	115	115
mip (mean indicated pressure lbs per square inch)	110 psi	112 psi
Length of engine	53 ft. 4 in.	45 ft. 6 in.
Weight of Engine	420 tons	375 tons
Number of turbo-blowers	2	2
Speed in service	14$\frac{1}{2}$ knots	14$\frac{1}{2}$ knots

The table shows that the main advantage was the reduction in both length and weight of the new engine for the same output and speed.

Troubled times for the Engineering Subsidiary

On 30 June 1953 William Hamilton Purdie retired as the Director and General Manager of the Engine Department. He received an O.B.E. in the following New

185. The Montana. The first ship fitted with a 'P' engine.

Year's Honours for his services to marine engineering. He was succeeded as General Manager of the Engineering subsidiary by Arthur Storey (1906-c1994), but remained as a part time consultant and a Director of Doxford until 31 December 1958.

Arthur Storey was born at Hetton-le-Hole, Durham, and was the son of a housebuilder. He fought to achieve a career in engineering against great odds, but managed to gain an apprenticeship at NEM in 1920. He remained with them for thirty two years before coming to Doxford on 1 July 1953. He was appointed Managing Director and a member of the Board under Dr. Andreae's Chairmanship.

186. Arthur Storey, Managing Director, Doxford Engineers, 1953-1958.

On 25 March 1956 Storey presented a paper to the NECIES on the Doxford Engine, in which he described the progress made on boiler fuels and in supercharging the engine.[29] He had the prescience to see that the engineering facilities at Pallion were inadequate to significantly increase production and to accommodate the larger engines now being demanded by shipowners. He also wanted to develop his technical support, to challenge that provided at continental engineers. This required major

219

investment and, in 1956, he put a scheme to Andreae, who was supportive. The Board took the decision to set aside £347,000 for new facilities but, before work started, Andreae retired and Gebbie took the chair. Gebbie immediately vetoed the full expenditure, reducing it to £150,000. This ultimately led to Storey's resignation in early 1958. In the early 1990s, Arthur Storey gave an interview to Anthony Slaven and Philip Taylor. This was later edited for publication in the series Research in Maritime History as 'Crossing the Bar'. Storey stated:

> "If I had been allowed to develop the engine as I wanted to and to extend production of it, it could have remained the best-selling engine, But, Dr. J. Ramsay Gebbie put the block on it in 1957. He told me that I could forget about extending the Engine Works because Doxford built ships."

Sadly, only six ships a year were leaving the yard at that period, generating a maximum profit of £350,000, whilst the Doxford engine department could turn out eighteen engines, and was making over £1.6m per annum, from its own production and from that of its licensees. The money that the Board under Gebbie allocated was not sufficient to greatly increase output.

By the beginning of the following year, Storey's relationship with the Board had deteriorated beyond hope. On 11 March 1958, he resigned,[30] moving to Vickers Engineering at Barrow, where he was appointed a Director in 1959. He later returned to Sunderland as Managing Director of Austin & Pickersgill, where he oversaw production of the successful SD14 standard cargo ships.

A significant discussion took place at the Board Meeting held on 28 April 1958, just a month after Storey's resignation. Headed: 'Policy in regard to Licensees of William Doxford & Sons (Engineers) Ltd.', the minute reads [sic]:

> "The Chairman read to the Meeting letter in French received from Monsieur Audouard, Director of Société des Chantiers et Ateliers de Provence of Marseille, in which Mr. Audouard indicated certain new buildings in which his Company were interested required larger powered engines. The letter instanced that these were available from the following engine builders: - Sulzer, Burmeister & Wain, M.A.N., and Fiat. These companies were offering engines up to 24,000 bhp.

> It was pointed out that larger engines of these powers were not required by William Doxford & Sons (Shipbuilders) Ltd. and would, in fact, seldom be required by outside local shipbuilders.

> After discussion it was resolved to confirm the opinion referred to the Meeting by the Board of William Doxford & Sons (Engineers) Ltd. to the effect that the policy to be followed should be directed towards the construction of engines up to 15,000 bhp, the maximum bore in the

meantime not to exceed 750 mm, it being unanimously agreed that the opposed piston engine was not suitable for powers above about 15,000 BHP."

This attitude was one of the factors that led to the closure of the Doxford Engine Works in 1984.

Gebbie also had a poor relationship with Storey's replacement as Managing Director of the Engineering Subsidiary. Robert Atkinson was born at Tynemouth on 7 March 1916, the son of a civil engineer. He read engineering at university and then joined the Royal Naval Reserve. During WWII, as a lieutenant commander, he commanded naval corvettes and received three D.S.C.s during this service. He joined Doxford in 1957 and was appointed Managing Director of Doxford Engineers in late1958 on a three year contract, following the resignation of Arthur Storey. On 4 January 1961, towards the end of his contract with Doxford, the Times published Atkinson's response to the report by Department of Scientific and Industrial Research on research within the shipbuilding industry. His opinion, which is where he may have clashed with the Board of Doxford, was that "research is of value only to the extent that its results are incorporated into efficient ships and engines, efficiently produced." In the event, he decided not to renew his contract in March 1961, shortly

187. Robert Atkinson, Managing Director, Doxford Engineers, 1958-1961.

before the creation of Doxford & Sunderland Shipbuilders and Engineers Ltd. Although there is a suggestion that he was 'pushed', it seems from Board minutes that he had planned to leave some months beforehand. He wrote to Gebbie on 14 October 1960 to reiterate his request of 19 September to be released from his "contractual obligations with the Company to take up another appointment", and that this request was accepted. He gave his date of resignation as 28 February 1961 and continued: "I will take this opportunity to assure you of my personal loyalty to you and the Firm, as well as my willingness to assist to the limit in furthering the interests of the Company to the moment I leave."[31] He was replaced on the Board by Gerald C. L. Thompson (b 1910), the son of E. C. Thompson, the Company's solicitor.[32]

During his lifetime, Atkinson published a number of papers on shipbuilding and engineering. He also gave a lengthy interview in 1990 to Anthony Slaven for 'Crossing the Bar'. In this he was critical of the industrial situation in the late 1950s, when shipbuilders felt they differed from newer industries. When an order was received, each ship was treated as a separate entity. It was designed and produced by the different departments, with little interchange of ideas. Management was treated as an appendage to the real business of building the ship, whose costs must be kept as low as possible.

He commented that the Chief Draughtsman and his Drawing Office staff:

> "designed the ship, did the estimating, ordered the materials etc. There was no management structure as you would know it today. What departments there were, were all under the drawing office. There was absolutely no marketing or personnel department."

'Sales' was then treated as a dirty word in the industry, as orders were taken from the existing client base, rather than being sought from new clients by a fully trained sales force. Atkinson was also an ardent proponent of standardisation. He wanted ship owning companies to run cost efficient ships, developed by the shipbuilding companies, rather than the shipowners dictating the specifications, with the resultant barrier to productivity. He advocated separating the design and production side, to promote innovation in the latter. He was heavily critical of management's approach to the workforce. Increases in productivity were resisted by the shop floor, in case they led to redundancy. He urged management to work out a new charter that addressed this, whilst dealing with compensation and re-skilling as a path to higher earnings.

Atkinson left the shipbuilding industry and worked elsewhere for some years. During this period he specialised in closing unprofitable industrial subsidiaries and disposing of others, in order to keep the parent company alive. He was Chairman of Aurora Holdings, a steel maker in Sheffield, when he was appointed Chairman of the national body, British Shipbuilders, in September 1980, with a brief for rationalisation and closure. By then, proper compensation for redundancy was an integral part of the process. This is where his path crossed once more with Doxford. (See Chapter Sixteen)

In 1959, Percy Jackson, by then Director of Research and Engineering, brought John Francis Butler into the department from Harland & Wolff in Belfast, as Technical Manager. J. F. Butler had lost a leg in early manhood through a motorcycle accident, but refused to let this slow him down. He was agile in negotiating the ladders on a ship, and sailed on a number of maiden voyages. In 1959, Butler became Technical Director. He stayed at Doxford Engineers through the parent Company's many changes of structure and was a vice president NECIES in 1970.[33]

Chapter Fifteen

1961-1978
Changes in Company Structure and New Engines

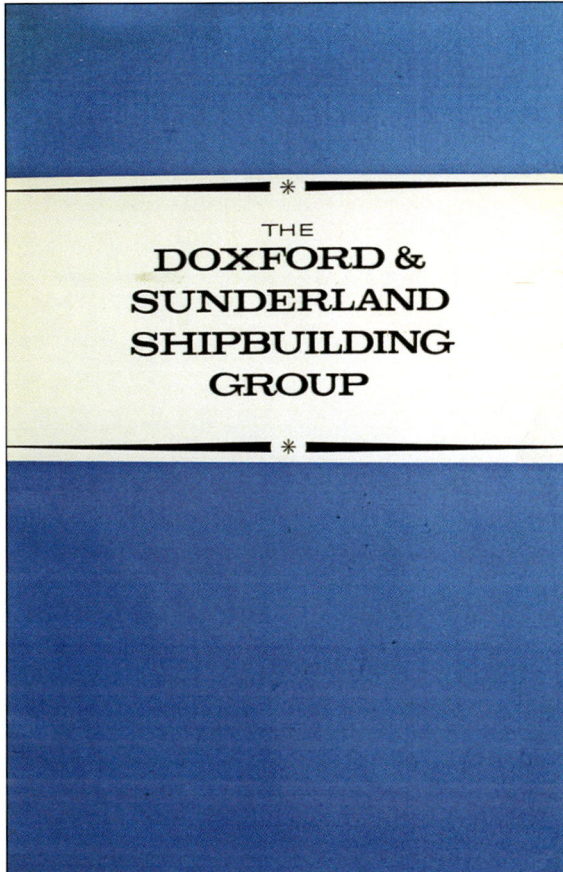

188. The Publicity Brochure issued in 1961 by the new Group. Courtesy of Ian Buxton.

This Chapter covers a period of intense politicisation of British industry. Shipbuilding and marine engineering were in no way sheltered from the pressures of foreign competition and political ideology. The name under which the Pallion yard was administered changed at least four times between 1961 and its final closure in 1989. However, Doxford shipbuilders and engineers managed to achieve successes during their last twenty seven years, even if profitability escaped their Directors. I have outlined the changes in ownership up to 1974 in this Chapter and the output from both the shipyard and the engineering division, before returning to the structure of the concern in the final Chapter of this history. One of the striking issues that I have noticed is that the key leaders from 1961 to 1983 were all born in the first twenty years of the 20th century.

1961-1972 Doxford & Sunderland Shipbuilding and Engineering Company Ltd.

At the start of the 1960s, orders were becoming thin on the ground, and the Doxford Board decided that the Company needed a better structure to remain competitive in the emerging global shipbuilding and marine engineering industry. Many of the Sunderland shipbuilders had already gone to the wall. Short Bros. had recently closed. Austin had merged with Wm. Pickersgill as Austin and Pickersgill in 1954. Bartrams were still independent, but 1954 had also seen the establishment of the Sunderland Shipbuilding, Dry Docks and Engineering Company Ltd. (SSDDE) as a collaborative concern, bringing together two shipbuilding yards on the Wear: J. L. Thompson and Sir James Laing, and three other associated businesses. Each company functioned independently, but with cross directorships, under a single holding company with a capital of £3m. Discussions began between SSDDE and William Doxford & Sons to form a larger conglomerate. Dr. J. R. Gebbie was the Chairman of Doxford during the negotiations, and Dr. Andreae, his predecessor, was also a key player, as the issues were challenging. By early 1961, discussions were faltering on the final terms. The Doxford Board were intransigent and the Board of SSDDE feared that their profits would be siphoned off to support the two businesses at Pallion. It was Andreae who eventually brokered the deal. Doxford offered five of their shares for six of the former conglomerate and to pay a 5% first dividend on ordinary shares immediately, plus a further 15% on acquisition. A 10% dividend would then be paid on 1 November 1961. Preference shareholders voted 94% in favour and the deal went ahead. On 14 June 1961, the Holding Company took the name Doxford & Sunderland Shipbuilding and Engineering Company Ltd. (DSSE), but the SSDDE delayed its own winding up until its accounting year ended on 31 March 1962. As before, the yards and associated businesses continued as independent Companies within the new group, though this structure ceased in 1966.

They were:

- * William Doxford & Sons Ltd. (the holding company and the shipbuilding and engineering subsidiaries)
- * J. L. Thompson & Sons Ltd., shipbuilders
- * Sir James Laing and Sons Ltd., shipbuilders
- * John Lynn & Co. Ltd., manufacturers of marine auxiliary machinery
- * Sunderland Engineering Equipment Co. Ltd.
- * Sunderland Forge and Engineering Co. Ltd.
- * Wear Winch and Foundry Co. Ltd., iron castings
- * T. W. Greenwell and Co. Ltd., ship repairers
- * Wolsingham Steel Co. Ltd., steel castings, forgings and fabrications

Dr. Gebbie took the chair of the new group on an interim basis, but retired in July 1962, aged 73. His role was assumed by Sir Henry Wilson Smith (1904-1978), a long serving civil servant who had turned to industry, who was Chairman of the Powell Duffryn (mining) Group. Wilson Smith was born in Newcastle. As a civil servant he had served mainly in the Treasury. He had an exceptionally keen mind and held a number of directorships. Whilst chairman of DSSE he was appointed a Director of the Bank of England, which he served from 1964-1970. He conducted leadership on a strategic, general policy level, rather than operational. Having steered the group through the 1960s, he retired from the chairmanship in 1969, but remained on the board until 1972.

189. Sir Henry Wilson Smith. Chairman, Doxford & Sunderland Shipbuilding & Engineering Co., 1962-69.

Wilson Smith's first Board was formed of directors of Doxford and of the other two of the shipyards in the group. Allan James Marr (1907-1989) was the Managing Director of Sir James Laing. Marr was the grandson of Sir James Marr, who had acquired the Company from the Laing family. Robert Cyril Thompson (1908-1967) was Chairman and Managing Director of J. L. Thompson. In November 1962, J. G. Hugall was appointed Financial Controller and Managing Director of the holding company. The holding company was dissolved and the two Doxford subsidiaries continued to have their own boards at this point: Tom Abell (1910-1983) and Clem Stephenson were made chairmen of these. The other constituent companies also retained their own boards.

A Committee of Management was appointed. Its members were A. J. Marr, R.C. Thompson, J. G. Hugall, C. Stephenson, T. W. D. Abell, N. C. Marr, J. V. Thompson, T. A. Greenwell and A. L. Marr. Issues that were addressed were joint bulk purchasing, the advertising policy, insurances, welfare and sports facilities, plus the Group policy on rating. A comprehensive capital expenditure policy was set in train, all projects to be examined by the Management Committee. The first decision was to extend one of the berths at J. L. Thompson and to purchase an additional crane at an estimated cost of £22,000.

Doxford Shipbuilders 1961-1973

At the merger with the Sunderland shipbuilding and engineering companies in 1961, Stephenson was Managing Director of William Doxford & Sons (Shipbuilders) Ltd. Whilst retaining this position, he also assumed the role of Chairman of the subsidiary. Stephenson was born at Whitburn, just north of Sunderland and obtained a scholarship to Sunderland Junior Technical School, after which he attended Sunderland Technical College. He served his apprenticeship as a draughtsman at Wigham Richardson and, through evening classes, qualified as a naval architect. After a period at Swan Hunter, in 1936 he joined the design staff at Doxford and became their naval architect in 1943. In 1951 he was appointed the Shipyard General Manager. In 1965, he was Chairman of the Wear Shipbuilders' Association, at a time of intense pressure from foreign competition. There were then approximately 6,000 shipyard workers on the Wear, and contracts were being agreed at a loss to obtain orders.

Stephenson remained as Chairman of Doxford Shipbuilders until DSSE was taken over by Court Shipbuilders. It seems from the board minutes that he had wished to step down two years earlier, but was persuaded to stay until the merger was completed in 1973.

190. Clement Stephenson (1913-2001) Chairman and Managing Director of Doxford Shipbuilders.

During the 1960s, Doxford Shipbuilders worked mainly for their existing customers, but were innovative in developing ships to meet changing circumstances. One of their long standing customers was the Charente Steam Ship Co. Ltd., owned by T. & J. Harrison. In December 1961, as the new chairman of Doxford Shipbuilders, Stephenson presented a lengthy paper to the NECIES on the Heavy Lift Vessel: Adventurer (C834), 8,925 grt, 450 feet in length, 65 in breadth and just under 38 depth, completed in February 1960 for this company.[1] In the post war period the Harrison Line began to specialise in heavy transportation of oil refinery equipment, including large diameter steel pipes for oil lines (each over forty feet in length), generators for power stations, heavy transport vehicles etc., whilst their ships still continued to carry general and bulk cargo and passengers. This diversity of needs set particular problems for the ship designer, who had to achieve ease of cargo handling, comfort for passengers and stability of the ship. The earlier ships had five

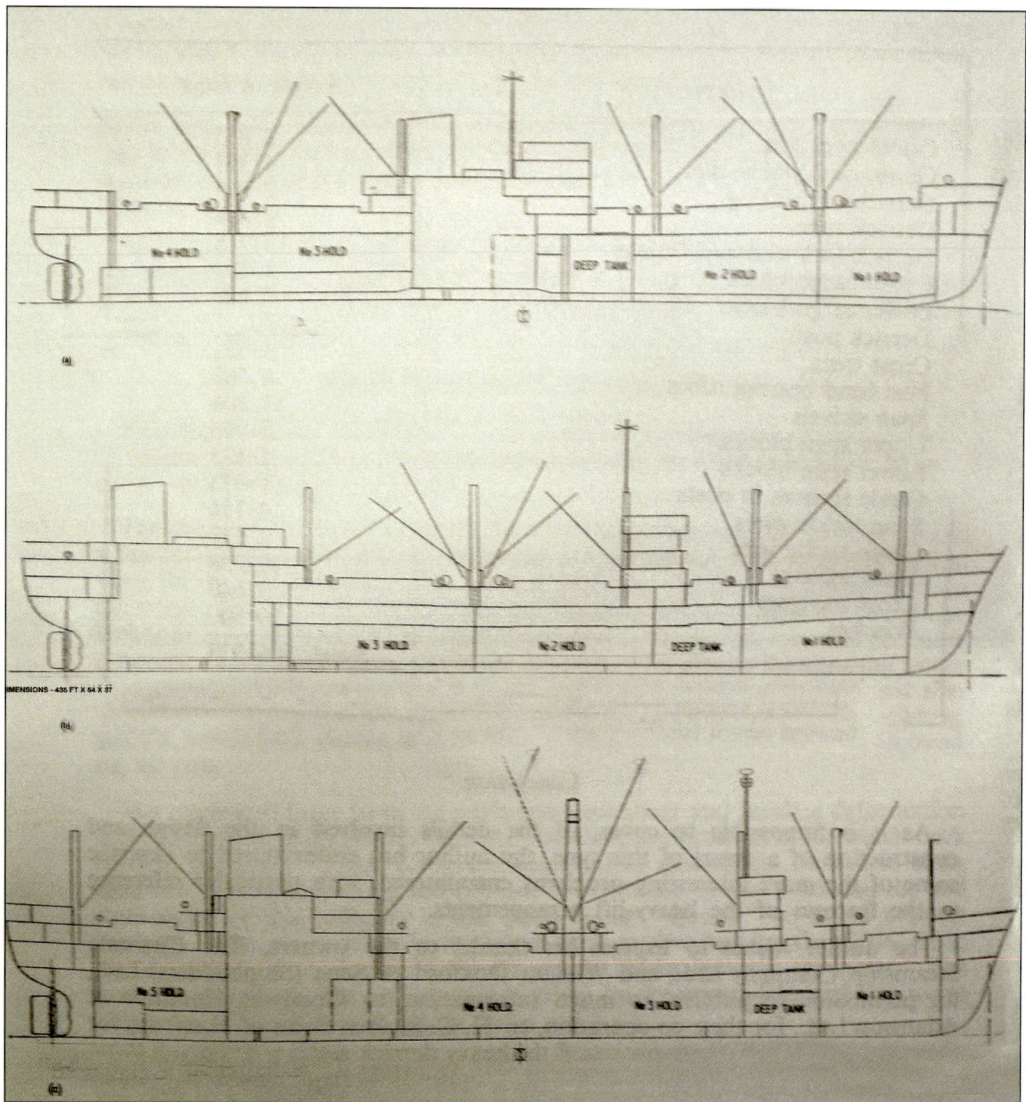

191. Adventurer, C834, changes to the design of a Doxford heavy lift vessel, 1959-1960.
From a paper presented by Clement Stephenson to the NECIES 11 December 1961.

cargo holds with engines amidships. The lifting gear was twin seventy ton derricks fore and aft. With loads increasing substantially, this design proved inadequate for the tasks required. After working up a number of options, the engines were moved to a position further aft, and the beam was increased from 59 feet to 65. The controls were moved forward and extra derricks were added to facilitate discharge. This image shows the process in redesigning the hull shape and general layout of the Adventurer; the design at the bottom eventually going into service.

However, the demands of ship owners to have such multi-use vessels demonstrates the problems faced by British shipbuilders. It led to them becoming less competitive, as they continued with their existing relationships rather than seeking new world-wide purchasers. Despite this, Doxford Shipbuilders responded to the increasing demand for bulk carriers and tankers. These formed the main output during the 1960s and early 1970s. At this time, ships were being converted to take containers. The process eventually led to the vast container ships that now sail the oceans. Doxford were unable to respond effectively to the demand for longer ships though. One of the constraints at Pallion was the length of the berths. The gross tonnage of the Company's ships remained below 12,000 up to December 1973.

Doxford Engineers

Following Robert Atkinson's resignation, T. W. D. Abell was appointed Managing Director of William Doxford & Sons (Engineers) Ltd., taking up post on 1 August 1961. He was the son of Sir Westcott Stile Abell, K. B. E., professor of naval architecture at the University of Liverpool and chief ship surveyor at Lloyd's Register of Shipping. From 1935 to 1940 Tom Abell served with the Southern Railway Company in their marine division and then joined the Dover and Folkestone harbour authority. He was seconded to a number of different ports during WWII.[2] With good credentials as an engineer he later worked on the Tyne at PAMETRADA (Parsons and Marine Engineering Turbine Research and Development Association),[3] He had also been in Canada with the Doxford licensee, Canadian Vickers. Immediately prior to joining Doxford Engineers, Abell was managing director of David Rowan & Co. Ltd., Glasgow. As Chairman of the Institute of Marine Engineers (Scottish Section), he strongly advocated the merger between shipbuilding and engineering companies to reduce costs and match the competitive prices of foreign competitors. Abell arrived with the challenge of developing a Doxford engine to meet the new market demands and to compete effectively with their continental rivals.

Abell was appointed a member of the DSSE Board. He was also Chairman of four other companies in the conglomerate: Sunderland Forge, Wolsingham, John Lynn and Wear Winch. His brief was to bring them all into profitability. Under his direction, Percy Jackson and his team succeeded in this challenge with the 'J' Engine. Abell took the leading role in marketing the engine. However, the politics of working within a large combine eventually defeated him. It seems that poor labour relations may have brought him down, as his last months were marred by a prolonged strike.

192. T.W.D. Abell, Chairman and Managing Director of Doxford Engineering Subsidiary, 1961-1966. From The Motor Ship July 1961

The decision was taken at a DSSE Board Meeting held on 30 March 1966 to absorb the trading activities of all the eleven subsidiary companies into the parent company, but no prior notice was given to Abell and he was not present. The chairman had written to him two days earlier, on 28 March, dismissing him from the board of DSSE. Abell does not seem to have accepted his dismissal, as two meetings of the board of directors were held on 13 April 1966. The first approved and ratified the letter dismissing him from the board and from his post as Chairman and Managing Director of the engineering subsidiary. The second meeting, held five minutes later, confirmed the validity of the decisions passed on 30 March.[4] The press was kept in the dark about these decisions for a further week. The Newcastle Journal reported on 20 April that Abell, as Chairman and Managing Director of William Doxford & Sons (Engineers) had just been appointed a vice president of NECIES. The very next day, the Company was forced to issue a statement that he had ceased to be a Director of the group and its subsidiaries.[5] Abell didn't go quietly. Two years later he brought a case of wrongful dismissal, loss of earnings and loss of pension rights in the High Court against the Company, who counterclaimed that losses of £1.5m were his responsibility. The case proceeded for eleven days before both parties withdrew.[6]

Abell was replaced by T. A. (Anthony) Greenwell (1922-1987), managing director of one of the group members, T. W. Greenwell & Co., ship repairers. Greenwell had a long track record in establishing good relationships with the workforces on the North East Coast. He was the Chairman of the Labour Relations Board of the Shipbuilders and Repairers National Association. As President of the Shipbuilding Employers' Federation that year, he succeeded in bringing the strike to a mutually agreed end. On 10 August 1967, Greenwell achieved a national agreement with the Confederation of Shipbuilding and Engineering Unions that set out procedures aimed at rapid settlement of industrial disputes. He became the first Managing Director of William Doxford & Sons Shipbuilders and Engineers Ltd., and of the Doxford & Sunderland Group. He held this position until Doxford and Sunderland were taken over by Court Shipbuilders Ltd.

Another key employee throughout this troubled period was J. F. Butler, who was the Technical Manager with Doxford Engineers. He led the development of the Doxford-Seahorse engine at the start of the 1970s.

193. J.F. Butler, Technical Director, Doxford Engines. Courtesy of The Motor Ship.

Health and Safety

Right through the 1960s ships continued to be built beneath the gantries designed by Robert Doxford Junior in 1904 and, although modern means of construction were now used, the shipyard was still a basic and dangerous place in which to work. New methods were constantly sought to improve efficiency and to lower operating costs, but health and safety rules lagged behind innovations. The worst tragedy in the history of the company happened on 30 October 1966 when seven men died in a fire whilst working within the propeller shaft tunnel of Toronto City (C875). She was under construction for Bibby Bulk Carriers, Liverpool. William Bendelow, the shipyard installation manager at the engine works, gave evidence to the inquest, held only six weeks later. He described the scenario that caused the conflagration. The men were testing a new oil system using pressure. The pipes had been fitted incorrectly and caused an intake of air, followed by a partial blockage. The pipe joint then came apart, resulting in an escape of oil. This shot as a spray right down to the other end of the propeller shaft, where a worker was using an acetylene cutter. A spark caused ignition and six Pallion shipyard workers, together with a marine engineer employed by a contractor, died from asphyxia due to carbon monoxide poisoning. The fire brigade were rapidly on site, but the position of the fire deep inside the ship made rapid rescue impossible, and it took many hours to bring the bodies out. Despite what would now be judged serious managerial failings, as a naked flame was operating close to a potential oil spill, a verdict of accidental death was recorded by the coroner on 17 December 1966. It was a great shock for the whole community, who responded by setting up an emergency fund for the widows and their children.[7]

Information Technology

It was at this time that the company began to embrace information technology. June Miller, of South Hylton, was then working for the Sunderland Technology College. Her role was to visit the yards of a number of Sunderland shipbuilding and engineering companies to train operatives as they developed their technology systems. This meant, at last, that more women were employed in a trained position in the shipbuilding industry. In the early days the information was punched into cards that were then fed on to tape. The tape had to be carried manually to Edinburgh, as there was no local facility for printing them locally. A junior member of staff travelled by train to Scotland in the morning, returning with the print outs that evening. They were then ready for the relevant drawing office the following morning. There was as yet no Computer Aided Design, so all designs were still drawn by hand, whether a small modification to the design of a ship's hull or major changes to its interior, its fittings or its engine. It was not until virtually the end of shipbuilding on the Wear that CAD was widely used. The Drawing Offices were therefore amongst the largest departments, and the Chief Draughtsman was a senior member of staff. A wooden extension had been added to the roof of the General Office at the turn of the century, where blueprints were produced by exposing

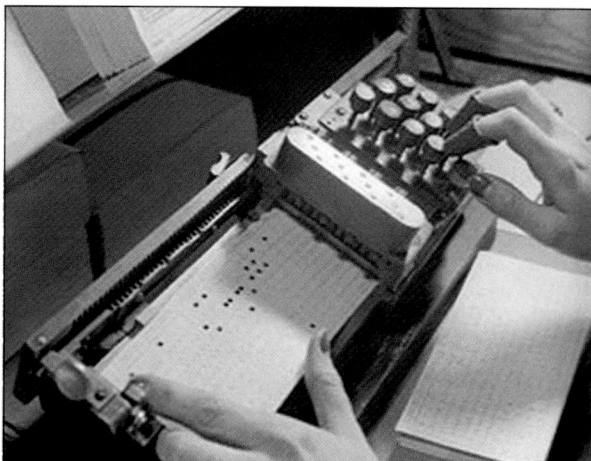
194. Punch card machine in operation.

sensitised paper to natural light. This room was still in use until the 1960s, though by this time machines produced white prints, i.e. positive rather than negative.

The financial problems of the 1960s

The new conglomerate rapidly ran into financial difficulties, due to lack of orders and the problems of managing such a wide range of separate ship-building and engineering businesses. Despite cost-cutting exercises, few of the smaller subsidiaries made profits, and they dragged down the rest of the group. By 1963 berths in all three shipyards were either lying empty or had no orders to refill them once the current ship was launched. Their worldwide competitors undercut their prices. This was partly due to lower wages, but also because the Far Eastern yards were of modern construction and offered better delivery times. Orders were only won at or below cost, leaving no cushion to improve facilities. Despite this, the Doxford yard completed six ships in 1963 and a further five the following year, though only one ship left the Laing yard at Deptford in these two years. The Thompson yard at North Sands completed two ships in 1963 and three in 1964. Two were less than 11,000 grt, but the largest was the tanker Borgsten, 49,311 grt (86,800 dwt). It was against this background that Doxford were developing the 'J' engine, described below in this Chapter. It is understandable that the J. L. Thompson yard were keen to participate by providing the ship in which to install the new engine. Unfortunately, the huge development costs of the 'J' engine were another drain on the consortium.

A problem in the mid-1960s was that modern industries were springing up in the North East, benefiting from the pool of experienced engineering operatives. Men moved from traditional work in the yards and engine shops into clean new factories, leading to a shortage of labour and slippage of delivery times. The works at Pallion were also out of date. The overhead gantries in the East Yard were sixty years old and even the welding sheds had been erected fifteen years earlier. Additionally, the long established shipyards still provided few comfortable facilities for their workmen: no hot water, changing facilities or decent restrooms. Workers were not even provided with work overalls. They wore their own clothes to work until the yard was modernised in 1973, though hard hats and other safety gear were standard protection. Photographs of the seventies that show men in clean, comfortable work clothes are a far cry from those taken in earlier times. Meals were sometimes heated over a small furnace in the oil engine shop that was normally used to harden injector spindles. The spindles were replaced by pies to warm for lunch. The first canteen in the engineering department was for staff members. Workers were not allowed to use this for some years. In this, Doxford was behind the times, as shipyards elsewhere had full service free canteens during the 1950s. At Pallion, the only free meals were to be had in the separate managers' canteen.

195. Doxford Works during the 1960's. Courtesy of Hilary Doxford.

In October 1964 Harold Wilson came into power with a Labour Government. Under his leadership the Board of Trade set up a committee in 1965, headed by R. M. Geddes, to inquire into the shipbuilding industry, which was beset by poor value orders, late deliveries and even worse industrial relations. J. F. Clarke recorded a note from page three of the report[7]: "As we began our inquiry, a supplier asked 'would you want your son to join this industry?' The question is a good one." The committee visited the twenty seven shipyards that came within its remit and issued its report in February 1966. It recommended a restructuring of the industry to rationalise facilities and management on as close a regional basis as possible and set up the Shipbuilding Industry Board. Doxford, of course, were by this time already in a conglomerate, but the remaining independent yards were now urged to join such organisations. Credit facilities were set up to encourage shipowners to buy from British yards, despite the yards' inability to build the size of ship that world markets demanded. The recommendations were included in the Shipbuilding Industry Act 1967.

On the Wear, a merger feasibility study was carried out in the autumn of 1967 by P. A. Management, with a view to persuade Austin & Pickersgill (A&P) and Bartram to join DSSE.[8] Negotiations foundered. The Times of 6 July 1968 reported that they had failed because the report found no possibility of expansion of business and recommended closing both the Bartram and Doxford yards. The Shipbuilding Investment Board threatened to withhold credit guarantees for ships from Wear yards unless they re-organised their resources, as they were entitled to do under the Act. This would deny orders from British shipowners. At the end of 1968 A & P merged with

Bartrams, both having repudiated joining the DSSE because this would have meant an effective takeover of the smaller yards. Their main incentive to merge was to obtain the credit guarantees. A&P Bartram were together for the next decade, but the Bartram yard closed in 1978. It was not until 1986 that the surviving two Wear shipyards: Southwick (A&P) and Pallion (Doxford) became a single entity. (Chapter Sixteen)

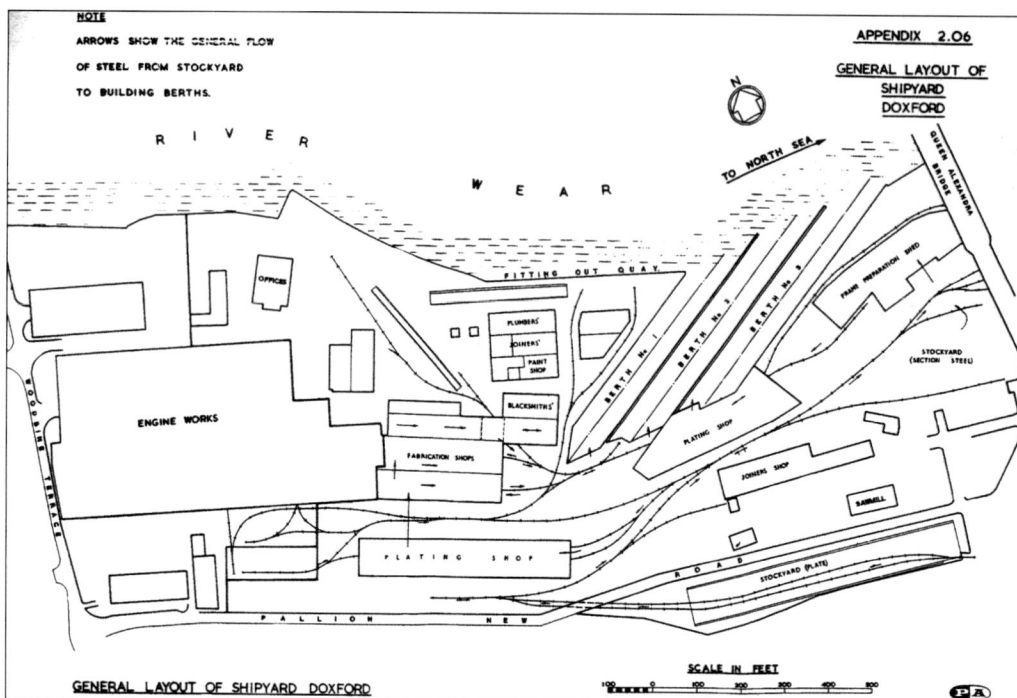

196. Plan of the Pallion yard in 1967. From Merger Feasibility Study, P. A. Management.

Although matters improved for DSSE during 1965 with an influx of orders, profitability turned down steeply the following year. Wilson Smith, although an extremely talented man, failed to find cost savings against such a tough background. This was despite the proximity of the yards, as recommended by the Geddes Report. He was unable to bring the new group into profitability and losses reached £3m in the year to June 1966. These were mainly because shipbuilders were forced to give fixed price quotations to clients in a time of inflation and rising employment costs. At the same time the Labour government reduced the working week from forty two to forty hours and established extra holiday entitlement. Wages had been expected to rise by 3-4% per annum, but far exceeded this. The decision was taken to integrate the separate companies under a single management. From then on trading and most other activities were carried out by the parent company. From this date all ships were built under the name of DSSE, though individual yard numbers continued in sequence.

The last ship to be launched as from William Doxford & Sons (Shipbuilders) Ltd. was, Coventry City (C873), for Bibby Bros, Liverpool. The following ship, Shirrabank (C874), 10,623 grt, was delivered to the Bank Line of Glasgow in September 1966 as from DSSE. The Bank Line were one of Doxford's most loyal customers. During

197. Coventry City, C873, the last launch from William Doxford & Sons (Shipbuilders Ltd.)
Photographed 1970. Shipspotting.com (frtrfred)

the 1960s, fifty three ships left Pallion. Of these, eighteen were built for the Bank Line, a third of production. Only twelve were supplied to foreign buyers. These were mainly based in Europe, but the People's Republic of China commissioned two cargo vessels in 1967: Dunhuang (C876), 11,422 grt and Jinsha (C878), of a similar size. I am told that whilst under construction the ships had communist banners draped from them and the Chinese held parties for the shipyard workers in the canteen where Mao Tse Tung's 'Little Red Books' were distributed. These vessels were fitted with Sulzer engines, rather than the just launched 'J' engine. Sulzer at that time were expanding fast, and had begun to make sales to the U.S. market, as well as to European buyers. The remaining twenty three ships were sold to just seven British firms and, of these, Bibby Bros. of Liverpool also favoured the Sulzer engine.

The development of the 'J' engine and the Doxford Shipyard in the 1960s

Throughout the change of structure Doxford Engines continued to supply engines at home and abroad. They completed thirteen 'P' type engines during 1961, totalling 104,560 ihp. Six were installed in ships built in other shipyards.[9] The largest, at 9,200 bhp, was for the Gorjistan, built by John Readhead & Sons for the Strick Line. However, despite significant interest, Percy Jackson and the new Doxford and Sunderland Group realised that a more powerful engine was needed to compete in the rapidly changing market, and that the 'P' design could not be adapted sufficiently to create the necessary higher power/weight ratio. Their shipowners were also demanding that Sulzer engines be fitted to Doxford ships, so there was a strong incentive to take back the initiative.

The Doxford engineers were hampered by one of the final decisions made by the main Board in 1961. A Japanese consortium visited Pallion just after the merger. They indicated that they were willing to build crankshafts for Doxford and also offered to take a licence to build the proposed 'J' engines. Gebbie, as chairman and as a shipbuilder through and through, vetoed this. Percy Jackson's team were left to go it alone, without the cost savings that such collaboration might have achieved.

233

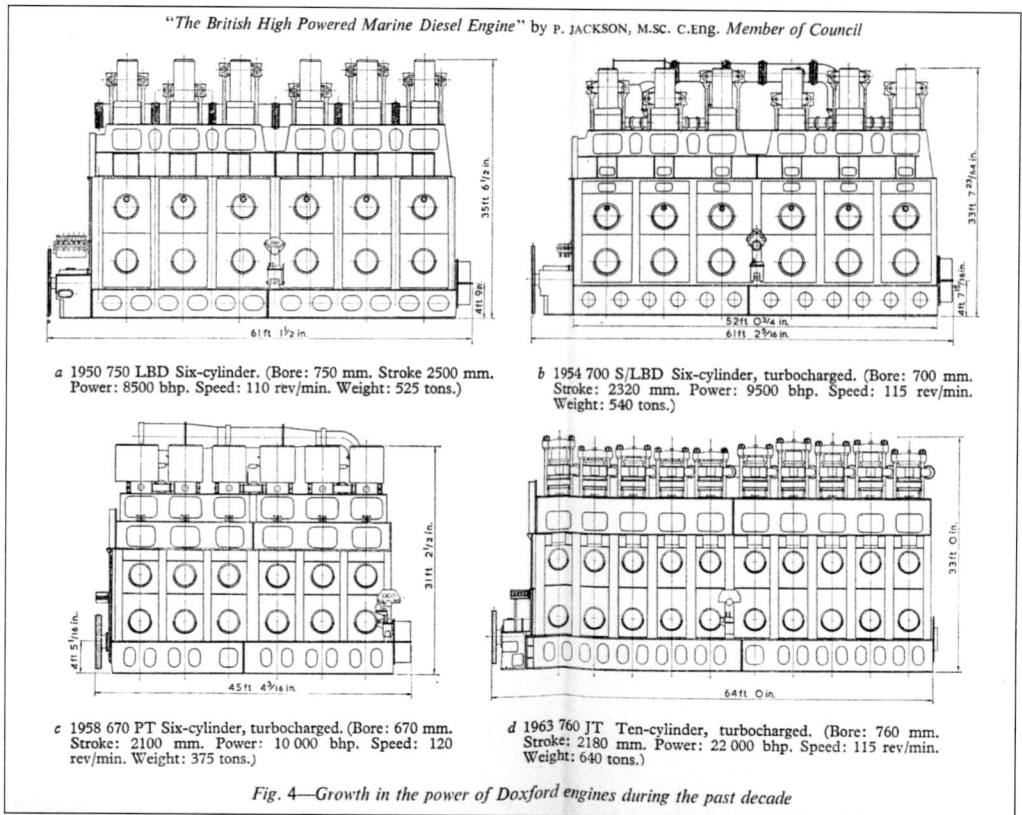

a 1950 750 LBD Six-cylinder. (Bore: 750 mm. Stroke 2500 mm. Power: 8500 bhp. Speed: 110 rev/min. Weight: 525 tons.)

b 1954 700 S/LBD Six-cylinder, turbocharged. (Bore: 700 mm. Stroke: 2320 mm. Power: 9500 bhp. Speed: 115 rev/min. Weight: 540 tons.)

c 1958 670 PT Six-cylinder, turbocharged. (Bore: 670 mm. Stroke: 2100 mm. Power: 10 000 bhp. Speed: 120 rev/min. Weight: 375 tons.)

d 1963 760 JT Ten-cylinder, turbocharged. (Bore: 760 mm. Stroke: 2180 mm. Power: 22 000 bhp. Speed: 115 rev/min. Weight: 640 tons.)

Fig. 4—Growth in the power of Doxford engines during the past decade

198. Illustration from page 101 of paper for the Institution of Mechanical Engineers, 1963, by Percy Jackson, entitled: The British High Powered Marine Diesel Engine.

The team pressed on. One of the prototypes is illustrated here from a paper written by Percy Jackson for the Institution of Mechanical Engineers.[10] In this he gave a comparison of Doxford engines since 1950. The engine in the bottom right corner was a 1963 10-cylinder 760 JT prototype. It developed 22,000 bhp, nearly three times the power of the 750 LBD 6-cylinder engine of 1950. However, it weighed 120 tons more.

At this period, because of the limitations of the 'P' engine Doxford were not able to bid for engines to be installed in ships above a certain size. Jackson recognised the urgency of bringing a more powerful engine into service. Rather than building a single cylinder test engine for the 'J' design, he persuaded the Board to build a full sized, 9-cylinder prototype engine and to commission a suitably sized ship to house this from one of Doxford's sister companies in DSSE. The order was facilitated through finance provided by the Labour Government[11] under its Credit Guarantee Scheme. It was intended for the ship to be chartered out and thus demonstrate the engine's capabilities to the market. The prototype was designed to develop 20,000 bhp at 115 rpm. The bore was 760 mm with an upper stroke of 520 mm and lower stroke of 1,660 mm, giving a total stroke of 2,180 mm. The prototype was given the designation 76J9 and was engine no. 367 on the Doxford book. It was comprehensively tested over 1,000 hours on the company's floating test bed at the massive cost of £800,000. J. L. Thompson built the tanker North Sands, 39,842 grt,

234

199. *View along the huge 'J' engine installed in the North Sands. Courtesy of The Motor Ship Jan 1966, p 111.*

as their yard list 715. The ship, named after the Thompson yard, was 800 feet in length, with a breadth of 110 feet. She had a dead weight of 65,450 tons. Both the 'J' engine and the ship were greeted with interest by the shipping press. The Motor Ship of January 1966 managed to sell a wide variety of advertisements for components installed in both ship and engine. The one here demonstrates the shape of the new bearings developed by Jackson's team.

The North Sands started her sea trials on 1 November 1965 and was chartered to Shell International Marine Ltd. for ten years. Her maiden voyages led rapidly to nineteen orde rs,[11] valued at £6m, and the ship was found to be remarkably free of vibration. One of the challenges in producing a new engine was to set up a chain of repairers throughout the world's shipping lanes. Otherwise a ship could be stuck in port, waiting for a spare part to arrive and to be fitted. This chain was fully in place by the end of 1965.[12]

She was one of a series of similar tankers built at the J. L. Thompson yard. Of these, British Commerce, Daphnella, and Donacilla were fitted with Sulzer engines, whilst Trident (registered by DSSE) had a Doxford 76J8, i.e. eight cylinders. The prototype

200. *Advertisement in the January 1966 edition of The Motor Ship. p 90.*

235

engine fitted in North Sands was, in fact, slightly too powerful for the size of tanker. Its first captain complained that she was not an easy ship to manoeuvre.[13] As a result, only one other 76J9 was built. This was installed into the Orenda Bridge built at the J. L. Thompson North Sands yard in 1972 as their no. 730 and also registered by DSSE.

The North Sands had a somewhat troubled life. In April 1967 an explosion killed one sailor and badly injured another, leaving the giant ship drifting in the Atlantic, north east of the Canary Islands. A Spanish helicopter was scrambled to fly the injured man to hospital at Las Palmas. In 1970 she was sold to the Neptune Maritime Co., Monrovia and renamed the Aeolus. On 24 August 1974 her engine room flooded to a depth of seventeen metres whilst fully loaded and at anchor outside New York harbour and she grounded. The Doxford service engineers reported that the cofferdam doors had been removed, allowing the flooding. In 1977 she was sold once again, this time to Myrmidones Compania Naviera S.A., Piraeus and renamed Nedi. A further Doxford service engineer's report of 12 December 1979 said:

> "The writer has never come upon such an ill-kept, ill maintained engine room and experienced such a lack of spares as on this ship. In thirty years he has never been in such a dirty, filthy engine room. Not only is there a lack of spares, but also a lack of tools to do any maintenance. Work benches with broken down vices. How can engineers work under these conditions when even the most essential facilities are not working or available?"

During his inspection a fire broke out in the engine room. The engineer asserted that had he not been present to raise the alarm, the consequences would have been

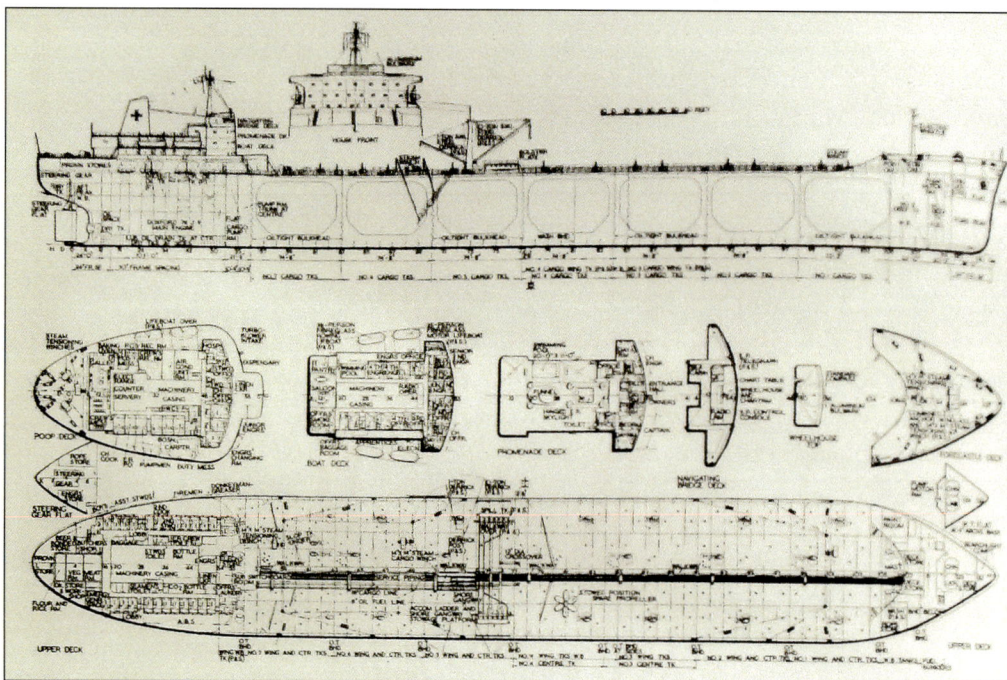

201. Plan of MV North Sands, built by J.L. Thompson to house the first 'J' Engine. The Motor Ship, *Jan 1966, p 474.*

catastrophic. The engine was said to be a serious fire hazard, and the report concluded that the incident "exposed the dangerous conditions under which the engine was operated." However, the former North Sands, with its prototype 'J' engine still in situ, survived for another eight years, latterly under the Panama flag, before being broken up on 27 June 1987. This was only a year before Doxford itself finally went out of existence.

The later 1960s

The Managing Director of Doxford Engineers during the latter part of the 1960s was T. A. Greenwell, with J. F. Butler as his Technical Director. Butler's senior engineering team was Bryan Taylor, Works Manager, George G. Jackson, Drawing and Design Office Manager and Dr. Finn Ørbeck, Technical/Test Office Manager.

In the Drawing Office G.G. Jackson was assisted by John Jordan and Harry Gold, plus about thirty drawing assistants and twelve tracers, who were women. These last two posts gradually reduced as computer aided design became the norm. Jackson was not related to Percy. He was a generalist, but produced papers on the development of the Doxford Slow Speed Engine in 1978 and 1979.[14] Shortly after this the team began to break up. Butler had retired and his replacement, Henry Henshall, reorganised the department. Jackson trained apprentices before moving to Swan Hunter shortly before his own retirement. John Jordan also left Doxford at this time, taking a post with British Shipbuilders at Benton.

202. Launch of the North Sands from the J.L. Thompson yard. Courtesy of Tom Scott.

Finn Ørbeck (1930-2008) came to Britain as a young man and obtained a degree in engineering at Glasgow University. He then returned to Norway, where he worked for some years at Norske Veritas, the Norwegian equivalent of Lloyd's Register. He was recruited to Doxford by Percy Jackson in 1959, because of his experience on electronic computing. He specialised in reducing torsional and axial vibration in marine oil engines, and the lack of vibration was one of the selling points of the 'J' engine. Ørbeck and Butler were granted patent no. 980333 under William Doxford (Engineers) Ltd. for 'Improvements in or relating to vibration reducing devices' from 1962-5. Ørbeck, Butler and Jordan, under Doxford and Sunderland

203. Finn Ørbeck, Technical Design Director.
Courtesy of John Jordan.

Ltd, were granted a further patent for 'Improvements in or relating to opposed piston two-stroke cycle internal combustion engines' in 1971-2, and Patent no. 1391268 was granted solely to Ørbeck under Doxford and Sunderland Ltd. for 'Improvements in or relating to cranks and crankshafts' from 1972-5. He also published a number of technical papers. Two referred to the development of a 3-cylinder engine from 1977-9, the second being in collaboration with his new boss, Henshall.[15] Ørbeck led two small divisions from his office, the technical/calculation side and the test side. He remained at Pallion until all activity closed in 1989. After this he set up his own design organisation on Wearside.

With regard to the 'J' engine, he altered the disc-type side crank webs, so that they became main bearings. This innovation led to the development of a crankshaft of 1,150 mm diameter, reducing the engine length. The more compact 'J' engine coped with much higher powers and proved to be the lightest of its type. Ørbeck was innovative, but was not a hands on engineer. Some of his calculations, whilst seemingly correct, proved impractical in service.

At Doxford Shipbuilders, Stephenson's Technical Director was Derek Camsey, followed by Brian Tebbutt, both of whom also acted as Chief Designer. Tebbutt remained with Doxford into the 1980s, and was appointed to the Board of its final successor company, North East Shipbuilders Ltd. The team was responsible not only for the design of the ships: general cargo vessels, bulk carriers and tankers, but also the equipment, fittings and furnishings within the hull. The gross tonnage range was generally between 8,500 and 11,500 at this period. Only Tudor Prince (C842) topped 12,000 grt at 12,958. Fifty five ships were delivered in total during the 1960s, twenty five being less than 9,000 grt. They also built small ships to demand. Two were Baltic Venture (C866), 1,581 grt, and Baltic Vanguard (C872), 1,903 grt, both for the United Baltic Corporation, London. They were general cargo ships, with a M.A.N.

204. Baltic Venture (C866), 1965. Photograph by Richard Cox. From The Sunderland Site.

engine, rather than one built by Doxford Engineers and both were later converted to take containers. The Baltic Vanguard had a long and varied life. She sailed on a number of world routes and was lengthened in 1976 by eighty feet on conversion to a container carrier. She finally ended her life in 2011.[16] The most loyal ship owning companies were still the Bank Line (19 orders), Charente SS Co. Ltd. (T & J Harrison) (6), Monrovia Tramp Shipping Co. (5) and Bibby Line (4).

Wilson Smith retired in 1969 and the Chairmanship of DSSE was assumed by Cuthbert Wrangham, former chairman of Short Brothers, the aerospace company, merged with Harland and Wolff. Wrangham had left Belfast in 1967 after clashes with the Labour Government, who had a controlling interest. Rumours of a takeover of DSSE were now recurring, causing the shares to fluctuate, though they remained consistently beneath the twenty shilling mark. Dividend payments were suspended after the tax year 1969/70, with little possibility of a distribution in the near future. To mitigate the situation, Wrangham simplified the group's name to Doxford & Sunderland Ltd. (D & S) and fully aligned the management of the constituent companies in 1970. He resigned at the beginning of 1971 due to clashes with his fellow directors over industrial relations. The Boilermakers' Union was in dispute with employers on a number of occasions between 1969 and 1971 and agreement was not finally achieved until March 1971. A strike dragged on for three months in 1970, closing all three yards, and this had a badly detrimental effect on profits. In his leaving statement Wrangham said that what Britain needed was:

> "much better industrial relations so that the man working on the shop floor or in the shipyard has a much better appreciation of what is going on elsewhere; how profits are made, or the losses; how the orders are got, and whether there is enough money to pay the wages, or more wages .... A major objective must be to break down the 'them and us' attitude common among both employees and employer."

239

Sadly, his hopes were not achieved during the 1970s, and rampant inflation led to yet higher wage demands. Hostile attitudes on both sides became even more entrenched.

John George Hugall (1911-1993), was appointed deputy chairman of D & S on 2 January 1970 and took over as Chairman on an interim basis when Wrangham resigned. Hugall had joined Doxford as their Chief Accountant in 1944 and served for many years as Financial Director. He was the Financial Controller of D & S. Wilson Smith re-joined the board, also on an interim basis. Hugall came into post at a time of industrial and financial crisis within the group and it was he who was given the unenviable task of finding the multi-million pound group a new owner. Although under his leadership the dispute with the Boilermakers' Union was settled, in mid-1971 D & S shares dropped by nearly a fifth to just 40 new pence,

205. John George Hugall, Interim Chairman Doxford & Sunderland.

decimal currency having just been introduced, though it later rebounded. The group became the subject of debate in Parliament, the Government now being led by Edward Heath. At the time the workforce numbered 7,000, so the group was of national importance.[17] In Hugall's first year as Chairman, D & S made a loss of £1,250,000. With a Conservative administration in power, if the group were to be sold the expectation was for it to remain in private ownership.

1972-1976 Sunderland Shipbuilders Ltd under Court Line - Nationalisation

By the spring of 1972 rumours increased that D & S were looking for a bid. Its stock rose £1 in early May, to £2.75 (from a quoted price of 44p at the start of the year) as 'vultures' began to circle the embattled shipbuilding and engineering group. Unemployment in the North East was rising. The Times of 15 May noted,

> "With the Government now seemingly prepared to do anything to avoid escalating unemployment in areas like the shipyards where it is already intolerable, the future is to some extent underpinned."

The business correspondent continued:

> "Admittedly there is little that shipbuilding yards can be used for apart from building ships, since in most cases they are not particularly well placed for anything else. But assets are attractive to firms like Court Line, the favourites to bid for Doxford, Furthermore, a successful management must be confident it can eventually return at least 10 per cent on turnover. That would suggest a pretax profit for Doxford of over £2m and, of course, accumulated losses would leave very little for the taxman in most cases." [18]

The Conservative Government pressed British shipowners to order from British yards and were, in turn, asked to subsidise the industry by a further £150m over the coming years. The U. S. Government of the day, for instance, gave grants of up to 43% to generate shipbuilding orders. Freight rates were so low that shipowners were laying up their vessels rather than run them at a loss. They were certainly not making new purchases. D & S failed to win a new order once investment grants were scrapped.[19] The long established shipping and charter holiday company, Court Line, were expected to make an offer in the near future, but this was, of course, categorically denied by the interim Chairman.

Court Line was founded in 1905 as a shipping company, but had diversified into providing services for holiday makers. In 1965 it had acquired Autair, a charter airline based at Luton, and developed a close relationship with companies such as Clarksons Holidays and Horizon. These flew holidaymakers to the Mediterranean, deeply undercutting rivals. It had also acquired a shipyard at Appledore, near Barnstaple, Devon in 1966, and had substantially rebuilt this in 1970.[20] The managing director of Court Line in the early 1970s was John Young. His right hand man in the takeover of D & S was James (Jim) Venus, the managing director of Appledore. Venus was a local man, who had been born in Newcastle-upon-Tyne. Whilst denials were being made by the D & S board, Court Line were carrying out a review of its businesses, with Government encouragement. They put in a takeover bid in June 1972, the offer being worth over £10m. Shareholders were offered two Ordinary 25p Shares in Court Line for each £1 Ordinary Share in D & S, plus a 15% dividend payable in the financial year. Court Line also pledged to renovate the yards, which were all in need of modernisation. Hugall and his board recommended acceptance, and the deal was agreed on 10 July. Court Line changed the name of the Wear combine to Sunderland Shipbuilders Ltd. (SSL). In November 1972 the name of the shipbuilding subsidiary became Doxford Shipbuilders Ltd. (DSL) and that of the engineering subsidiary to Doxford Engines Ltd. (DEL), a name retained until final closure in 1984.[21]

Jim Venus (1920-1992) and Anthony Greenwell were of a similar age and briefly became joint Managing Directors of SSL. As Venus also assumed the role of chief executive, he was in affect the senior of the two. The Directors of the new group were Venus, Greenwell, Young, M. I. Makins, financial controller of Court Line and M. Hall, financial director of North-East Coast Ship Repairers.[22] The inaugural Company Secretary was John Walton Holey, but he immediately tendered his resignation and left on 30 April 1973. The two principals fell out and Greenwell resigned in March. He became the President of the Shipbuilders and Repairers National Association and was later the managing director of Lawson-Batey Tugs, Newcastle and of the Blyth Tug Company.

Greenwell's post as Managing Director of DEL was taken by D. B. Stables, who had been 'head hunted' by Venus. David Stables (b. 1925) had joined Doxford in 1958 and had been Doxford Engines General Manager, with a particular brief for sales.

He had worked on and promoted both the 'P' and 'J' engines. After leaving Doxford he became managing director of Crossley Premier Engines Ltd. at Manchester and in 1972 was chairman of the British Marine Equipment Council. He was to manage the Doxford Seahorse engine project below.

Sadly, the takeover took place just as the economy faltered even further, and economic sentiment went into reverse. The 1973 energy crisis blew up, leading to high inflation. Within a year both Clarksons and Horizon were on the verge of collapse. Court Line, with Venus now their Chairman, were forced to acquire them, for a nominal £1 in the case of Clarksons. 1974 became the worst year ever for the holiday trade. Heath's government introduced the three day week in January, cutting both production and money in pockets. He called an election in February, but failed to achieve a majority. In March, Harold Wilson formed a minority Labour Government and negotiated with Court Line to take their empire into public ownership. Court Line agreed, as its high gearing of debt on the two travel companies could not withstand the pressure. They ceased trading on 15 August 1974.

Holiday makers were left stranded, as aircraft and liners were impounded in foreign ports. The Halcyon, under Captain Brian Greenwood, slipped quietly away from her berth at Come-by-Chance, Newfoundland, avoiding Canadian police boats (and a potential $300,000 docking and fuel fee charge), to return rapidly to Britain. He told the press on his arrival at Tilbury that his obligation was to look after his crew's welfare and he felt his action was both legal and honourable, though the fifty one members of crew were forced to remain on board until the ship was sold.

It was a sad time for the Wearside yards, from which they never fully recovered. The culmination of the nationalisation did not reach a conclusion until 1977, when the British Shipbuilders' Corporation came into being, as described in Chapter Sixteen. The years between were times of uncertainty. However, Appledore Shipbuilders remained independent under Venus, who had already set up a consultancy company with Austin & Pickersgill in 1971 that focussed on ship design and shipyard construction. After the nationalisation of A&P in 1977, A&P-Appledore International was acquired by its management and, as A&P Group, still operates as one of the two remaining large commercial ship repair companies in the United Kingdom.[23] The Appledore shipyard, latterly in the ownership of Babcock International, finally closed in March 2019.

1973-76 Modernisation of the Shipyard

One of the positive actions taken by Court Shipbuilders was that the gantried East Berths were demolished. Court Shipbuilders put in £3m and the Government gave a £9m loan under the aegis of the 1972 Industry Act to build a 'ship factory' at Pallion. Work started in 1973. Despite the parent company's collapse, the development of an all-weather construction hall proceeded and the office and shipyard buildings were updated. The factory was capable of building two ships of

206. Plan of the Pallion Yard after modernisation in 1977. from Modern Shipyard Developments, Franks & Paton, 1978. Courtesy of Ian Buxton.

30,000 dw simultaneously and obviated the need for engines to be installed post launch. The completed ship left the yard on to the river with its engine not only in situ, but its machinery potentially able to run. The yard numbers were restarted, with Cedarbank receiving the first number, C1. She is seen here being towed out onto the Wear on 26 May 1976.

207. MV Cedarbank (C1), 11,282 grt, the launch on 26 May 1976, the first to leave the new ship factory at Pallion. Courtesy of Ian Buxton.

1970-1978 Doxford Hawthorn Research Services Ltd.
- The Doxford-Seahorse engine

By the end of the 1960s vessels, particularly tankers, were exceeding 250,000 tons displacement. Marine engineers were tasked to design engines that could reach or better 48,000 bhp at speeds varying between 90 and 110 rpm to power such large ships. In 1969 the largest Doxford engine was the 76J9C, which had a maximum power of only 27,000 bhp at 119 rpm.[24] The cost of developing a larger engine was beyond the financial capability of William Doxford and Sons (Engineers) Ltd. (DE). In 1968 Frank Butler approached one of the company's longstanding licensees, Hawthorn Leslie at Hebburn. He and E. P. (Ben) Crowdy, Managing Director of Hawthorn Leslie, came to an agreement that led to the incorporation of Doxford Hawthorn Research Services Ltd. (DHRS).

Its purpose was to develop a new engine that could compete with market rivals. Continental companies were already producing single engines that could drive the huge ships now afloat, but these were suffering from lack of reliability. The Hawthorn and Doxford engineers saw an opportunity to drive these ships with twin engines that were smaller but more reliable and the ship could still run with one out of action. Jack Butler and Ben Crowdy set to work with enthusiasm. They had known each other for some time, as the two companies had worked closely together.

The new engine was intended to be more flexible by running at medium speed and allowing for gearing. It was designed to have from 4 to 7 cylinders. The new engine could be geared down to turn the propeller as slowly as 67 rpm. This was claimed to save up to 9% in fuel costs on a large ship compared to a single direct drive engine running in excess of 100rpm. The test engine was given the designation 58G4 (580 mm bore, G for geared and 4 for four cylinders). They named it the Doxford-Seahorse engine, a seahorse being the Hawthorn Leslie logo.

208. Hawthorn Leslie Seahorse logo. Courtesy of Tom Scott.

The 58G4 was a development of the opposed piston marine oil engine, rather than a complete breakaway. It ran on the common rail system as before. Butler gave a presentation to the Institution of Marine Engineers on its development and this was printed in their transactions of 1972, Vol. 84. In this he described an engine which could develop 2,500 bhp per cylinder at 300 rpm, i.e. medium speed, this being suitable for both marine propulsion and electricity generation in power stations. One change was splitting the exhaust to drive two turbo chargers, one for the forward cylinders and one for the aft. This was to improve gas flow and achieve 10% more scavenge air at full power.[25] However, problems arose with actually achieving this.

DHRS was incorporated on 8 June 1970 with an authorised capital of £1,000 in £1 shares. It was fully funded by equal contributions from the two parent companies.

209. Full sized model in wood of Doxford Seahorse 58G4 engine displayed at Earls Court. With Frank Butler and Ben Crowdy. Courtesy of the Doxford Engine Friends Association.

Its first Chairman was Rear Admiral Sir Matthew Slattery, K. B. E., C. B. (1902-1990), Chairman of Hawthorn Leslie. Slattery was a naval officer, a military aviator and latterly a businessman. He had been the Managing Director and Chairman of Short Brothers and Harland & Wolff, and Chairman of British Overseas Airways Corporation before coming to Hawthorn Leslie. The other founding directors were J. G. Hugall, SSL, J. F. Butler (DE Tech. Dir), E. P. Crowdy (Hawthorn MD), T. A. Greenwell (DE MD), Admiral Sir Horace Law, D. G. Ogilvie (Hawthorn). John Walton Holey, Company Secretary to SSL, undertook the same work for the new subsidiary for its first three years.[26]

During the development of the Doxford Seahorse engine, Court Line became the parent company, but work continued as before. By 19 September the total expenditure, less grants, had grown to £655,375. The two parent companies loaned a further £21,465 to continue the research. It was at this point in 1972 that David Stables became Managing Director of the newly renamed Doxford Engines Ltd. (DEL) and also of DHRS. Admiral Sir Horace Law replaced Slattery as Chairman of the research company in 1974, but rarely seems to have attended meetings.

Stables proved an effective manager and revitalised the work on the Doxford Seahorse engine, which had been struggling. The test engine underwent trials shortly after he came into post and proved to be extremely economical on fuel. However, during testing, a number of modifications were found necessary, because the engine was designed to reach very high powers with a low

210. D.B. Stables, Managing Director, Doxford Engineers, Managing Director of DHRS.

245

number of cylinders. Financial problems continued to dog the project. The cost of the trials was very high, especially due to inflation and DHRS were unsuccessful in obtaining Government grants. Doxford Engines also struggled to win orders for their existing engine production and had to lay off 200 men in January 1974. This was a fifth of the workforce. To minimise costs, in 1975 DEL signed an agreement with M.A.N. of Augsburg to rationalise the supply of engine parts and after sales service. There were hopes that a second new engine would be built co-operatively between the two companies in the future, but this failed to materialise.

By mid-1976 the engine was ready for marketing, but Court Line had collapsed and Sunderland Shipbuilders and Doxford Engines had been taken into public ownership. Additionally, the recession was at its deepest. The huge tankers for which the engine was designed were in oversupply and being laid up, thus dooming the project. Although the group were under Government control, the structure had not yet been finalised, and this was a further barrier to sales. After five years of concentrated research and development, and an outlay of about £5m from the joint sponsors, but minimal government grants, not one engine was ordered. Only three engines went into production and none went into active service. Sadly, no Pallion built ship ever ran with a Doxford Seahorse engine. The test engines were dismantled. Approaches were made to a number of companies over their use as a static source of power, without success.[27] The prototype was sold to Young's Scrapyard in Sunderland and some Doxford-Seahorse castings and components were used in the later 58JS3 engines described in Chapter Sixteen.[28] The DHRS became a shell company until 1981 and was renamed British Shipbuilders Engineering Technical Services Ltd. Unsuccessful efforts were made to diversify its operations.

Chapter Sixteen

1974-1988
The Final Years of the Pallion Yard

1974-1979 Public Ownership under British Shipbuilders

The 1970s were a stressful time for British industry as a whole. The shipbuilding and ship repairing companies were under particular strain, not only on Wearside but throughout the United Kingdom and Northern Ireland. A resolution was tabled by the Boilermakers' Society at the 1971 Labour Party Conference to nationalise the shipbuilding industry and in May 1973 a policy statement was agreed. When a Labour government came into power in 1974 Anthony Benn, as Trade Secretary, announced that a bill would be presented to Parliament on the issue. Court Line had collapsed early that year, so the Government took Sunderland Shipbuilders Ltd. into public ownership, pending legislation. The Chairman Designate of the entity was Admiral Sir Anthony Griffin (1920-1996), who was then Controller of the Navy. He was nominated in 1975. Griffin and his fellow nominees, however, endured a period of political uncertainty until the Corporation was finally inaugurated two years later. Two potential joint Deputy Chairmen were appointed: Graham Day, a Canadian, who was also to be Chief Executive, and Kenneth Griffin (with the same surname as the Chairman), who was a retired union official then acting as industrial advisor at the Department of Industry. Day resigned after some months, due to frustration at the protracted negotiations. He was replaced by Michael Casey, on secondment from the Department of Industry. Kenneth Griffin, however, served two terms as Deputy Chairman.

The nationalisation of twenty seven shipbuilding and marine engineering companies in England and Scotland was passed under the Aircraft and Shipbuilding Industries Act, 1977. The government created a state owned entity, British Shipbuilders Corporation (BS), to manage and rationalise these companies. 97% of merchant ship production and 100% warship output came under the Corporation's umbrella. The exception was Harland & Wolff in Belfast. This was already publicly owned, but did not form part of the group. Ship repairing companies remained in private ownership. On 2 September 1976, towards the end of the process, Sunderland Shipbuilders Ltd. briefly assumed yet another name as Sunderland Shipbuilding and Engineering Ltd. The company's interests were then simultaneously trans-ferred to two of its subsidiary companies: Sunderland Shipbuilders Ltd. (SSL) retained the shipbuilding and engineering interests and T. W. Greenwell & Co. Ltd. operated separately as ship repairers. SSL formally joined BS on 1 July 1977.

The BS headquarters was established at Benton, Newcastle-upon-Tyne. The brief under Griffin's Chairmanship was to reduce capacity significantly and to bring the shipbuilding industry back to profitability. The first objective was achieved. Between

1977 and 1980 shipbuilding capacity contracted from 630,000 grt to 400,000 cgrt (compensated gross registered tonnage, a measure that takes account of the complexity of different ship types). The national shipbuilding workforce reduced from 38,000 to 18,000 over the same three years. BS also put pressure on companies to rationalise their operations.

Despite the upheavals, between 1968 and 1978 the three shipyards in SSL, at North Sands, Deptford and Pallion, produced over 1.5m gross tonnage of shipping. However, between 1978 and 1984, shipbuilding employment declined sharply on the Wear. J.F. Clarke noted that in 1978 there were 7,535 men and women working on the river, of which 4,612 were in the SSL group and 2,923 at A&P Bartram. After this employment fell each year. The J. L. Thompson North Sands yard was closed for shipbuilding in 1979, though its fitting out quay was still used by SSL. The Bartram yard closed in 1978. By 1984 SSL had lost 2,272 workers but, because of their successful SD14 cargo ship, the reduction at A&P was only 820. The employment figures that year were SSL: 2,340 and A&P: 2,103. The two companies were now of a similar size.

SSL's fitting out quay at North Sands closed in 1985 and the yard was made redundant. A further casualty was the engine works at Pallion. In 1979 Griffin took the controversial decision to stop new engine production. Between 1980 and 1984 only repair and maintenance work was undertaken by Doxford Engines. Surprisingly, this proved to be a successful enterprise, bringing much needed work to SSL. The engine works were completely rebuilt in 1983, at a staggering cost of £4m. Despite this, the decision was taken in June 1984 to cease all engineering at Pallion. This was heavily criticised by the former Chairman of British Shipbuilders, Sir Robert Atkinson, who called for a public inquiry into the decision.[1]

1979 Conservative Administration

Despite these measures, the second objective for BS to achieve profitability proved elusive. The early delays in setting up the Corporation did not help. By 1979 Griffin had been Chairman for only two years and his contract was extended, though this proved a poisoned chalice. The General Election in May delivered a Conservative administration under Margaret Thatcher. Her Industry Secretary, Sir Keith Joseph, announced cuts in subsidies of £3-4bn to industry as a whole. Shipbuilding subsidies were agreed at £100m per year, but losses in the industry exceeded this. Griffin also failed to provide the Government with robust financial information on the subsidiary companies within BS. Despite this his chairmanship was extended the following March to run until his successor was found. It must have been with some relief that he handed over the reins only three months later.

On 1 July 1980 Robert Atkinson, the former Managing Director of William Doxford & Sons (Engineers), took over as BS Chairman. He was on a three and a half year secondment from Aurora Holdings, steel makers at Sheffield. BS now had a hands-on leader with an understanding of engineering. Atkinson was unable to restart new engine production at Pallion but, under his direction, the works were profitable and that is why they were rebuilt in 1983. He also ensured that labour relations throughout the shipbuilding industry improved and that productivity grew within the remaining shipyards. He brought in Maurice Phelps, an industrial relations expert, to concentrate on minimising disputes. During the first three years of BS progress had already been made over collective bargaining. Whereas in the 1950s employers had 168 separate organisations to negotiate with, by 1967 talks were conducted with just one: the Confederation of Shipbuilding and Engineering Unions. Credit was due to Anthony Greenwell of Doxford Engines who had established a better framework for disputes. Between 1980 and 1983 two national pay and productivity deals were agreed.

Sadly, Atkinson could not ignore the Conservative Government's brief to reduce the shipbuilding industry, and rationalisation continued. By 1982 half the BS shipyards had closed and, at the end of his tenure, Atkinson's despair was apparent as he urged support for shipbuilding. By this time the Government were considering whether to hive off warship building to the private sector. This was the only profitable part of the industry, due to lack of overseas competition for orders. Quotations for merchant vessels from Japanese and Korean shipyards were up to 30% lower than those offered by British yards.

Atkinson received a knighthood at the New Year's Honours of 1983 but was not offered a second term. He returned to Aurora Holdings and was succeeded as Chairman of BS by J.G. Day, the putative Chief Executive in 1975. Graham Day was a Canadian lawyer, at that time in charge of Dome Petroleum's shipbuilding interests. He was only forty nine when he took over as Chairman and Chief Executive (replacing Michael Casey) on 1 September 1983. His dual role commanded a salary of £80,000. This was the highest in the public sector at that time. Griffin had been paid £44,000.[2] It was Day's task to deliver the Conservative Government's agenda to combine the remaining companies within BS. He first closed or sold the remaining ship repairing businesses and during his time in office Doxford Engine Works and the North Sands Yard also closed. The upheavals led to further industrial action in the mid-1980s. This was the time of the miners' strike and further weakened the industry. By mid-1984 Day was ordered by the Government to prepare all warship building for privatisation the following year, even though some of the yards, such as Swan Hunter, were mixed. The timetable slipped somewhat but all seven such yards were privatised in March 1986. In his first two years Day reduced the Corporation's huge losses and disposed of virtually all the peripheral businesses. The former Laing yard at Deptford launched its last ships in 1985 and closed in 1986. A&P's Southwick yard merged with the former Doxford yard at Pallion, the last remaining shipyard of the former SSL. The new BS subsidiary took the name North East Shipbuilders Ltd. (NESL) and the new Board took up their positions on 1 March 1986.

1977-1987 The SSL shipyards output under British Shipbuilders Corporation

Sunderland Shipbuilders Ltd. continued to produce bulk carrier and general cargo ships, with each yard retaining its numbering system. Twenty three ships followed the Cedarbank from Pallion up to 30 January 1987. (C10 was not used, so the final ship was C25.) Under NESL, yard numbers restarted at 3001.

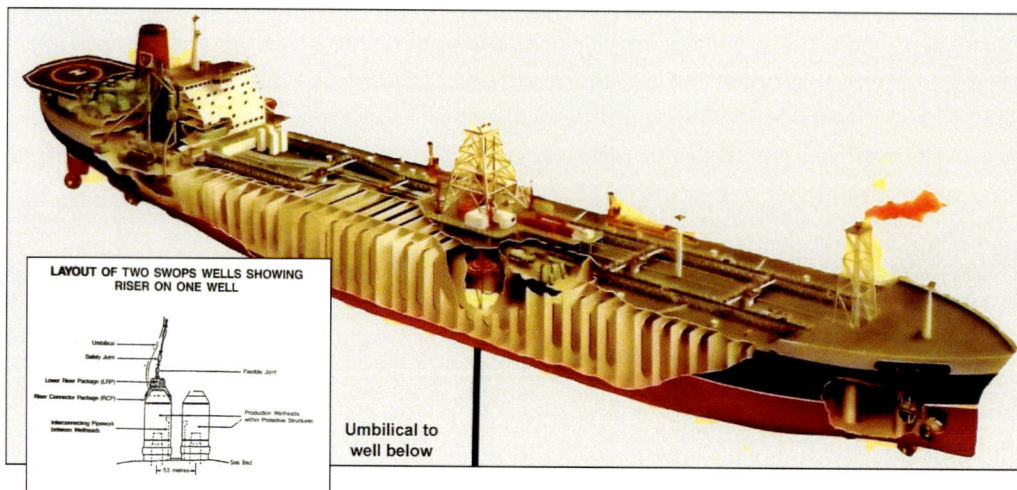

211. & 212. The layout of a SWOPS - showing the oil line to the well below. Inset shows riser connected to one of two wells. Courtesy of the Doxford Engine Friends Association.

By 1980, the operating divisions of BS were merchant shipbuilding, warship building, engineering, ship repair and offshore. The Pallion yard built for this last category. Ships that left the yard had the designation Single Well Oil Production System/Vessel (SWOPS). An umbilical oil line was attached from the ship to a well on the seabed and this was then drained over a period of time. The line was then removed and attached to neighbouring wells in sequence, before returning to the original well, which by then had refilled. The separate compartments shown here enabled the product from individual wells to be identified.

213. Sunderland Shipbuilders Nosira Sharon (C18), 1981. Her bow was added at Palmers Hill Quay, Courtesy of Tom Scott.

*214. Canadian Pioneer the ship that held no. 477, the last Doxford 'J' Engine built at Pallion.
Photograph Courtesy of Marc Piché.*

Unfortunately, by the early 1980s the length of the covered hall proved inadequate for the longer ships under construction. They had to be launched without a bow, which was added at the Palmers Hill fitting out quay. The photograph opposite shows the Nosira Sharon (C18), 18,040 grt, just after her launch on 22 September 1981. She was one of three bulk carriers built for the Nosira Shipping Co. Ltd., London, and managed by Bolton Maritime Management Ltd. Nosira was the name of the owner, Ted Arison, spelt backwards.

The 1980s brought further difficult conditions. Only one ship was delivered from Pallion in 1983. This was the Darya Ma (C21), 17,720 grt, a bulk carrier sold to the Litak Shipping Co. Ltd. Hong Kong, managed by Patt Manfield & Co. Ltd.

When the bulk carriers Alberta (C22), and Radnik (C23), both 17,882 grt, were built in 1984, their engines were by Burmeister & Wain. They were the last Wear-built ships to have opposed piston engines installed. The final two contracts, Stena Seawell (C24) and the Stena Wellservicer (C25), were diesel-electric deep-sea vessels. As such they were electrically driven, with six diesel generator sets supplied by Hedemora. The delivery times for C24 and C25 were much delayed. The man hours rose well above the projected 1,130,000 per ship as problems arose over the equipment, and much of it had to be replaced. C24 was eventually launched at the end of 1986, but was not accepted by Stena Offshore Ltd. until sixty defects had been remedied. She was finally handed over on 16 March 1987. Stena Wellservicer was launched at the end of June 1987 but was not accepted by Stena until 1989.

1976-1984 the Doxford Engine Works

During the development of the Doxford-Seahorse engine, Pallion-built ships were equipped with either a 4 or 6-cylinder 'J' engine. The last 'J' engine installed at Pallion was No. 469, a 4-cylinder 76J4 developing 12,000 bhp. This was for the Tenchbank (C12),[3] launched on 5 October 1979 for the Bank Line. Six ships were fitted with these engines by other shipbuilders. The last two Doxford engines actually built at Pallion were both 'J' type. No. 476 was a 76J4C, fitted to the Badagry Palm (North Sands, number 741), owned by the Palm line. This ship

215. Michael Richardson and John Clayson, right, with the 58JS3C at the Regional Museum Store, Beamish.

had her sea trial on 9 November 1979. She was a general cargo, later a container ship. The last engine built at Pallion was no. 477, a 76J4CR. This was installed in Canadian Pioneer, 24,113 grt, a bulk carrier built by Seaway Marine & Industrial at Port Weller Drydock, Ontario, as number 67. Her sea trials took place on 28 October 1981. She was owned by Upper Lakes Shipping and was later renamed Pioneer.

In 1977, as the Doxford-Seahorse project drew to a close, Doxford Engineers developed a new 3-cylinder 'Economy' engine designated 58JS3C (580mm bore, 'J' type, Supercharged, 3-cylinders, Constant pressure). This had a service rpm of 220, delivering 1,833 bhp per cylinder and was aimed at smaller sized container vessels, such as those operating in the Mediterranean for the Ellerman Line and the Weir Group (Bank Line). The engine was broadly based on the Doxford Seahorse 58G4, but the main change was that the centre crosshead lubrication and upper piston cooling water, which had both proved problematic in the earlier engine, were re-designed to be delivered by telescopic pipes with a semi non-return valve fitted. Ten of these engines were built of which seven were fitted to ships. The first of these was engine 460, fitted to the City of Plymouth, built by A&P Appledore, their yard number 121. However, Doxford Engines had little chance to carry this project through as within two years the decision was taken to cease new engine production.

Meanwhile, in 1981, British Shipbuilders renamed the now defunct Doxford Hawthorn Research Services as British Shipbuilders Engineering Technical Services

Ltd. (BSETS). Efforts were made to diversify the appeal of the research services into work on power stations and in re-engineering ships currently in service. The technical workforce was limited and BSETS had a limited life.

The final years of Doxford Engines were governed by very few meetings, with only two (BS-appointed) Directors present. F. E. Noah was the Chairman, (P. C. M. Thompson replaced him in 1985) and J. M. Blyth was the second Director. M. Day acted as the Secretary. The engine works carried out maintenance and repairs and acted as a spare parts supplier. As referred to above, the works were rebuilt a year before closure in 1984. The Annual Meeting held on 16 December 1985 resolved

216. The cover of the Auction of Doxford Engineers plant, 1986.
© Tyne & Wear Archive Service, DS.DOX/2/88/2.

that as the Company was dormant no auditors would be appointed and confirmed that Doxford Engines had not traded during the year to 31 March 1985. The last AGM of the dormant company took place on 24 June 1988.[4]

After the engine works closed a sale of equipment took place on Saturday, 26 February 1986, under the directions of Sanderson, Townsend & Gilbert, of Middlesbrough.[6] Over 200 lots came under the hammer, including huge items such as boilers, pattern drills, and borers of various types. Three unsold 58JS3C engines were sold at scrap value. John Clayson, of the Tyne and Wear Archive Service, arranged for one of these to be bought for preservation. This engine is now at the Regional Museum Store at Beamish, Co. Durham. Clayson later encouraged a group of retired engineers to restore the engine. The Doxford Engine Friends Association was inaugurated in January 2003. Its first president was Iain Doxford (1932-2006), grandson of Charles David Doxford. Hilary Doxford assumed this role after her father's death and Francis Hanson Doxford Budden, great-great grandson of William Theodore, is on the Committee. There is still interest in the many engines built by William Doxford & Sons Ltd. and its successor companies. Owen Scraggs, a past employee of Doxford, bought the goodwill of the spare parts department and ran this successfully into the twenty first century, sourcing parts for engines still in service.

1986-1989 North East Shipbuilders Ltd.

North East Shipbuilders Ltd. (NESL) was established by British Shipbuilders Corporation. It comprised the former Doxford yard at Pallion and the former A&P yard at Southwick. The Directors were appointed by Graham Day, as Chairman of BS. The Newcastle Evening Chronicle of 12 February 1986 expressed concern that many of the appointees were "favoured British Shipbuilders management", and that experienced directors from outside the group had been overlooked. Chris Finnerty, the national negotiating officer for the Engineers' and Managers' Association feared that the same bias would apply to the next tier of appointments.

Finnerty seems to have had some basis for his allegations. A BS Board Member since 1978, Dr. Peter A. Milne, became the first Chairman, with additional responsibility for shipbuilding. Milne had been the Managing Director of A&P. George H. Parker, an engineer, and the Managing Director of BS, was appointed to the same role at NESL. The background of the other appointees was similar. The Finance Director was David Armstrong, who also retained his position as a director at BS. Graham Schuil-Brewer, the Company Secretary, came from BS and had recently acted as Financial Controller of A&P. Dr. Brian Varney, A&P's Commercial Director, also joined NESL. Sunderland Shipbuilders, i.e. the Pallion yard, were represented on the Board of NESL by Brian Tennant, the Project and Production Services Director. Tennant had been a director at SSL, so was also a continuity appointment.

217. A ship in production in the Pallion Ship factory in the 1980s.
Photograph by George Taylor. From J. F. Clarke, Part II, p. 475.

The inaugural meeting of the new Board was held on 7 March 1987. Operational issues were addressed on 21 April, when the Board were concerned that BS had prevented NESL from producing a corporate plan and had instead prepared one for them. At the June meeting it was reported that both companies within the group were operating at a great loss—over £20m in the case of A&P (£6.6m greater than forecast) and nearly £23m for SSL (£8m higher). The deficits for both companies were exacerbated by additional labour costs in shipbuilding, credit problems from purchasers and faults with subcontractors' equipment. BS had ordered 925 redundancies for A&P, so provision was included in the figures. The workforce at A&P was now 1,196 and that at SSL was 1,753. (2,949 combined). This was slightly higher than had been projected. Average Government support for each NESL employee was over £9,000, but at Pallion yard this was £9,890. On top of the permanent staff figures, 116 manual workers were at SSL on short-term contracts and 84 at A&P. Overtime in the production area had been restricted to 10% to alleviate costs and a Quality Assurance Department set up.[6] However, the situation was becoming desperate, especially when the Government pulled the plug on the Govan yard without warning. Uncertainty hindered the company's ability to win orders. To address future deficits labour transfers were arranged between the two companies to keep the shipbuilding programme to time. Buildings at Southwick, Deptford and North Sands were vacated in the early autumn and demolished or sold.

The yard list numbers changed once again. Twenty six roll on roll off ferries were allocated NESL contract numbers C3001 to C3026. These ships were given the prefix 'Superflex' and, like the Stena ships, were electrically driven with multiple diesel generator sets. The odd numbered contracts were built at Pallion and those with even numbers at Southwick. The contracts were with Vegnmards Ruten AS/S, Denmark (later renamed V.R. Shipping Aps). John Landels researched these contracts when compiling the yard list for William Doxford and its successor companies. He established that the contracts were later taken over by P. Z. Trading Aps, Denmark. By 1987 more financial problems arose and some of the Superflex ships changed

218. One of the final launches from the Wear, in 1988. Courtesy of Ian Buxton.

hands whilst still under construction. Others were refused acceptance as 'not to specification' or 'late delivery'. Construction proceeded very slowly and some of the ships were left in a basic state and laid up.[7] C3015-3022 were cancelled after the two yards closed in 1988. C3023-C3026 onwards were allocated to ships to be built at Appledore Shipbuilders, but only the first in the series was completed.

George Parker resigned as Managing Director of NESL in February 1987. Dr. Milne took on his role and became Executive Chairman. By this time employee numbers had dropped further. On 22 April 1987 the figures were A&P: 913, SSL: 1,485 (2,398). This was 551 less than in 1983.

In July 1987 the decision was taken to merge the two companies and, in November 1987, W. Scott replaced Milne as Executive Chairman of NESL. His first decision was to merge staff employment: 1,636 hourly paid workers and 630 staff (2,266 in total). This was half the number employed in the two shipyards in 1974. Despite the strains of the situation, absence levels were very low, at 5% for manual workers and just 3% for staff. Manual workers undertook 17% overtime and staff 12%. Even with better health and safety rules there were still thirteen reportable accidents per month.

The NESL was in operation during most of 1988, but the writing was on the wall. The Newcastle Journal of 8 June 1988 contained an article describing a campaign to save the Wearside based company and that it had gained support from all three political parties: "not because they are anxious to prop up a 'lame duck' outfit but because they share the belief that the company has a role to play in Britain's future." NESL were then hoping to win a contract from Cuba worth around £100m, but this would only be profitable if the Government agreed to invoke the European Intervention Fund procedure. This gave a subsidy of up to 28% of the contract cost to match that available to shipbuilding companies in other countries.

The local press and community were right to be anxious. At the beginning of December 1988, the Government announced that the remaining three shipyards within NESL, at Pallion, Southwick and North Sands (already redundant) would be decommissioned. The former Doxford yard was closed just a few days later, on 7 December. The decision and closure were greeted with dismay in the area, as there had been an understanding that a private buyer was being sought. Discussions had been held in mid-1988 with a Dutch consortium, led by Alex Copson, which intended to build waste disposal vehicles in the SSL yards. It later emerged that agreement had been made some months earlier with the European Union to reduce shipbuilding in the UK, thus ensuring the viability of yards on the Continent. The Government now switched its support to the new Nissan factory at Hylton and men were given training for this and other work. Those in their forties managed to find alternative employment, though not always in the North East, but the closure was particularly hard on workers in their late fifties and early sixties. Jobs were also lost in the associated businesses in the region. As people moved away community and family ties were loosened.

On 9 December 1988 Superflex Mike (NESL C3113) left Pallion. She was handed over in April 1989 to Mercandia Liniere, Copenhagen, managed by Oer Henriksen who renamed her Mercandia II.[8] Thus ended shipbuilding and engineering from this once proud company.

Once the last merchant shipyards on the River Wear had been closed British Shipbuilders became a shell company. In 1989 the remaining assets were sold and liabilities settled.

And the aftermath for Pallion

There is still activity at Pallion, though much of the site is now bare. Many of the buildings were demolished, but Pallion Engineering Ltd. currently produce fabricated steel in the engineering shops. Other businesses are using the office and workshop areas. The covered building dock has been used for demolition of some ships. This photograph was taken from the opposite bank of the Wear, just below the Queen Alexandra Bridge. At North Sands the Sunderland Corporation constructed new buildings for the University and the National Glass Museum and housing developments have sprung up at the mouth of the Wear. However, the Corporation have put an embargo on development of the southern bank of the Wear, including the Pallion site, as their intention is to drive a dual-carriageway through the land, giving easy access for heavy goods vehicles to Sunderland Docks, with the hope of their revival.

219. The Doxford Ship Factory, taken from below Queen Alexandra Bridge, March 2019.
Photograph by Patricia Richardson.

The photograph here shows the former ship factory on the site of the old transporting gantries, surrounded by ancillary buildings. The sloping nature of the site is still apparent from the height of the houses on the horizon.

220. Photograph c. 2002, by Hilary Doxford,
great-grand-daughter of Charles David Doxford

Since the early 1990s, when we began our researches into the Doxford family history, Michael and I have observed the iconic West Entrance Gate at Pallion Shipyard become more and more decrepit. This photograph, taken by Hilary Doxford in 2002 looks sad enough, though the building still retains curtains in the upper rooms, but the one below shows the aftermath of a fire that broke out in

257

221. The West Gate to Pallion Shipyard 18 September 2018. Nature is returning, as the few remaining buildings in the vicinity have been demolished. Photograph by Patricia Richardson.

2017. The gatehouse became a dangerous shell, with the original brickwork covered in decaying stucco. At the time of writing it was proposed to save just the gates and their arches. The plan was for them to be dismantled and re-erected nearby, next to a planned dual carriageway that will run from the new Northern Spire Bridge to the City centre. However, there was still opposition to the demolition of the last building standing from this great industry of the River Wear.

So ended 150 years of outstanding shipbuilding and marine engineering by William Doxford and Sons on the River Wear, from hesitant beginnings to one of the largest concerns in the British marine industry. As with so much of British industry it was

222. View across Pallion Shipyard towards Queen Alexandra Bridge. Photograph by Patricia Richardson, 18 September 2018.

taken over by large conglomerates, nationalised when the conglomerates proved unable to run it and then sacrificed to suit the convenience of government. Proper support for the sections of the shipbuilding industry that might have had a future on the global stage, such as Doxford engines, could have made use of the expertise built up on the Wear and still be prospering. Instead there is hardly a visible trace in Sunderland of the industry that led the world for many years from the smallest and physically most unlikely of rivers. The only visible remains left in the city is the old Austin's dry dock which is now home to a few small dinghies.

The saving of the last Doxford engine to the Tyne and Wear Museum's regional store at Beamish has happened by the personal endeavour of a few individuals and largely in spite of those organisations which might have been expected to save and cherish the Wear's spectacular industrial heritage. The saving of the single cylinder Doxford test engine from the scrapyard was also a last minute effort by a few individuals. It is currently at the Anson Engine Museum, as yet not re-assembled. The only other Doxford engine in existence is on the oil well drilling ship Aban Ice, working in the Indian Ocean, west of Mumbai. The ship is mostly stationary so her engine has lasted but she could be scrapped at any time, ending her days driven up onto an Indian shoreline for dismantling.

Notes on the Chapters

Chapter One: The Doxford Family of Northumberland

1. Corder's substantial manuscript books are held by the Tyne and Wear Archives. I studied them during my researches in the 1990s and have found them to be generally accurate, but with this one exception.
2. Vol. 1, p 262. Sir Nicolas was a respected historian, who collated the letters written by Horatio Nelson and published them in eight volumes.
3. Duke of Northumberland MSS.
4. Family Search.Org website.
5. Find a Grave Index, through Ancestry.co.uk.
6. Corder notes.
7. 1881 Census.
8. University of Leicester project on local directories: Ward's 1850, Hagar's 1851, Census info.
9. The development of this area in the 1850s and 1860s is described in Chapter 2.
10. Sunderland Daily Echo and Shipping Gazette announcement. All provincial newspaper reports come from the British Newspaper Archive online.
11. Short obituary in the Shields Daily Gazette, 9 Jan 1871 and 1866 report on the Building Society.
12. Electoral and burial records, through Ancestry.co.uk.
13. 1841 Census.
14. Corder, p 106, B3.
15. Ward's Directory 1850, pp 288, 341 and 352.
16. Durham Probate Records, DPRI/1/1855/D27.

Chapter Two: 1812-1882: William Doxford of Pallion

1. The 1796 bridge was the second to be built after Ironbridge in Staffordshire. It was reconstructed in 1857 by Robert Stephenson, removing the bow. The current Wear Bridge was built in 1929.
2. Sunderland Daily Echo, 6 Apr 1903.
3. Newspaper report in Yorkshire Post and Leeds Intelligencer, 24 Dec 1925.
4. From 'Ritsons' Branch Line' by Malcolm Cooper. Introduction.
5. These comprehensive lists are held at the World Ship Society's library at the Historic Dockyard, Chatham , Kent. Sheets can be purchased from the Society.
6. Darlington Northern Echo, 27 Dec 1882. Unfortunately, these figures are hard to read, but the addition for the gross registered tonnage seems faulty at 212,491, and also that for the H. P. at 19,522. George Almond's manuscript treatise on William Doxford & Sons, held by the Sunderland Antiquarian Society. He studied the originals and gives figures for grt on p 21-22: Total Wear grt: 212,464, Doxford grt: 22,231.
7. A schooner has the main driving sails rigged up the two masts, without yards. This was a popular rig for American built ships.
8. Lloyd's Register. There are two distinct businesses with regard to Lloyd's of London. Lloyd's Register began in 1760, when the Society for the Registry of Shipping was set up by customers of Edward Lloyd's Coffee House in Lombard Street, with the aim of giving merchants and insurance underwriters information on the quality of their vessels. It was the first of its kind in the world. Lloyd's underwriting was already in operation by the 1730s, as its genesis was

at the end of the 17th century.

9.   Clarke, Building Ships on the North East Coast, Part 1 (of 2).
10. Meaning a petty trader or merchant.
11. Census records.
12. Newcastle Courant, 29 Dec 1841.
13. London Gazette, p 3364. From its website.
14. Manuscript agreement.
15. Howick Street, Monkwearmouth was a terrace built in 1811 (it had this date on its street sign). It was demolished in the late 1950s, so spanned the boom years of Sunderland shipbuilding.
16. Clarke, Part 1, p 105.
17. www.searlecanada.org.
18. Pallion Hall was an early 19th century property that replaced an earlier building on the site. Joseph Swan, the inventor of the electric light bulb, was born there in 1829. Webster died in 1894, and his widow, the sister of Sir James Laing, in 1899. The Hall was demolished in 1901. This was to be the fate of a number of substantial Sunderland properties in the first three decades of the 20th century.
19. Corder, Commercial Volume, p 203.
20. Oswald also built rolling mills at Castletown, on the north bank of the Wear, to produce iron for his shipyard. He created a new village for his workers, which was abandoned when the mill failed, but later rebuilt. Oswald was declared bankrupt in 1870, and Short Bros took over his yard. (Where Ships are Born, p 48).
21. Pallion Station opened as a branch line on 1 June 1853. It stood firstly in open land, but housing quickly spread around it. It closed to passengers on 4 May 1964 and to freight a year later.
22. Clarke, Part 1, p 92.
23. Sturgess, R. W., ed., The Great Age of Industry in the North East: Chap 4, Shipbuilding on the River Wear 1780-1870, p 83.
24. Sturgess, p 94.
25. www.crimeanwar-veteranswa.com/ships/belgravia/.
26. The Perth Gazette of 6 Jul 1866 states that the doctor on board was on his third voyage in her.
27. The last convict ship, the Hougoumont, arrived in Western Australia on 10 Jan 1868. c. 164,000 convicts were transported to the Australian colonies between 1788 and 1868 in 806 ships. I believe that only one of these was built by Doxford, as William only restarted at Pallion in 1857.
28. With thanks to Diane Oldman, who also provided me with a short biography of Samuel Speed.
29. Sturgess, p 93.
30. Newcastle Courier, 27 Aug 1864.
31. A roughly squared timber beam. Oxford English Dictionary.
32. Reported in a number of provincial newspapers.

Chapter Three: 1882-1900: Three Doxford brothers develop Turret Ships

1.   Nominal horsepower. This bore little relationship to the power actually generated, according to Dr. Ian Buxton.
2.   Sunderland, River Town and People, pp 33-44 section on Shipbuilding by J. F. Clarke.
3.   From The Ship, the Life and death of the Merchant Sailing Ship, Basil Greenwood, p 32.
4.   Sunderland, J. F. Clarke, p 41.
5.   www.flotilla-australia.com.
6.   The Mamari was sold to the Houston Line in 1903 and renamed Hesione. She was captured by the German U-41 and sunk by gunfire on 23 Sep 1915, 86 miles off Fastnet, Ireland.
7.   Grace's Guide.

by the German U-41 and sunk by gunfire on 23 Sep 1915, 86 miles off Fastnet, Ireland.

8. www.plimsoll.org and www.wrecksite.eu.
9. DS.DOX/1/5/1, p 2. First meeting of Directors, 19 Jan 1891. The Doxford file (DS.DOX) is held at Tyne & Wear Archives Service, Newcastle upon Tyne.
10. DS.DOX/1/5/1, p 17, minutes of meeting of 2 Mar 1891.
11. Sydney Morning Herald, 18 May 1891, Trove website.
12. Charles W. Wetmore was a business associate of MacDougall.
13. DS.DOX/2/5/2. Notebooks of W. T. Doxford. 1891 onwards.
14. McIlwraith, McEacharn & Co., shipping agents, coal bunkerers, etc. were founded in Scotland in 1875, by Andrew McIlwraith and Malcolm McEacharn. They opened an office in Melbourne in 1888 to develop their interests in the local coal industry. Sir Malcolm McEacharn became a Federal Member of the House of Representatives. His brother, John McIlwraith (1828-1902) was his partner. R. P. Doxford's daughter married Christopher McIlwraith.
15. DS.DOX/1/5/1, p 65. Directors' Minutes of 15 Feb 1892.
16. Ibid. Minutes of 25 Apr 1893.
17. Ibid. p 113, Minutes of Jan 1895.
18. DS.DOX/2/26/1. Patent applications.
19. The hull cost £16,250, builder's margin: £1,000 and royalty: £1,000, plus the cost of machinery. The ship was sold for £26,000. Clarke, Part 1, p 199, including footnote.
20. Clan MacDonald was the second of this name. The first was built in 1883, but sold in 1897 to the Dene Steamship Co., Newcastle-upon-Tyne and renamed Briardene. Clan MacDonald II was sold in 1922 to Hokoyu Kisen Kabushiki Kaisa, Japan and renamed Hokuyo Maru. A third Clan Macdonald was built in 1928.
21. DS.DOX/1/4/1, p 37.
22. Ibid. p 38. Extraordinary General Meeting held on 8 May 1899.
23. Ibid. pp 39-44. Annual Meeting held at Pallion on 26 Mar 1900.

Chapter Four: The early 20th Century

1. Table in Where Ships Are Born, p 53. I have not included the whole table as this omits Bartrams, so it may not be a complete record.
2. This was the family concern run by A. O. Hedley's father.
3. Sunderland Daily Echo, 11 Sep 1901 and other newspapers the following days.
4. The description is taken from 'The Birthplace of the Turret', in The Syren and Shipping, 3 Jan 1906.
5. DS.DOX/2/54/7, wages account for 28 Dec 1903.
6. The Blue Riband of the Atlantic was a similar unofficial accolade given to the single hull passenger ship that could cross the Atlantic in the westward direction in the shortest time, compared to its rivals. This was also awarded from the Edwardian period, and reached its most competitive period in the 1930s.
7. The Syren & Shipping, 3 Jan 1906, p 72, the Shipping Returns for 1905. Harland & Wolf built 9 much larger ships, with an average 9,476 grt (total 85,287 grt). Swan Hunter built 22 ships, but with an average 3,760 grt, (total 82,727 grt).
8. The Times report of 13 Mar 1908.
9. Gray & Lingwood, Doxford Turret Ships and Ship's Nostalgia website. Pat Kennedy's description on the website reads: "To maintain the fiction that the space above the original upper deck was still 'open', the shelter deck spaces were interconnected by openings and a small 'tonnage hatch' at the after end of the ship led to the shelter deck space. The tonnage hatch could not be permanently or substantially covered. This led to a concern for the safety of these vessels. The tonnage mark was introduced to encourage shipowners to close the tonnage openings.

This method was not popular with port and other authorities which derived their revenue based on the ship's tonnage."

10. Programme of the Visit of their Majesties, the King and Queen to the North-East Coast Shipbuilding and Engineering Works (The Wear), 15 Jun 1917. Courtesy of Francis Hanson Doxford Budden.
11. A battalion was commanded by a Lieutenant-Colonel and consisted of between 300-800 men. This demonstrates the size of the Doxford workforce, in that it continued to produce so many ships, both cargo and naval, despite losing volunteers to the conflict.
12. From 'Queen Mary, the Official Biography', J. Pope-Hennesy, 1955, p 505.

Chapter Five: Sir William Theodore Doxford (1841-1916)

1. NECIES Transactions are held at the Marine Technology Special Collection, Newcastle University. Their papers are at the Tyne & Wear Archives Service.
2. Forces War Records online.
3. From their website: hedleyssolicitors.co.uk.
4. Where Ships Are Born, p 47, Ancestry.co.uk and Wikipedia.
5. England and Wales National Probate Calendar (Wills & Administrations), 1858-1966.
6. 1911 census. This census gives the number of rooms in each dwelling.
7. Grindon Hall and grounds are described in Sir Theodore's will, lodged at Durham Probate Office.
8. The Times of 21 Aug 1916.
9. Obituary in the Transactions of the NECIES, Vol. 54, pp D233-4.
10. Commander Stack was a grandson of Rt. Rev. Charles Maurice Stack (1825-1914), Anglican Bishop of Clogher, Co. Donegal, Ireland. He served as acting Captain, R.N. during WWII.
11. Papers at National Archives, Kew.
12. https//grindonhall.org.uk.
13. Yorkshire Post, 5 Aug 1949.
14. Sunderland Daily Echo, 23 Feb 1954.

Chapter Six: Alfred Doxford (1842-1895)

1. Sunderland Daily Echo, 20 Oct 1884.
2. Ibid., 23 Oct 1888, the contact for responding to the advertisement was A. O. Hedley.
3. 1911 census shows the family living in a six roomed house at 72 Ormonde Street, Sunderland. He is noted in the wage books DS.DOX/2/54/7 etc. as a Doxford 'official', on £1 5s 10d per week.
4. 1901 Census record. The family were still in Scotland at the time of the 1891 census, but Mrs. Dalrymple died at Sunderland in July 1899.
5. Their parents' home at no. 38 is noted as empty at this time.
6. Oral information from Jack Jordan.

Chapter Seven: Robert Pile Doxford (1851-1932)

1. Sunderland Daily Echo, 9 Aug 1892.
2. Transactions of the Silksworth Historical Society, 1905.
3. From the Victoria County History on the development of Ashbrooke, Sunderland.
4. Sunderland Daily Echo, 5 Dec 1902.
5. Kelly's Directory for Hertfordshire, 1914, p 313.
6. Ward's Directory of Northumberland, 1916, p 448. This gives Burletson's residence as Silksworth Hall.

7. Ship's passenger list for Otranto, departure 8 Nov 1930.
8. This is the address given in the Indenture following the sale of William Doxford & Sons in 1919 to the Sperling Group The house was later extended and renamed Fyning Hill.
9. Kelly's Directory, 1926 and 1929.
10. Supplement to the London Gazette, Friday, 20 Nov 1953. This gives the names of all who took part and the route taken during the procession. Gold Stick and Silver Stick are honorary positions as guardians to the monarch. They take part in ceremonials such as a coronation and state opening of parliament. The assistant to Silver Stick (who holds the rank of Colonel) is known as the adjutant.
11. For the history of Broomleaf kennels visit www.solidcolourcockers.co.uk/.
12. US subscription website: www.fold3.com.

Chapter Eight: Charles David Doxford (1856-1935)

1. C. D. Doxford's obituary states that he was educated at Durham, but he is not included in their alumni. It was his son, also named Charles, who went to Durham School (in 1903).
2. Sunderland Council Planning application 80/1725.
3. The Motor Ship, Feb 1935, p 383.
4. The Tatler, Wednesday, 25 Dec 1918, p 32, British Newspapers Online.
5. Burdon House still stands. It is used as offices, but a home is also on the premises.

Chapter Nine: The Doxford Opposed Piston Marine Oil Engine

1. Clarke, Part 2, pp 95-105.
2. Available through the Doxford Engine Friends Association.
3. Scandinavian shipbuilders were the first to explore this fuel for marine engines.
4. Clarke, Part 2, note on p 85.
5. DS.DOX/2/54/7.
6. Sir John Knott was elected a Member of Parliament for Sunderland in 1910. He was created a baronet in 1917.
7. Clarke, Part 2, p 95.
8. Held at Tyne and Wear Archives Service, Newcastle.
9. Whitakers Red Book, 1914.
10. DS.DOX/1/5/3, Meeting of Board of Directors of 21 Feb 1926 recorded the termination of licences and assignment of patents.
11. DS.DOX/2/26/23, Patent application no. 5330/16 for 'Improvements in or relating to fuel-injection devices for internal combustion engines' is held by Tyne and Wear Archives.
12. The engine categories are: L: Long Stroke, LB: Long Balanced and SB: Short Balanced, LBD: Long Balanced with Diaphragm, 'P' and 'J': engines designed by Percy Jackson. T: Turbo-charged, S: Super-charged, C: Constant Pressure, G: Geared. The number before the letter refers to the bore in millimetres (but without a zero), the number after the letter/s refers to the number of cylinders. Thus: 76LBD6S means 760mm bore, Long, Balanced with a Diaphragm, six cylinders, supercharged.
13. Indicated horse power.
14. Tom Scott, member of the Doxford Engine Friends Association.
15. From the website www.sunderlandships.com.
16. Jordan and Cartridge, Notable Points in the Design History of the Doxford Opposed Piston Engine, p 63.
17. World Ship Society List and The Ships' List, Furness Withy's Fleet.

18. The Motor Ship, 1971, '60 years of the Doxford Opposed Piston Engine'.
19. DS.DOX/2/26/25-28.
20. DS.DOX/2/26/30-37.
21. Held at Tyne and Wear Archives Service.

Chapter Ten: 1918-1923: The Sale of William Doxford & Sons Ltd.

1. Press notice in Yorkshire Post, 19 Nov 1915, p 10.
2. This ship was ordered as HMS Whitby, but was renamed in error. This was not corrected, and she carried out her service under the name HMS Whitley. She served into WWII, and was badly damaged by a German dive bomber. She was destroyed by friendly gunfire to prevent her falling into enemy hands.
3. I am assuming that this was for both the Shipyard, Engine Works and Management.
4. DS.DOX/1/5/2.
5. Stephanie Diaper, 'Capitalism in a Mature Economy', Essay on the Sperling Combine, p 76. She consulted the Bank of England supervision department record card at the Guildhall Library Ms 20,120 and Ms.21, 799 and noted the correspondence of E. C. Grenfell.
6. Diaper, p 75. Plus birth & death dates researched on Ancestry.co.uk and elsewhere.
7. With Messrs. Montgomerie and Workman. Founded in 1849, they were incorporated in 1913. They also acted as agents for the Ellerman shipping line, whose papers (1888-1950) are held at Glasgow University. Ref: GB 248 UGD 131/7.
8. Diaper, p 74.
9. The merchant bank that later became Kleinwort Benson traded under this name from 1888.
10. Hatry set up Amalgamated Industrials to acquire three small Clyde shipyards and other companies during WWI. He ceded control to John Slater in 1920, but remained an advisor. The company overextended and became insolvent in 1929. Hatry later spent a period in prison for fraud.
11. There was an earlier SS Peruviana, built in 1909, also owned by Furness Withy, which they sold to the Russian Government in 1922.
12. Northumberland SBC yard list 4D, World Ship Society.
13. London Metropolitan Archives: CLC/B/140/KS04/03/18/007. Kleinwort papers covering the purchase of the NSBC 1917-1924.
14. Minutes of 10 Jan 1919, pp 426-7. The pages contain the full list of names and number of shares transferred.
15. DS.DOX 1/16/1 includes a copy of the Indenture dated 10 January whereby the members of the Doxford family agreed to sell their shares, but retain certain rights. A further copy of extracts from the Agreement, endorsed 13 Nov 1922, and the Indenture dated 1 May 1919, confirm the names of all the original shareholders as being eligible for these payments.
16. London Metropolitan Archives: CLC/B/140/KS04/03/18/007. Kleinwort papers.
17. Esplen's obituary in The Times, 8 Feb 1930.
18. James Lambe Yeames (1873-1960) was born in Russia to a British father and Russian mother. As a child, he modelled the young Charles II for the painting 'When did you last see your father' by the artist William Frederick Yeames, who was his uncle. He trained at University College, London, became a member of the Institution of Mechanical Engineers in 1899. He was with Harland and Wolff, Belfast after which he spent some time in the Argentine. Returning to Belfast, he married in 1901. In later life, he returned to Northern Ireland, where he died. He and Keller appear to have clashed.
19. Murphy, note 27, Stock Exchange Official Intelligence 1920.
20. DS.DOX 1/16/1.
21. Reported in the Minutes of 16 Oct 1919.

22. CLC/B/140/KS04/03/18/007 Kleinwort papers held at the London Metropolitan Archives. Correspondence re the purchase of the NSBC, including the prospectus, and marked 'For Private Circulation Only'.
23. Their mother was Sofie Charlotte Kleinwort, sister of the founder of the bank.
24. Wake: Kleinwort Benson: the History of two families in Banking, p 238.
25. DS.DOX/1/5/2, pp 473-474.
26. Ibid. pp 517-19 – its ownership is revealed in the Minute of the new Board of 9 April 1924.

Chapter Eleven: 1923-1939: The Company survives two Depressions

1. The following year, in November 1925, Sir Edward Mackay Edgar was declared bankrupt through the failure of the British Controlled Oilfields Ltd., of which he was the Chairman. At this point he resigned all positions that he held at Messrs. Sperling & Co. It was a terrible year for him, as in July his only son was killed in a car accident.
2. Transactions of the Institution of Naval Architects, Vol. 81, 1939, pp 347-8 and portrait.
3. DS.DOX/1/5/3. Minutes of the Board of Directors.
4. Ibid. pp 3-4. Minutes of meeting held on 4 Apr 1924.
5. Ibid. p 5. Minutes of the Meeting of Directors 9 Apr 1924.
6. Ibid. pp 22-44. Minutes of Meeting of Directors of 28 Jan 1925.
7. DS.DOX/1/8 contains the Directors' annual reports and accounts.
8. Herbert Pike Pease (1867-1949) was Unionist MP for Darlington from 1898-1923, after which he was elevated to the peerage. His son, the second Baron died unmarried in 1994.
9. DS.DOX/1/5/3, p 48, Meeting of the Board of Directors 8 Nov 1926 gives details of engine contracts with Workman, Clark and with Swan Hunter & Wigham Richardson.
10. Ibid. pp 79-80, 6 Sep 1928. Page 83 records the transfer of the shares to Horace George Dumford and James William Mitchell, as nominees of the Commissioners of Inland Revenue.
11. DS.DOX/1/5/3, Minutes of Directors' Meeting, 12 Sep 1927, p 63.
12. Grace's guide.
13. TNA BT31/32792/218009. Plus research by Stephanie Diaper, note 72 on p 94.
14. The Times, 18 Nov 1945, p 9. Announcement of closure.
15. Although this dividend seems high, it was paid on the £1 nominal amount of the shares. The yield was therefore less than 5%.

Chapter Twelve: The Pallion Yard in the Interwar period.

1. Clarke, Part 2, p 296.
2. His wife, Wilhemine Vera, was Theodore and Margaret Doxford's youngest daughter.
3. DS.DOX/2/9/1. Letters from Robert Haswell to Charles Doxford dated 19 Sep 1924 and 22 Oct 1924.
4. Clarke, Part 2, pp 499-500.
5. Wikipedia, with source: William Miller Jr. (2001). Picture History of British Ocean Liners 1900 to the Present. Mineola, NY: Dover Publications, p 49. Also numerous press reports between 1931 and 1933.
6. From Shipbuilding Conference records held at the Marine Technology Special Collection, Newcastle University.
7. The unescorted MV Cingalese Prince was torpedoed and sunk on 20 Sep 1941 off St Paul Rocks, West Indies, with the loss of her captain, 48 crew members and 8 gunners. The remaining 15 crew and 3 gunners were rescued after 12 days by a Spanish merchant ship, and landed at St. Vincent, Cape Verde Islands.
8. DS.DOX/1/5/3, pp 54-5. Directors Meeting 4 Apr 1927.

9. Clarke, Part 2, pp 240-1.
10. www.marinerslist.com: Essex Line ships.
11. 1939 Register for Sunderland.
12. Information from a table given in the Sunderland Daily Echo, in an article on Wear shipyards published 27 Dec 1938.
13. Notes on contract details of engines supplied to other shipbuilders, compiled by Ian Rutherford, Doxford Engine Friends Association.
14. From '60 years of Doxford Opposed Piston Engine Development', T.A. Greenwell, The Motor Ship, 1971, p 49.
15. From the website 'Ships Nostalgia', the contributor's father, William Redvers Forster (1900-1975), was 2nd Engineer, later promoted to 'Chief'.
16. D. C. E. Burrell, 'Scrap and Build', p 27.
17. Note from Dr. Ian Buxton.
18. Report of 46th AGM, for year ending 30 June 1938. The Times, 31 Oct. 1938.
19. Clarke, Part 2, p 239.
20. Admiralty orders were not included in the figures, and these ships were large and complicated. (Dr. Ian Buxton)

Chapter Thirteen: 1939-1945: The Second World War

1. www.searlecanada.org.
2. John Botwright served with Doxford for over 30 years, from 1920 to 1951. He became Manager of the Engine Works in 1942, when W. H. Purdie succeeded Keller as Director.
3. Another long serving employee of Doxford. Harry Jeans joined in 1895 on a wage of 4 shillings per week. He retired from his post as Personnel Manager in July 1948.
4. www.searlecanada.org.
5. Extracted from W. H. Purdie's obituary in the Transactions of the NECIES.
6. Clarke, Part 2, p 323. This was a joint panel of employment exchange, trade union and employers' representatives that examined nine separate trades, but excluded shipwrights.
7. DS.DOX/1/4/2.
8. Ibid.

Chapter Fourteen: 1945-1961: Post war boom and bust

1. Note from Dr. Ian Buxton.
2. Sunderland Daily Echo, 15 Mar 1946, p 4 and illustration p 8.
3. The name of this company, founded in 1908 to exploit the oil reserves in Iran, was firstly the Anglo-Persian Oil Company. The name changed to the Anglo-Iranian Oil Company, then to British Tankers and finally to British Petroleum Ltd. in 1954.
4. www.sunderlandships.com. Wear Built Ships.
5. Information from the Texaco Overseas Tankship Association.
6. Sunderland Daily Echo report on the inquest, 15 Dec 1951.
7. Stephenson, Clement, 'A Shipyard re-organization for welded pre-fabricated construction.' Presented to the North Eastern (Tyneside) Branch of the Institution of Welding, 17 Apr 1952. Subsequently published in the Transactions of the Institution of Welding.
8. DS/DOX/1/5/4, p 177.
9. Figures given in The Journal of Commerce, 'British Shipbuilding Accepts a Challenge', 25 Sep 1959.
10. DS.DOX/1/5/4, p 202.
11. Information on subsequent career from www.sunderlandships.com.

12. From press reports. His appointment to the Board of Trade was in 1949.
13. Directive of the Main Board attached to the minutes of the Shipbuilding subsidiary Directors' Meeting of 18 Sep 1956. Held at the Marine Technology Special Collection, Newcastle University.
14. Verbal anecdote from Jack Jordan.
15. Frontispiece of 'Where Ships are Born'.
16. The Times report of 9 Oct 1958 detailing his expected statement of 30 October.
17. Biographical notes from Clarke, Part 2, p 405.
18. Sunderland Daily Echo, 20 Jan 1954, p 2.
19. Transactions of the Institute of Marine Engineering, Feb. 1960.
20. Jordan & Cartridge, pp 161-4.
21. Short report of the start of testing of this engine in Shipbuilding & Shipping Record, 16 Dec 1954.
22. www.clydeships.co.uk.
23. The Motor Ship, March 1961, pp 544-48, contains a pull-out plan of ship and plan of the engine room.
24. Having served its purpose, the engine was presented to the South Shields Marine College in 1966. The Anson Engine Museum at Poynton, Cheshire acquired the engine in 2006 and intend to restore it to working order, but at the time of writing this work has only just begun.
25. DS.DOX/1/5/4, p 30.
26. The Montana remained with her first owners for only two years. She was sold to a Bulgarian company in 1963, and renamed Dunav. Having changed ownership again, she was broken up in 1987.
27. Newcastle Journal, 21 Dec 1961.
28. The Motor Ship, Jul 1961, pp 188-192.
29. NECIES 072:0327-360. The Doxford [2-stroke opposed-piston diesel] engine: progress and development [inc. boiler fuels & supercharging].By A. Storey ([William Doxford & Sons Ltd]). Read to the Institution on 23 Mar 1956.
30. DS.DOX/1/5/4, p 215. The meeting of the Board of Directors held on 12 Mar 1958.
31. DS.DOX/1/5/4, Board Minutes.
32. As a reminder, they were unrelated to the Thompson family of shipbuilders of Sunderland.
33. Newcastle Journal, 15/07/1970

Chapter Fifteen: 1961-1978: Changes in Structure and New Engines

1. Transactions of the NECIES, paper written 10 Feb 1961.
2. Whitstable Times & Herne Bay Herald, 10 Jan 1948.
3. PAMETRADA was created in 1944 as a research and development organisation through the collaboration of 19 shipbuilding and marine engineering companies. In 1965 it provided the turbine designs for QEII. It merged into the British Shipbuilding Research Association and was closed down in 1967.
4. DS.DOX/1/5/6, p 295. Confirmed in the DSSE Board minutes of 13 Apr1966. And the second meeting held that day, p 296.
5. Newcastle Evening Chronicle, 21 Apr 1966, p 1. The Times, 22 Apr 1966, p 18, and others.
6. The Toronto City was completed within a month and sailed under the Bibby Line until 1971, when she was sold to the Bristol City Line. In 1974 she was sold once more to Brandts Ltd. and renamed Ilkon Polly.
7. Clarke, Part 2, note on p 445.
8. DSSE Board Minutes 1967.
9. The Motor Ship March 1962. Ihp, or indicated horse power, was an ideal figure. The bhp (brake

horse power) would have been lower, but the Motor Ship was there to promote British engine production (Dr. Buxton's comment).

10. Later reprinted in the Transactions of NECIES 1966.

11. Harold Wilson's government fell in July that year, and Edward Heath then led a Conservative administration.

12. Sadly, Doxford Engineers struggled to supply these on time, due to a lack of manpower.

13. Newcastle Journal, 25 Nov 1965, report by D. B. Stables, General Manager, Doxford Engines.

14. Ken Dawson is a member of the World Ship Society and a volunteer at their library at the Historic Dockyard at Chatham.

15. DS.DOX/6/4/177 and 180. Papers, 'The Doxford Slow Speed Engine' and 'Progress on the Development of the Doxford Oil Engine', 1978 and 1979.

16. These are at Tyne and Wear Archives Service, under DS.DOX.

17. www.sunderlandships.com.

18. Newcastle Journal, 27 Jul 1971.

19. The article also stated that Court Line were capitalised at £25m against Doxford & Sunderland at £6m.

20. Newcastle Journal, 14 Jul 1972.

21. Court Line redesigned the shipyard in 1970, at great cost. However, Appledore survived the upheavals of the late 20th century, partly through supplying the Ministry of Defence. The final owners were Babcock International. It finally closed in March 2019, as this history was being written.

22. DS.DOX/1/5/5. Minutes of Meeting of the Directors of Doxford & Sunderland, held on 30 Nov 1972.

23. Newcastle Journal, 19 Nov 1972, p 13.

24. Notes from Wikipedia and from Venus's obituary in the Independent, 2 Nov 1992.

25. Jordan & Cartridge, p 289.

26. Ibid. p 290.

27. The Minutes of the Directors' Meetings and its Annual Reports (16 Jun 1970-20 Jan 1978) are held at the Marine Technology Special Collection, Newcastle University. Ref: 03578/4.

28. Butler wrote 'Industrial application of the Doxford Seahorse engine' in 1972 for the Diesel Engineers and Users Association.

29. Information from Tom Scott.

Chapter Sixteen: The Final Years

1. Newcastle Journal, 21 Jun 1984.

2. The Times, 18 Mar 1980, p 17.

3. After the new covered yard was opened, yard numbers recommenced at 1 (Cedarbank).

4. Minutes of Doxford Engines 1983-1988, held at the Marine Technology Special Collection, Newcastle University.

5. DS.DOX/2/88/2.

6. DS.NES/1/1. Board Minutes of North East Shipbuilders Ltd. from 7 Mar 1986 to 9 Jul 1990.

7. Notes written by John Landels beneath WSS yard list 256 (Doxford and successors).

8. The Superflex numbers were C3001-3014. Odd numbers were built at Pallion and even at Southwick.

Bibliography

Books

Armitage, A., *Shipbuilding at Belfast: Workman, Clark and Company, 1880-1935*,
    From Wheelhouse to Counting House, ed. L.R. Fischer, Liverpool University Press, 1992

Brett, Alan, *On the Banks of the Wear,* Black Cat Publications, Roker, Sunderland, 2018

Burrell, D.C.E., *Scrap and Build,* World Ship Society, 1983

Cameron, K., *English Place Names,* William Clowes, London, 1961-1977

Clarke, J.F., *Building Ships on the North East Coast, A Labour of Love, Risk and Pain, Parts 1*
    (1640-1914) and 2 (1914-present), Bewick Press, 1997

Cooper, M., *Ritsons' Branch Line,* World Ship Society, 2002

Dougan, D.J., *The History of North East Shipbuilding,* George Allan & Unwin Ltd., 1968

Fletcher, R.A., *Steam ships and their Story,* 1910 (full text online at archive.org)

Fordyce, W., *The History and Antiquities of the County Palatine of Durham, 2 vols,* Fullerton, 1857

Gray, L. and Lingwood, J., *The Doxford Turret Ships,* World Ship Society, 1975

Greenhill, B., *The Ship: The Life and Death of the Merchant Sailing Ship. 1815-1965,* Her
    Majesty's Stationery Office, London, 1980

Hopkins, C.H.G., *Pallion 1874-1954, church and people in a shipyard parish,* Sunderland, 1954 Keys, R.E.,
    Dictionary of Tyne Sailing Ships, A Record of Merchant Sailing Ships Owned,
    Registered and Built in the Port of Tyne from 1830 to 1930, 1998

Lingwood, J., *SD 14, The Great British Shipbuilding Success Story,* World Ship Society, 1976

Middlemiss, N.L., *British Shipbuilding Yards, Volume 1, North-East Coast,* Shield Publications, 1993

Milburn, G.E. and Miller, S.T., ed., *Sunderland, River, Town and People, A history from the 1780s,*
    Sunderland Borough Council, 1988

Nicolas, N.H., *The Synopsis of the Peerage of England,* London, 1831 (Google Books)

Parker, G.H., *Astern Business: 75 Years of U.K. Shipbuilding,* World Ship Society, 1996

Rain, J., ed. Clay, Milburn and Miller, *An Eye Plan of Sunderland and Bishopwearmouth 1785-1790,*
    Frank Graham, Newcastle, 1984

Reaney, P.H., *The Origin of English Surnames,* Routledge and Kegan Paul, London, 1967

Slaven, A. and Murphy, H., ed., *Crossing the Bar: An Oral History of the British Shipbuilding, Ship*
    repairing and Marine Engine Building in the age of decline 1956-1990.
    From Research in Maritime History, No. 51, St. John's, Newfoundland, 2013

Smith, J.W, and Holden, T.S., *Where Ships are Born,* Sunderland, 1947

Sturgess, R.W. ed., *The Great Age of Industry in the North East, (Chapter 4: Shipbuilding on*
    the River Wear, 1780-1870, J.F. Clarke), Durham County Local History Society, 1981

Van Helton, J.J. and Cassis, Y. ed., *Capitalism in a Mature Economy, Financial Institutions: Capital Export and*
    British Industry, 1870-1939, New Business History Series, Elgar Publishing, 1990

Wake, J., Kleinwort Benson: *The History of Two Families in Banking,* Oxford University Press, 1997

Booklets, Academic Papers and Pamphlets

Doxford publicity, *The Birthplace of the Turret Ship,* Sunderland, 1906

Doxford publicity, *William Doxford & Sons: Shipbuilder and Engineers,* Sunderland, 1921 and later
    editions

Franks, M.L. and Paton, D.S., *Modern Developments with Special Reference to Pallion Ship Factory*
    Project, Paper to NECIES, 11 December 1978

Greenwell, T.A., *60 years of Doxford Opposed-Piston Engine Development,* Motor Ship, 1970, pp 47-50

Ker Wilson, W., *The balancing of oil engines,* 1929

Murphy, Prof. H., University of Glasgow, *An anatomy of speculative failure: Wm. Doxford & Sons Ltd., Sunderland, and the Northumberland Shipbuilding Company of Howdon on Tyne, 1919-1945*, The Mariners Mirror, Society for Nautical Research, 2018

Roberts, N.A., *The Turret Deck Vessel,* Norwegian Yearbook of Maritime History, 1966

Stephenson, Clement, *A Shipyard Re-Organization for Welded Pre-fabricated Construction,* paper read to the North Eastern (Tyneside) Branch of the Institute of Welding, 17 April 1952. Published in the Transactions of the Institute of Welding, August 1952, p 101

Stephenson, Clement, *The Heavy Lift Vessel "Adventurer",* NECIES, 1961

Magazines and periodicals

Journal of Commerce, *British Shipbuilding Accepts a Challenge,* article on Doxford titled Pioneers in New Forms of Merchant Ships, 25 September 1959

Ships in Focus

Ships Monthly

Syren and Shipping, early 20th century, long articles, with illustrations on Doxford, 3 January 1906 and 2 January 1929

The Motor Ship journal, early 20th century to present day

The Shipbuilder, early-mid 20th century

Web sources (some of them)

Ancestry.co.uk, subscription service

International Maritime Organization. Boisson, Philippe, Safety at Sea. Policies, Regulations and International Law, Paris, 1999, extract online

British Newspaper Archive: Britishnewspapers.com, subscription service

Gale Vault of 19th century newspapers, subscription service

Grace's Guide to British Industrial History

London Metropolitan Archive Catalogue online

National Archives Catalogue

Searle Canada's Sunderland site: www.searlecanada.org/sunderland/sunderland001.html

Shipspotting.com – registration service

Sunderland Echo: sunderlandecho.com

The Times Archive, subscription service

The Wreck Site

Tyne and Wear Archive Service catalogue search

Tyne built ships: www.tynebuiltships.com

University of Leicester, local directories in their special collections section, www.specialcollections.le.ac.uk/

Wear Built Ships: www.sunderlandships.com

Wikipedia

Index of the ships
recorded in the text

General Index